CISSP (ISC)² Certification Practice Exams and Tests

Over 1,000 practice questions and explanations covering all 8 CISSP domains for the May 2021 exam version

Ted Jordan, MSc, CISSP

BIRMINGHAM—MUMBAI

CISSP (ISC)² Certification Practice Exams and Tests

Group Product Manager: Wilson D'souza

Publishing Product Manager: Shrilekha Malpani

Senior Editor: Arun Nadar

Content Development Editor: Mrudgandha Kulkarni

Technical Editor: Nithik Cheruvakodan

Copy Editor: Safis Editing

Project Coordinator: Shagun Saini

Proofreader: Safis Editing

Indexer: Pratik Shirodkar

Production Designer: Nilesh Mohite

First published: August 2021
Production reference: 1220721

Published by Packt Publishing Ltd.
Livery Place
35 Livery Street
Birmingham
B3 2PB, UK.

ISBN 978-1-80056-137-3

www.packt.com

Thank you Cheryl, Theo, and Aria for allowing Daddy time to complete this work.

Thanks to Cass Tech HS teachers Max Green and Walter Downs, a Tuskegee Airman who felled 6½ WWII enemy aircraft, for giving me my "serious fun" teaching style.

Dr. Green and Dr. McKeachie of Kettering U showed me how to simplify tough concepts for students.

Dr. Stark and Dr. Tomizuka of UC Berkeley introduced me to UNIX, which has taken me further than I imagined.

Contributors

About the author

Ted Jordan, MSc, CISSP, CSSLP, CEH, Security+, Cloud+, CTT+, Linux+, has over 30 years of cybersecurity experience. He studied info security at UC Berkeley and Kettering U. As an engineer, he used agile SDLC principles at GM, SGI, CAVE AR/VR, and SUN.

He is president of the successful start-up JordanTeam, which provides ethical hacking and education solutions. He has trained hundreds to attain their CISSP, CSSLP, CEH, Security+, and other certifications at Training Camp, ACI, NetCom, Training Assoc, Learning Tree, Global Knowledge, TechnoTraining, iKue, and more.

Follow him on Twitter and YouTube at @JordanTeamLearn.

This book is dedicated to my parents, Gwen and Ted Jordan, who helped me find my passion and teach others "how to fish."

About the reviewers

Dharam Chhatbar is a seasoned InfoSec professional with more than 11 years of experience in various verticals of InfoSec, delivering impactful and high-quality risk-reducing work. He has helped secure many banks and retail firms, and is currently working in a Fortune 500 company. He holds a master's degree, is a fervent learner, and has earned several global certifications, such as CISSP, GSLC (GIAC), CCSP, CSSLP, GMOB, and some certifications related to the cloud, such as Azure (AZ500), GCP (PCSE), and AWS (SAA). His key competencies include vulnerability management, application security, cloud security, VA/PT, and managing teams/vendors. Reach him on LinkedIn at @dharamm.

> *I would like to thank my parents, Bina and Jagdish; my wife, Chaitali;*
> *and my sister, Hina, for their continued support and encouragement with*
> *everything that I do, and for motivating me to always achieve my ambitions.*

Wade Henderson holds an MBA in international business and several IT, project management, and business-related certifications. His career spans over 15 years in the project management field, as well as mentoring and teaching in these areas. Wade is a professional project management consultant and has provided services to a wide range of business types, from multinational corporations to start-ups. Being a lifelong learner, he is continuously involved in many forms of education as a daily pursuit of personal development.

Table of Contents

Preface

I

Scheduling the CISSP Exam

1

Security and Risk Management Domain 1 Practice Questions

2

Asset Security Domain 2 Practice Questions

3

Security Architecture and Engineering Domain 3 Practice Questions

4

Communication and Network Security Domain 4 Practice Questions

5

Identity and Access Management Domain 5 Practice Questions

6

Security Assessment and Testing Domain 6 Practice Questions

7

Security Operations Domain 7 Practice Questions

8

Software Development Security Domain 8 Practice Questions

9

Full Practice Exam Exam 1

10

Full Practice Exam Exam 2

Other Books You May Enjoy

Index

Preface

Congratulations on taking this next step toward completing your **International Information System Security Certification Consortium, o**r (ISC)², **Certified Information Systems Security Professional** (**CISSP**) certification. This certification preparation guide contains over 1,000 practice questions covering all eight domains of the CISSP exam. The content is complete, up to date, and covers the latest CISSP exam topics released on *May 1, 2021*. Take the exam with confidence, fully equipped to pass the first time.

Who this book is for

This book is for the information technology professional who seeks to gain the (ISC)² CISSP certification.

You should have at least 2 years of experience in one of the following areas: **governance, risk, and compliance** (**GRC**), change management, network administration, systems administration, physical security, database management, or software development.

What this book covers

Chapter I, Scheduling the CISSP Exam, is where you will learn about where to schedule and take the exam.

Chapter 1, Security and Risk Management Domain 1 Practice Questions, has 100 practice questions covering GRC management and security requirements.

Chapter 2, Asset Security Domain 2 Practice Questions, has 100 practice questions covering asset handling and the data life cycle.

Chapter 3, Security Architecture and Engineering Domain 3 Practice Questions, has 100 practice questions covering security models, systems security, encryption, and physical security.

Chapter 4, Communication and Network Security Domain 4 Practice Questions, has 100 practice questions covering network architecture security and network component security.

, Access Management Domain 5 Practice Questions, has 100 practice
multi-factor authentication, single sign-on, and federation.

ty Assessment and Testing Domain 6 Practice Questions, has 100 practice
ring vulnerability assessments, penetration testing, disaster recovery, and
ntinuity.

7, Security Operations Domain 7 Practice Questions, has 100 practice questions
ing investigative techniques, threat intelligence, foundational security concepts, and
dent management.

Chapter 8, Software Development Security Domain 8 Practice Questions, has 100
practice questions covering the software development life cycle, software configuration
management, open source software, and secure coding practices.

Chapter 9, Full Practice Exam 1, has 100 practice questions as an exam simulation
covering all eight domains.

Chapter 10, Full Practice Exam 2, is an exam simulation, to be timed like a real exam,
with 100 practice questions.

To get the most out of this book

The use of a timer is very important while taking practice questions. The goal is to read
and correctly answer each question within 60 seconds.

Access to the internet and a web browser is important to research scenarios and get
more details as to why specific answers are correct. The web browser can be run from a
computer or tablet.

Software/hardware required	Operating system requirements
Web browser	Windows, macOS, or Linux
Tablet or computer	Android or iOS

Candidates without 5 years of work experience should continue accruing security
experience to complete their CISSP and move toward getting the Associate of (ISC)²
certification. As an associate, you have 6 years to fulfill the 5-year requirement.

Conventions used

There are a number of text conventions used throughout this book.

`Code in text`: Indicates code words in text, database table names, folder names, filenames, file extensions, pathnames, dummy URLs, user input, and Twitter handles. Here is an example: "The `sudoers` file is a database of users allowed to use `sudo` and which elevated commands they can run."

Bold: Indicates a new term, an important word, or words that you see onscreen. For instance, words in menus or dialog boxes appear in **bold**. Here is an example: "**Two-factor authentication** (**2FA**) asks for two different types of verification."

Get in touch

Feedback from our readers is always welcome.

General feedback: If you have questions about any aspect of this book, email us at `customercare@packtpub.com` and mention the book title in the subject of your message.

Errata: Although we have taken every care to ensure the accuracy of our content, mistakes do happen. If you have found a mistake in this book, we would be grateful if you would report this to us. Please visit `www.packtpub.com/support/errata` and fill in the form.

Piracy: If you come across any illegal copies of our works in any form on the internet, we would be grateful if you would provide us with the location address or website name. Please contact us at `copyright@packt.com` with a link to the material.

If you are interested in becoming an author: If there is a topic that you have expertise in and you are interested in either writing or contributing to a book, please visit `authors.packtpub.com`.

Share Your Thoughts

Once you've read *CISSP (ISC)² Certification Practice Exams and Tests*, we'd love to hear your thoughts! Scan the QR code below to go straight to the Amazon review page for this book and share your feedback.

https://packt.link/r/1-800-56137-7

Your review is important to us and the tech community and will help us make sure we're delivering excellent quality content.

1
Scheduling the CISSP Exam

The CISSP exam is seen as one of the world's most respected cyber security certifications. Fortune 1000 companies, the US Federal Government, and the US Department of Defense require individuals to have the certification to advance their career in cyber security. The United Kingdom's National Academic Recognition Information Centre states that the CISSP qualification assessment of knowledge and skills is as good as a master's degree (learn more here: `https://www.mercurysolutions.co/blog/cissp-certification-is-equivalent-to-masters-degree-now`).

In this introductory chapter, we provide the steps to schedule the exam, find a testing center, and best use this book to put you in the greatest situation for passing and achieving the CISSP certification. We will cover the following:

- Creating an (ISC)² account
- Finding a nearby Pearson Vue testing center
- Maintaining your CISSP certification
- The CISSP experiential requirements
- How to use this book

Creating an (ISC)² account

The first step to scheduling the exam is to create an account with the testing provider, Pearson Vue Testing Services. Pearson Vue has over 25 years of certification testing experience and works with (ISC)² so that you can schedule and take your exam at one of their many partner testing provider centers.

The first step is to create an account with (ISC)² on the Pearson Vue partner page here: `https://home.pearsonvue.com/isc2`.

Finding a nearby Pearson Vue testing center

After your Pearson Vue/(ISC)² account is created, log in and select **View Exams,** and then select the **CISSP: Certified Information Systems Security Professional** exam to schedule. (There is an option for **Online Exams** to take at home, but this is not available for the CISSP exam.)

Select your preferred language, and review the testing policies as needed. These will contain information pertaining to COVID-19 and mask-wearing while at the testing center. Also, the candidate needs to bring *two pieces of identification* to the testing center; otherwise, the candidate is failed without a refund.

Look your best at the testing center because, as stated in the testing policies, they will take a photograph and a palm vein scan that stays with your (ISC)² account.

The testing policies also include information about rescheduling and cancellation fees. Find the full list of terms and conditions here: `https://www.isc2.org/uploadedFiles/Certification_Programs/CBT-Examination-Agreement.pdf`.

If you need an accommodation, let them know ahead of time as stated in the testing policies. For example, let (ISC)² know before you arrive if you have mechanical parts on your body, for example, for dialysis; otherwise, you may not be able to take the test on your scheduled day. To request an accommodation, visit this link: `https://www.isc2.org/Register-for-Exam`.

Next, complete the exam eligibility form with employer information, your address, languages, degrees attained, and whether you are selecting the **Associate** option.

After this step, choose a convenient testing center. A calendar will pop up for you to choose a convenient date and time to take the exam.

Pay the *US$749* exam fee at the checkout and you will then be scheduled to take your exam.

Exam day has arrived

You have studied, taken hundreds of practice questions, and are now ready to sit the CISSP exam. Arrive at the testing center at least 30 minutes early. There may be others taking exams, so the Pearson Vue proctors may need time to check you in.

They will ask you for two pieces of identification. A driver's license and a signed credit card are fine. They will also accept a passport or common access card.

You are not allowed to take anything into the testing room, so they will ask you to turn your phone off, and put it in a locker with your keys, wallet, and study notes. They will provide earplugs if desired.

They provide a sheet or two of notepaper to use, but you have to return it to them at the end of the exam.

They will inspect your glasses, pants pockets, mask, and might ask you to frisk yourself.

Next, you enter the exam room and sit at a computer where the exam is displayed. The first screen shown is the terms and conditions. **You must accept the terms and conditions before the 25-minute timer runs out; otherwise, you'll fail without a refund.** *Avoid T&C failure (terms and conditions)* by reading them before taking the exam on the (ISC)² website: `https://www.isc2.org/Exams/Exam-Agreement`.

The exam is over

You will get your score after you exit the testing room. Once you have *provisionally* passed, you still need to provide (ISC)² with a sponsor that can vouch for your security experience. If you have trouble finding one, (ISC)² can assist, but check your LinkedIn account first for fellow (ISC)² members.

Within 4 to 6 weeks, you will receive your Certified Information Systems Security Professional certification diploma in the mail. Also included in the shipment will be the following:

- A welcome letter
- Information about joining your local (ISC)² chapter
- Information about where and how to obtain Continuing Professional Education hours
- Information about assisting as an exam developer for future exams
- A list of member benefits
- A certified membership identification card
- A certified membership pin

Now that you have received your diploma, you can publicly let the world know that you are an official certified CISSP!

Maintaining your CISSP certification

The certification is not a lifetime credential and expires after 3 years. There are two options to retain the certification beyond that period. Either take the exam every 3 years or complete **Continuing Professional Education hours (CPE hours)**. Details are found here: `https://www.isc2.org/-/media/ISC2/Certifications/CPE/CPE---Handbook.ashx`.

Continuing professional education credits are granted for the following:

- Attending information system security related training classes
- Reading or publishing information system security related articles or books
- Attending information system security conferences
- Attending information system security classes
- Preparing to teach a course on information system security
- A work-related project that is not part of your normal work duties
- Taking a higher education course
- Volunteering in information system security for non-profit organizations
- Self-study preparing for a certification exam

To track your CPE hours, first, join `https://www.isc2.org` and become a member. The annual dues are *US$125*. Then, to maintain the CISSP, acquire 120 CPE hours over 3 years. One website that automates the CPE process is *BrightTALK*, at `https://www.brighttalk.com`. After registering on their website, watch their information security related videos to earn CPE hours. They will automatically inform (ISC)² of the titles, descriptions, and CPE credit hours so you don't have to.

The CISSP experiential requirements

Not only does the candidate need to pass the exam, but they must meet the CISSP experience requirements found here: `https://www.isc2.org/Certifications/CISSP/experience-requirements`.

Candidates must have at least 5 years of work experience in at least 2 of the 8 domains. If the candidate does not have the work experience, they may become an Associate CISSP and are allowed up to 6 years to achieve the 5-year work experience requirement. Also, a college degree and some certifications count toward 1 of the 5 years of work experience.

The eight domains are as follows:

- Domain 1: Security and Risk Management
- Domain 2: Asset Security
- Domain 3: Security Architecture and Engineering
- Domain 4: Communication and Network Security
- Domain 5: Identity and Access Management (IAM)
- Domain 6: Security Assessment and Testing
- Domain 7: Security Operations
- Domain 8: Software Development Security

Don't think that you need to have *Security* in your job title, or need to have worked in a **Security Operations Center** (**SOC**) to attain the work experience requirement. Security includes backing up computers, setting up networks, programming firewalls, installing IOTs, and testing for malware.

Are you a computer programmer? Security includes reviewing source code for vulnerabilities, adding input sanitization features, being part of the software development lifecycle team, and so much more. See where your experiences qualify toward CISSP certification by reviewing the detailed outline on the (ISC)² website here: `https://www.isc2.org/-/media/ISC2/Certifications/Exam-Outlines/CISSP-Exam-Outline-English-April-2021.ashx` or refer to the list of topics covered, given in the following sections for your convenience.

Domain 1: Security and Risk Management

1.1 Understand, adhere to, and promote professional ethics:

- (ISC)² Code of Professional Ethics
- Organizational code of ethics

1.2 Understand and apply security concepts:

- Confidentiality, integrity, and availability, authenticity, and nonrepudiation

1.3 Evaluate and apply security governance principles:

- Alignment of the security function to business strategy, goals, mission, and objectives
- Organizational processes (for example, acquisitions, divestitures, governance committees)
- Organizational roles and responsibilities
- Security control frameworks
- Due care/due diligence

1.4 Determine compliance and other requirements:

- Contractual, legal, industry standards, and regulatory requirements
- Privacy requirements

1.5 Understand legal and regulatory issues that pertain to information security in a holistic context:

- Cybercrimes and data breaches
- Licensing and **Intellectual Property** (**IP**) requirements
- Import/export controls
- Transborder data flow
- Privacy

1.6 Understand requirements for investigation types (such as, administrative, criminal, civil, regulatory, or industry standards)

1.7 Develop, document, and implement security policy, standards, procedures, and guidelines

1.8 Identify, analyze, and prioritize **Business Continuity** (**BC**) requirements:

- **Business Impact Analysis** (**BIA**)
- Develop and document the scope and the plan

1.9 Contribute to and enforce personnel security policies and procedures:

- Candidate screening and hiring
- Employment agreements and policies
- Onboarding, transfers, and termination processes

- Vendor, consultant, and contractor agreements and controls
- Compliance policy requirements
- Privacy policy requirements

1.10 Understand and apply risk management concepts:

- Identify threats and vulnerabilities
- Risk assessment/analysis
- Risk response
- Countermeasure selection and implementation
- Applicable types of controls (for example, preventive, detective, or corrective)
- Control assessments (security and privacy)
- Monitoring and measurement
- Reporting
- Continuous improvement (for example, risk maturity modeling)
- Risk frameworks

1.11 Understand and apply threat modeling concepts and methodologies

1.12 Apply **Supply Chain Risk Management** (**SCRM**) concepts:

- Risks associated with hardware, software, and services
- Third-party assessment and monitoring
- Minimum security requirements
- Service level requirements

1.13 Establish and maintain a security awareness, education, and training program:

- Methods and techniques to present awareness and training (for example, social engineering, phishing, security champions, or gamification)
- Periodic content reviews
- Program effectiveness evaluation

Domain 2: Asset Security

2.1 Identify and classify information and assets:

- Data classification
- Asset classification

2.2 Establish information and asset handling requirements:

- Information and asset ownership
- Asset inventory (for example, tangible or intangible)
- Asset management

2.3 Provision resources securely

2.4 Manage the data life cycle:

- Data roles (for example, owners, controllers, custodians, processors, and users/subjects)
- Data collection
- Data location
- Data maintenance
- Data retention
- Data remanence
- Data destruction

2.5 Ensure appropriate asset retention (for example, **End-of-Life** (**EOL**) or **End-of-Support** (**EOS**))

2.6 Determine data security controls and compliance requirements:

- Data states (for example, in use, in transit, or at rest)
- Scoping and tailoring
- Standards selection
- Data protection methods (for example, **Digital Rights Management** (**DRM**), **Data Loss Prevention** (**DLP**), or **Cloud Access Security Broker** (**CASB**))

Domain 3: Security Architecture and Engineering

3.1 Research, implement, and manage engineering processes using secure design principles:

- Threat modeling
- Least privilege
- Defense in depth
- Secure defaults
- Fail securely
- **Separation of Duties (SoD)**
- Keep it simple
- Zero trust
- Privacy by design
- Trust but verify
- Shared responsibility

3.2 Understand the fundamental concepts of security models (for example, Biba, Star Model, and Bell-LaPadula)

3.3 Select controls based upon systems security requirements

3.4 Understand security capabilities of **Information Systems (IS)** (for example, memory protection, **Trusted Platform Module (TPM)**, and encryption/decryption)

3.5 Assess and mitigate the vulnerabilities of security architectures, designs, and solution elements:

- Client-based systems
- Server-based systems
- Database systems
- Cryptographic systems
- **Industrial Control Systems (ICS)**
- Cloud-based systems (for example, **Software as a Service (SaaS)**, **Infrastructure as a Service (IaaS)**, or **Platform as a Service (PaaS)**)

- Distributed systems
- **Internet of Things** (**IoT**)
- Microservices
- Containerization
- Serverless
- Embedded systems
- **High-Performance Computing** (**HPC**) systems
- Edge computing systems
- Virtualized systems

3.6 Select and determine cryptographic solutions:

- Cryptographic life cycle (for example, keys or algorithm selection)
- Cryptographic methods (for example, symmetric, asymmetric, elliptic curves, or quantum)
- **Public Key Infrastructure** (**PKI**)
- Key management practices
- Digital signatures and digital certificates
- Non-repudiation
- Integrity (for example, hashing)

3.7 Understand methods of cryptanalytic attacks:

- Brute force
- Ciphertext only
- Known plaintext
- Frequency analysis
- Chosen ciphertext
- Implementation attacks
- Side-channel
- Fault injection
- Timing
- **Man-in-the-Middle** (**MITM**)

- Pass the hash

- Kerberos exploitation

- Ransomware

3.8 Apply security principles to site and facility design

3.9 Design site and facility security controls:

- Wiring closets/intermediate distribution facilities

- Server rooms/data centers

- Media storage facilities

- Evidence storage

- Restricted and work area security

- Utilities and **Heating, Ventilation, and Air Conditioning** (**HVAC**)

- Environmental issues

- Fire prevention, detection, and suppression

- Power (for example, redundant or backup)

Domain 4: Communication and Network Security

4.1 Assess and implement secure design principles in network architectures:

- **Open System Interconnection** (**OSI**) and **Transmission Control Protocol/ Internet Protocol** (**TCP/IP**) models

- **Internet Protocol** (**IP**) networking (for example, **Internet Protocol Security** (**IPSec**) or **Internet Protocol** (**IP**) v4/6)

- Secure protocols

- Implications of multilayer protocols

- Converged protocols (for example, **Fiber Channel Over Ethernet** (**FCoE**), **Internet Small Computer Systems Interface** (**iSCSI**), and **Voice over Internet Protocol** (**VoIP**))

- Micro-segmentation (for example, **Software Defined Networks** (**SDN**), **Virtual eXtensible Local Area Network** (**VXLAN**), encapsulation, and **Software-Defined Wide Area Network** (**SD-WAN**))

- Wireless networks (for example, Li-Fi, Wi-Fi, Zigbee, and satellite)
- Cellular networks (for example, 4G, and 5G)
- **Content Distribution Networks (CDN)**

4.2 Secure network components:

- Operation of hardware (for example, redundant power, warranty, or support)
- Transmission media
- **Network Access Control (NAC)** devices
- Endpoint security

4.3 Implement secure communication channels according to design:

- Voice
- Multimedia collaboration
- Remote access
- Data communications
- Virtualized networks
- Third-party connectivity

Domain 5: Identity and Access Management (IAM)

5.1 Control physical and logical access to assets:

- Information
- Systems
- Devices
- Facilities
- Applications

5.2 Manage identification and authentication of people, devices, and services:

- **Identity Management (IdM)** implementation
- Single/**Multi-Factor Authentication (MFA)**
- Accountability

- Session management
- Registration, proofing, and establishment of identity
- **Federated Identity Management (FIM)**
- Credential management systems
- **Single Sign On (SSO)**
- **Just-In-Time (JIT)**

5.3 Federated identity with a third-party service:

- On-premise
- Cloud
- Hybrid

5.4 Implement and manage authorization mechanisms:

- **Role Based Access Control (RBAC)**
- Rule based access control
- **Mandatory Access Control (MAC)**
- **Discretionary Access Control (DAC)**
- **Attribute Based Access Control (ABAC)**
- Risk based access control

5.5 Manage the identity and access provisioning life cycle:

- Account access review (for example, user, system, or service)
- Provisioning and deprovisioning (for example, on /off boarding and transfers)
- Role definition (for example, people assigned to new roles)
- Privilege escalation (for example, managed service accounts, use of sudo, and minimizing its use)

5.6 Implement authentication systems:

- **OpenID Connect (OIDC)/Open Authorization(OAuth)**
- **Security Assertion Markup Language (SAML)**
- Kerberos
- **Remote Authentication Dial-In User Service (RADIUS)** or **Terminal Access Controller Access Control System Plus (TACACS+)**

Domain 6: Security Assessment and Testing

6.1 Design and validate assessment, test, and audit strategies:

- Internal
- External
- Third-party

6.2 Conduct security control testing:

- Vulnerability assessment
- Penetration testing
- Log reviews
- Synthetic transactions
- Code review and testing
- Misuse case testing
- Test coverage analysis
- Interface testing
- Breach attack simulations
- Compliance checks

6.3 Collect security process data (for example, technical and administrative):

- Account management
- Management review and approval
- Key performance and risk indicators
- Backup verification data
- Training and awareness
- **Disaster Recovery (DR)** and **Business Continuity (BC)**

6.4 Analyze test output and generate reports:

- Remediation
- Exception handling
- Ethical disclosure

6.5 Conduct or facilitate security audits:

- Internal

- External

- Third-party

Domain 7: Security Operations

7.1 Understand and comply with investigations:

- Evidence collection and handling

- Reporting and documentation

- Investigative techniques

- Digital forensics tools, tactics, and procedures

- Artifacts (for example, a computer, network, or mobile device)

7.2 Conduct logging and monitoring activities:

- Intrusion detection and prevention

- **Security Information and Event Management** (**SIEM**)

- Continuous monitoring

- Egress monitoring

- Log management

- Threat intelligence (for example, threat feeds or threat hunting)

- **User and Entity Behavior Analytics** (**UEBA**)

7.3 Perform **Configuration Management** (**CM**) (for example, provisioning, baselining, or automation)

7.4 Apply foundational security operations concepts:

- Need-to-know/least privilege

- **Separation of Duties** (**SoD**) and responsibilities

- Privileged account management

- Job rotation

- **Service Level Agreements** (**SLAs**)

7.5 Apply resource protection:

- Media management

- Media protection techniques

7.6 Conduct incident management:

- Detection

- Response

- Mitigation

- Reporting

- Recovery

- Remediation

- Lessons learned

7.7 Operate and maintain detective and preventative measures:

- Firewalls (for example, next generation, web application, or network)

- **Intrusion Detection Systems** (**IDS**) and **Intrusion Prevention Systems** (**IPS**)

- Whitelisting/blacklisting

- Third-party provided security services

- Sandboxing

- Honeypots/honeynets

- Anti-malware

- Machine learning and **Artificial Intelligence** (**AI**) based tools

7.8 Implement and support patch and vulnerability management

7.9 Understand and participate in change management processes

7.10 Implement recovery strategies:

- Backup storage strategies

- Recovery site strategies

- Multiple processing sites

- System resilience, **High Availability** (**HA**), **Quality of Service** (**QoS**), and fault tolerance

7.11 Implement **Disaster Recovery (DR)** processes:

- Response
- Personnel
- Communications
- Assessment
- Restoration
- Training and awareness
- Lessons learned

7.12 Test **Disaster Recovery Plans (DRP)**:

- Read-through/tabletop
- Walkthrough
- Simulation
- Parallel
- Full interruption

7.13 Participate in **Business Continuity (BC)** planning and exercises:

7.14 Implement and manage physical security

- Perimeter security controls
- Internal security controls

7.15 Address personnel safety and security concerns:

- Travel
- Security training and awareness
- Emergency management
- Duress

Domain 8: Software Development Security

8.1 Understand and integrate security in the **Software Development Life Cycle** (**SDLC**):

- Development methodologies (for example, Agile, Waterfall, DevOps, or DevSecOps)
- Maturity models (for example, the **Capability Maturity Model** (**CMM**) or the **Software Assurance Maturity Model** (**SAMM**))
- Operation and maintenance
- Change management
- **Integrated Product Team** (**IPT**)

8.2 Identify and apply security controls in software development ecosystems:

- Programming languages
- Libraries
- Tool sets
- **Integrated Development Environment** (**IDE**)
- Runtime
- **Continuous Integration and Continuous Delivery** (**CI/CD**)
- **Security Orchestration, Automation, and Response** (**SOAR**)
- **Software Configuration Management** (**SCM**)
- Code repositories
- Application security testing (for example, **Static Application Security Testing** (**SAST**) or **Dynamic Application Security Testing** (**DAST**))

8.3 Assess the effectiveness of software security:

- Auditing and logging of changes
- Risk analysis and mitigation

8.4 Assess security impact of acquired software:

- **Commercial-off-the-shelf** (**COTS**)
- Open source
- Third-party

- Managed services (for example, **Software as a Service (SaaS)**, **Infrastructure as a Service (IaaS)**, or **Platform as a Service (PaaS)**)

8.5 Define and apply secure coding guidelines and standards:

- Security weaknesses and vulnerabilities at the source-code level
- Security of **Application Programming Interfaces (APIs)**
- Secure coding practices
- Software-defined security

How to use this book

To best prepare for taking the CISSP exam, it is recommended you attempt practice exam 1 first, at the end of the book. Take 2 hours to complete the exam. Make sure to grade yourself.

Use the domain guide at the end of the exam, and determine which domains you need the most help with. Study further by reviewing the *Learn more* links that are provided with some of the questions to brush up on domains you are weak on.

This book has 100 practice questions for each domain, so review those practice questions to become stronger in those domains, and become better at test taking. For example, make sure to not spend more than 1 to 2 minutes per question so that when taking the real exam, you will not run out of time.

The real exam has up to 150 questions, with 3 hours to complete it, but if you demonstrate the required information security skills earlier, the exam may end at question 100, 120, or even 137. The exam ends once you demonstrate the required knowledge and experience.

Also, when taking the practice questions, try not to go back and change answers, because the real exam does not allow candidates to go back and correct wrong answers. Once a question is answered, you will never see that question again because you cannot go back. What if you realize you got an answer wrong a few questions later? It stays wrong. You are not allowed to go back and change answers.

Summary

To best prepare for the CISSP exam, study the practice questions in this book, and complete the full practice exams at the end of the book:

- The CISSP exam has a 5-year experience requirement, and if you have been working in information systems for at least 10 years, it should be straightforward to satisfy the work experience requirement.

- Once you earn the CISSP, you can retain it with CPE credit, or you can take the exam again in 3 years.

- Good luck on the exam, and please let us know how well you did on Twitter or YouTube: @JordanTeamLearn.

1
Security and Risk Management Domain 1 Practice Questions

Questions from the following topics are included in this domain:

- Basics of security and risk management
- Differing data roles and responsibilities
- Identifying administrative, physical, and technical controls
- Ethics of security professionals
- Administrative policies, procedures, and guidelines
- Object categorization and classification
- Importance of security training

To pass the **Certified Information Systems Security Professional** (**CISSP**) exam, you have to score high in the Security and Risk Management domain. Domain 1 has a 15% weighting on the exam and requires you to understand professional ethics, apply security concepts, understand how to apply security governance principles, and look at the big picture when it comes to compliance and other regulations, industry standards, or contractual and legal obligations. There is huge importance in understanding privacy security and keeping your customers' data protected.

If there are any corporate investigations due to a breach, these can follow administrative, criminal, civil, or regulatory investigations, and the security professional must be prepared. Management policies help reduce the risk of damage and litigation from incidents and other security threats.

Understanding how to implement **business impact analysis** (**BIA**) and knowing business continuity requirements are also important for Domain 1. Mastering this domain puts you a step ahead in preparing to pass the entire exam because it summarizes the other seven domains.

Questions

1. Dorian automatically backs up his smartphone nightly to the cloud. Does this represent safety, confidentiality, integrity, or availability?

    A. Confidentiality

    B. Integrity

    C. Availability

    D. Safety

2. Aisha just received an International Information Systems Security Certification Consortium (ISC)² certification. Her primary service as per their *Code of Ethics* is to:

    A. Shareholders

    B. Management

    C. Users

    D. Humanity

3. Ian's private data has been attacked and leaked on the internet. Which of the following is *NOT* his personally identifiable information (PII)?

   A. Password

   B. Facial photo

   C. Media access control (MAC) address

   D. Internet Protocol (IP) address

4. Gwendolyn completes all the backups for her cloud subscribers. What is her role at the company?

   A. Data owner

   B. Data subject

   C. Data custodian

   D. Data processor

5. Usain has lost his login and password for the *Verbal Co.* software-as-a-service (SAAS) system set up in 1999. The system is so old, he no longer has the email account to recover the password. *Verbal Co.'s* policy is to not provide credentials via technical support. What is his next *BEST* step?

   A. Scour the dark web for the credentials.

   B. Recover the login details from 1999 backup tapes.

   C. Continue emailing technical support.

   D. Give up—he has done everything he can do.

6. Quinonez, a CISSP security engineer with *SMR Tech*, has discovered that Mike and Dave, also CISSPs, colluded and harmed a contractor. How should she report this ethics violation to (ISC)²?

   A. Only with the sponsorship of another (ISC)²-certified individual

   B. By emailing `ethics@isc2.org`

   C. Through the (ISC)² ethics web page

   D. In a typed or handwritten letter

7. Elimu has installed firewalls to protect his users from outside attacks. This is a good example of what?

   A. Due diligence

   B. Due process

   C. Due care

   D. Regulatory requirements

8. Which of the following is it only recommended to follow?

   A. Policies

   B. Procedures

   C. Standards

   D. Guidelines

9. Wade is required to rebuild the organization and build an IT helpdesk infrastructure for customer support. Which framework and standards would help him *BEST* facilitate this?

   A. The IT Infrastructure Library (ITIL)

   B. The Committee of Sponsoring Organizations (COSO)

   C. International Organization for Standardization (ISO) *27001*

   D. Control Objectives for Information and Related Technologies (COBIT)

10. Montrie is required to destroy card verification value (CVV) codes after transactions have been completed. She is complying with which standard?

    A. The National Institute of Standards and Technology (NIST)

    B. ITIL

    C. COSO

    D. The Payment Card Industry Data Security Standard (PCI-DSS)

11. Teecee is running the computer sales department and sees that her team has sold $600,000 of their yearly goal of $1,000,000. What are the key performance indicator (KPI) and the key goal indicator (KGI)?

    A. The KPI is 60%, and the KGI is $600,000.

    B. The KPI is $600,000, and the KGI is 60%.

C. The KPI is $600,000, and the KGI is $600,000.

D. The KPI is -$400,000, and the KGI is $1,000,000.

12. Phillip is reviewing frameworks that would help him with the types of controls that should be in place to secure his organization. Which standard should he use?

A. ISO *27001*

B. ISO *27002*

C. ISO *27003*

D. ISO *27004*

13. Nina, a forensic accountant, suspects fraud within the organization, and implemented separation of duties (SoD) to mitigate the issues. Later investigation shows the fraud has appeared to continue. What is *MOST LIKELY* occurring?

A. Collusion

B. Miscalculation of taxes

C. Miscalculation of expenses

D. Miscalculation of net income

14. Nina, a forensic accountant, suspects fraud within the organization and implemented SoD to mitigate the issues. Later investigation shows the fraud has appeared to continue. What is her *BEST* next step?

A. Implement countermeasures

B. Implement business continuity

C. Implement job rotation

D. Implement data leak prevention (DLP)

15. What represents the indirect costs, direct costs, replacement costs, and upgrade costs for the entire life cycle of an asset?

A. Total cost of ownership (TCO)

B. Return on investment (ROI)

C. Recovery point objective (RPO)

D. Recovery time objective (RTO)

16. Negligence uses a *reasonable person* standard in cybersecurity measures, showing necessary due care when working with PII. This is also known as:

    A. Due diligence principle

    B. Due care principle

    C. Prudent person principle

    D. Measured negligence rule

17. Scoop loaned a job slot to the Systems Engineering (SE) department and stored the details using multi-factor authentication (MFA). The SE department refuses to return the job slot because Scoop cannot prove the loan agreement. What should he use combined with his personal identification number (PIN) to recover the detailed records of the loan agreement?

    A. Common access card (CAC)

    B. Password

    C. Mother's maiden name

    D. His birthday

18. Randi is an engineering manager who hires Percy, a senior engineer, to manage the *ASAN Corp* account in Cleveland. Bud, also a senior engineer, hears complaints from the *ASAN* customers and reports them to Randi instead of Percy. What is Randi's *BEST* next step?

    A. Thank Bud for being a great spy.

    B. Get feedback directly from the customer.

    C. Immediately transfer Percy to the Detroit office.

    D. Follow corporate policies on staff management.

19. Dito works in the Detroit office of the organization, and Greg states a management opportunity is soon opening and guarantees that Dito will get the job. Dito would feel more comfortable if the verbal guarantee came with a(n):

    A. Non-disclosure agreement (NDA)

    B. Contract

    C. Intellectual property (IP)

    D. Acceptable use policy (AUP)

20. Yaza is planning on selling COVID-19 masks online to the European Union (EU). Which regulation is the *most* important for her to consider?

    A. The Federal Trade Commission (FTC)

    B. Health Insurance Portability and Accountability Act (HIPAA)

    C. General Data Protection Regulation (GDPR)

    D. The Sarbanes-Oxley Act (SOX)

21. Trevor is considering transferring much of his organization's data to the cloud. Which vendor-neutral certification helps him to validate that the cloud provider has good security quality assurance (QA)?

    A. Cloud Security Allowance Security, Trust, Assurance, and Risk (CSA STAR)

    B. Azure certification

    C. Amazon Web Services (AWS) certification

    D. Red Hat (RH) cloud certification

22. Shewan's credit card information was stolen, and she realizes this occurred at the *AXQA store*. She believes the owner should go to prison. Which would *MOST LIKELY* occur?

    A. The PCI-DSS is a contractual agreement between the store owner and the credit card provider. At worst, the owner will lose the right to accept credit cards.

    B. The PCI-DSS is a federal regulation, violations of which are punishable by up to 5 years in federal prison.

    C. The PCI-DSS is an industry standard. At worst, the owner will lose their credit card license.

    D. The PCI-DSS is a legal standard, violations of which are punishable by up to 5 years in state prison.

23. Pat plans on outsourcing their Information Technology (IT) services so that they can focus on designing cars and trucks. Which is the *BEST* way for them to monitor the effectiveness of the service provider?

    A. Key risk indicator (KRI)

    B. KGI

    C. KPI

    D. Service-level agreement (SLA)

24. Tara's computer started performing very slowly, and then a popup locked her computer and notified her that unless she paid $300, she would never have access to her data again. Which of the following *BEST* describes this attack?

    A. Malware

    B. Ransomware

    C. Denial of Service (DoS)

    D. Man in the Middle (MitM)

25. Karthik receives a threatening email stating that they have a video of him performing lewd acts while watching porn. They will release the videos unless he pays them $1,000. This type of attack is *BEST* called:

    A. Social engineering

    B. Sextortion

    C. Ransomware

    D. Spam

26. Alexis is a security engineer and must secure her network from outside attackers. Which is the first *BEST* step she can take?

    A. Disable File Transfer Protocol (FTP) and Telnet services

    B. Install the latest security update patches

    C. Remove default logins and passwords

    D. Implement security-hardening standards

27. Zosimo works for *Maximo Smartphones*, and for years, their new smartphone plans have been leaked to the public 2 years ahead of time, hurting sales. What is the *BEST* administrative control he can use to stop this?

    A. Have employees sign an NDA

    B. Install DLP

    C. Install an internal proxy server

    D. Have guards scan workers' briefcases when they leave for the day

28. Angalina has noticed that several books have gone missing from the corporate library. She would like to install security controls but is on a budget. Which is the *BEST* solution for her?

    A. Add radio-frequency identification (RFID) to books.

B. Security guards

C. Dummy cameras

D. Security cameras

29. Coop, a security manager, practices decrypting secure documents. He has plain text of some of the files and needs to decrypt the rest. Which attack should he use?

A. Chosen plaintext

B. Known ciphertext

C. Chosen ciphertext

D. Known plaintext

30. Which of the following is *NOT* a directive control type?

A. Privacy policy (PP)

B. Terms of service (ToS)

C. Guard dog

D. Beware of dog sign

31. Ysaline has discovered her staff is spending over 80% of their time on IT-related issues, instead of designing and engineering smartphones. She wants to outsource IT-related issues to *AXQO Corp*. Which type of risk management is this?

A. Risk mitigation

B. Risk transference

C. Risk avoidance

D. Risk acceptance

32. Levi has purchased tablets for his staff for $2,000 each. Insurance will cover 50% if they are lost, stolen, or damaged. On an average year, five laptops are lost, stolen, or damaged. What would be the annualized loss expectancy (ALE) calculation?

A. $10,000

B. $5,000

C. $2,000

D. $1,000

33. Zulene has spent weeks collecting pricing, performance, and tuning data to conduct her risk assessment meeting. Now that she has all the data, her team will perform which type of risk analysis?

    A. Quantitative

    B. Qualitative

    C. Likelihood

    D. Impact

34. Zhenyu advises on security matters, helps draft security policy, and sits on the configuration management board. What is his role in the organization?

    A. Senior management

    B. Security director

    C. Security personnel

    D. Systems administrator

35. Bianca has already contacted *SGI News* regarding the use of her copyrighted images on their website, but they refuse to take them down. What is her *BEST* next step to have her images removed from the site?

    A. Use stronger watermarking procedures so that her images are not cloned.

    B. Consider that the SGI News posting gives her free publicity.

    C. Contact her lawyer to take immediate legal action.

    D. Submit a Digital Millennium Copyright Act (DMCA) takedown request to the hosting provider.

36. Roger, the chief financial officer (CFO) of *NUS Micro*, just received an email from his boss requesting he immediately wire $50 million to China to close a business deal. He calls his boss but cannot reach him. The email looks genuine, including the email address and domain name. He wires the money, only to find out later that his boss did not make this request. This represents which type of attack?

    A. Phishing

    B. Spear phishing

    C. Business email compromise (BEC)

    D. Whaling

37. Sloane received a phone call from her administrator to confirm an email received from her. She then gets a phone call from her CFO that he received a message from her to transfer $1 million overseas. What has *MOST LIKELY* occurred?

    A. Email account compromise (EAC)

    B. Spear phishing

    C. Phishing

    D. Whaling

38. Rafael, a systems administrator, notices that spam and phishing attacks are increasing. Which is the next *BEST* step he can take to safeguard the organization?

    A. Add additional firewall rules

    B. Implement training on spam and phishing attacks

    C. Modify the SpamAssassin rules

    D. Modify the external proxy server

39. Which of the following represents an acceptable amount of data loss measured in time?

    A. RPO

    B. RTO

    C. Maximum tolerable downtime (MTD)

    D. Work recovery time (WRT)

40. Individuals from all departments of the organization meet to prioritize risks based on impact, likelihood, and exposure. Which process is this?

    A. Business Continuity Planning (BCP)

    B. Disaster Recovery Planning (DRP)

    C. Incident Response Planning (IRP)

    D. BIA

41. Attacks such as dumpster diving, phishing, baiting, and piggybacking all represent a class of attacks called:

    A. MitM

    B. DoS

    C. Social engineering

    D. Doxxing

42. Unexpectedly, Coco has been given 2 weeks of paid time off. What is the security purpose of this event?

    A. Mandatory vacation as part of a healthy worker campaign

    B. Mandatory vacation to help expose fraud

    C. Mandatory vacation because she clicked a phishing email

    D. Mandatory vacation as part of a disaster recovery (DR) simulation

43. Simon needs to calculate risk. Which formula will he use?

    A. Risk = Likelihood * Exposure

    B. Risk = Threat/Vulnerability

    C. Risk = Threat * Vulnerability

    D. Risk = Exposure * Impact

44. Qiang has been assigned to find recovery sites as a result of the DR planning meeting. Her job is to find sites with heating, cooling, electricity, internet access, and power. The site will require no computers. Which type of recovery site is this?

    A. Mirrored site

    B. Hot site

    C. Warm site

    D. Cold site

45. Milos is the chief security officer (CSO) of the organization and is designing a policy that includes fences, secured parking, security policies, firewalls, account management, and patch management. This is an example of which strategy?

    A. Defense-in-depth (DiD)

    B. Use of physical controls

    C. Proper use of technical controls

    D. Combining administrative, technical, and physical controls

46. As part of a disaster strategy, Caty asks management for approval of deploying a warm site. Warm sites are which type of control functionality?

    A. Recovery

    B. Deterrent

C. Detective

D. Preventative

47. Arthur, chief executive officer (CEO) of *Funutek*, wishes to implement online purchasing via their website. The chief marketing officer (CMO) likes the idea because the new system can double sales. The CSO fears internet attacks and suggests *NOT* moving forward. How should Arthur proceed?

A. Implement the website once certain there is no risk of attack.

B. Implement the website after the CMO collects research on securing websites.

C. Implement the website and secure it within acceptable risk levels.

D. Listen to the CSO and do not implement the website.

48. NIST outlines security controls to put in place of federal agencies in which Special Publication (SP)?

A. *800-50*

B. *800-51*

C. *800-52*

D. *800-53*

49. Bud has just learned about hacking, knows a little about programming, and likes to bring misery to others. He decides to attempt hacking into his school website to change his grades. This puts him in which class of hackers?

A. Advanced persistent threat (APT)

B. Script kiddie

C. Ethical hacker

D. Internal threat

50. When it comes to dual-use goods (items that can be used by the military and ordinary citizens), there are special requirements and agreements for import and export. One that seeks to limit military buildup that could threaten international security is called *Conventional Arms and Dual-Use Goods and Technologies*, or the:

A. Arms Agreement

B. Wassenaar Arrangement

C. Dual-Use Agreement

D. Import/Export Law

51. Taylor just won her court case through the benefit of the doubt. Her case falls under which legal system?

    A. Contract

    B. Administrative

    C. Civil

    D. Criminal

52. Gael and his team have developed the perfect advertising algorithm so that when users search on his website, it leads them exactly to the information they need to reach. What is his *BEST* approach to assuring the secrecy of this algorithm?

    A. Trade secret

    B. Patent

    C. Copyright

    D. Trademark

53. Su-wei uses the Linux operating system, and freely copies it and gives it to friends. She is allowed to do this because of which of the following licenses?

    A. Shareware

    B. Commercial

    C. End-user license agreement (EULA)

    D. Academic

54. The area of United States (US) copyright law that makes it a crime to copy and distribute stolen software is called:

    A. DMCA

    B. EULA

    C. Privacy Act

    D. Business Software Alliance (BSA)

55. Fritz works with a document providing him step-by-step instructions. Which of the following is he working with?

    A. Policies

    B. Procedures

    C. Standards

    D. Guidelines

56. Naomi needs to calculate the TCO. Which of the following will she *NOT* use to complete the calculation?

    A. Support costs

    B. Cost to replace the unit

    C. Cost of maintenance

    D. Asset cost

57. Viktor is conducting a risk assessment and needs to determine the percentage of risk his organization would suffer if an asset is compromised. Which of the following signifies this aspect of risk?

    A. Safeguards

    B. Vulnerabilities

    C. Exposure factor

    D. Risk

58. Ons, a security manager, is working with her team to develop and update policies for staff and vendors. Controls in this area are considered which of the following?

    A. Management

    B. Operational

    C. Technical

    D. Logical

59. Which of these is *NOT* true?

    A. Procedures are the same as written directions.

    B. Strategic documents would be considered policies.

    C. Guidelines contain step-by-step instructions that must be followed.

    D. Standards can define KPIs.

60. Kei, a security manager, just completed a risk assessment with his team, and they determined that the new planned plant location was too dangerous, so they decided not to expand there. Which risk response did his team use?

    A. Mitigation

    B. Avoidance

    C. Transfer

    D. Acceptance

61. Molla, a project engineer, puts together a project, and she adds security according to which of the following life cycles?

    A. Requirements, planning, design, test, develop, production, disposal

    B. Planning, requirements, design, develop, test, production, disposal

    C. Design, develop, requirements, planning, test, production, disposal

    D. Planning, design, requirements, test, develop, production, disposal

62. Wilfried is the security administrator of a store and is preparing for the PCI-DSS audit. Which is *NOT* one of the PCI-DSS requirements?

    A. Configure switch settings

    B. Maintain the firewall

    C. Encrypt transmission of credit card transactions

    D. Use antivirus software

63. Vania, an administrative assistant, has discovered that her employer has been listening to her telephone conversations and reading her emails. She approaches her boss, and she shows her that she signed the reasonable expectation of privacy (REP) agreement. Which steps can Vania take next?

    A. Report the supervisor to human resources (HR).

    B. File a civil lawsuit.

    C. Nothing—she waived her rights to phone privacy while at work.

    D. Contact the police or federal authorities and open a criminal case.

64. Grigor fears he will lose his job if his employer learns of his cancer diagnosis. He does not want which of the following to leak?

    A. Health and Human Services (HHS)

    B. Health Information Technology for Economic and Clinical Health Act (HITECH)

    C. HIPAA

    D. Personal health information (PHI)

65. Martina seeks to press criminal charges against the CEO of *RMS Foods Inc.* because their employee stole her credit card. What happens next?

    A. The government will press charges against the CEO.

    B. Conflicts are managed under PCI-DSS agreements, not the government.

C. Conflicts are managed under ISO or NIST certification, not the government.

D. Conflicts are managed under GDPR laws, so there will only be fines.

66. Boris is working to complete a design project. He decides to hire a contractor to help complete the project on time. Which type of risk response is he using?

    A. Transfer

    B. Acceptance

    C. Division

    D. Avoidance

67. Petra uses her own secret formula to manufacturer her synthetic gut tennis string. This is then stolen by the SGI Strings Company. Which law or agreement has been broken?

    A. Patent

    B. Trade secret

    C. Copyright

    D. Trademark

68. As Bjorn leaves the office this day, Steffi tells him she overheard men starting to break in earlier that evening to steal documents. The men are later caught, and Bjorn is brought onto the witness stand in court to mention what he heard. This type of evidence is termed which of the following?

    A. Conclusive

    B. Admissible

    C. Hearsay

    D. Best evidence

69. Garbine performs inspections of whether security policies, procedures, standards, and guidelines are followed according to the organization's security objectives. What is her role for the firm?

    A. Auditor

    B. Chief information security officer (CISO)

    C. Information security manager (ISM)

    D. Data owner

70. Which is critical for proper incident response?

    A. Evidence handling

    B. Security information and event management (SIEM)

    C. Intrusion detection system (IDS)

    D. Incident response policy

71. Novak is preparing a DR exercise and emails the emergency task lists to the DR teams for review. Which type of exercise is he running?

    A. Full interruption test

    B. Parallel test

    C. Tabletop test

    D. Checklist test

72. Simona is a space fleet lieutenant putting together classifications for her computer system. Which of the following sensitivity systems will she follow?

    A. Confidential, private, sensitive, public

    B. Top-secret, secret, confidential, unclassified

    C. Highly sensitive, sensitive, classified, unclassified

    D. Top-secret, secret, classified, unclassified

73. Andre has provided his phone number, email address, and home address to *Pyramid Grocer* so that they can deliver groceries to his home. He is considered to be which of the following?

    A. Data owner

    B. Data custodian

    C. Data subject

    D. Data auditor

74. Venus needs an administrative control to enhance the confidentiality of data. Which should she choose?

    A. DLP system

    B. Fencing

    C. Security guards

    D. NDA

75. Juan plans to perform testing on his website and generate random input to see if it is vulnerable to which type of attack?

    A. Fuzzing

    B. DoS

    C. Malware

    D. Input validation

76. Victoria has worked in several departments of the company, including marketing, quality, and production. An audit found she still has privileges in all of her past departments even though she works in finance. This is called:

    A. SoD

    B. Collusion

    C. Privilege creep

    D. Least privilege

77. Stan wishes to set up secure authentication for his users. Which of the following is *NOT BEST* for authentication?

    A. Retinal scan

    B. Username

    C. Palm vein scan

    D. CAC

78. Billie needs to determine how much risk her organization can handle and still operate efficiently. She will first conduct a?

    A. Risk assessment

    B. Risk mitigation

    C. Risk acceptance

    D. Risk avoidance

79. Which of the following does *NOT* require an AUP?

    A. Consultant

    B. Contractor

    C. Employee

    D. Computer

80. Stefanos has just signed an SLA with *NUS Systems*. Which of the following is *NOT* part of the agreement?

    A. Financial credit for downtime

    B. Alpha services

    C. Covered service

    D. Service-level objectives (SLOs)

81. Madison received an email from Justine stating that $1,000 in funds had been transferred to her. Justine states she never sent the email. Which process would prove Justine sent the email?

    A. Fingerprinting

    B. Encryption

    C. Non-repudiation

    D. Hashing

82. Security education should be required for whom in an organization?

    A. Computer users

    B. Everyone

    C. Senior executives

    D. Security teams

83. Lleyton is planning on hiring 50 new engineers. What should be his *FIRST* step when reviewing new candidates?

    A. Make sure prospects pass lie-detector screening.

    B. Conduct thorough background checks.

    C. Follow the employment candidate-screening process.

    D. Perform drug screenings.

84. Non-compete agreements (NCAs) are generally unenforceable because:

    A. NCAs are illegal.

    B. Courts value a citizen's right to earn a reasonable income.

    C. Competition is covered in the NDA.

    D. NCAs are always enforceable.

85. Ana, a systems engineer, caught Bud stealing corporate financial documents and informed her manager. Which department handles Bud's termination?

    A. HR

    B. Security

    C. Engineering

    D. Finance

86. Daniil has finished a successful career with *DDA Motors*. As part of the exit interview, he's required to return everything *Except* for:

    A. Last week's paycheck

    B. Smart card

    C. Corporate smartphone

    D. Employee identifier (ID) card

87. Which of the following does *NOT* represent an asset for an organization?

    A. Sunk costs

    B. Computer

    C. Trademark

    D. Staff

88. Which is *BEST* represented as the product of a threat and vulnerability?

    A. Safeguard

    B. Exposure

    C. Risk

    D. Breach

89. What is the biggest threat to any organization?

    A. Pandemics

    B. Malware

    C. Clear text

    D. Disgruntled employees

90. Elina is interviewing risk consulting firms. What is the main item she should *NOT* look for in a qualified firm?

    A. Can assist in defining the scope and purpose of risk assessments

    B. Categorizes and prioritizes assets

    C. Helps in defining acceptable levels of risk

    D. Years of experience in bringing organizations' risk to zero

91. What represents the product of the asset value (AV) and exposure factor (EF)?

    A. Annual rate of occurrence (ARO)

    B. Single loss expectancy (SLE)

    C. ALE

    D. Annual cost of a safeguard (ACS)

92. An organization is initiating the qualitative risk analysis process. Which of the following is *NOT* part of the process?

    A. Cost versus benefit analysis

    B. Educated guesses

    C. Opinions considered

    D. Multiple experts

93. The Risk Management Framework (RMF) is also known as which NIST SP?

    A. *800-35*

    B. *800-36*

    C. *800-37*

    D. *800-38*

94. Feliciano has applied multiple risk mitigations to protect an asset. When should he stop?

    A. When risk reaches an acceptable level

    B. When the asset becomes unusable

    C. After purchasing insurance for the asset

    D. When the risk is reduced to zero

95. According to the *Cisco 2020 CISO Benchmark Report*, cyber (security) fatigue is defined as *virtually giving up on proactively defending against malicious actors.* What is the number 1 source of cyber fatigue?

    A. Malware

    B. Phishing attacks

    C. Shadow IT

    D. Password management

96. Sofia, a senior manager, needs to get a Linux update installed on her team's server. Central IT has not performed the update even after being asked three times. Sofia selects a team member to install it and work around the IT department. This is *BEST* referred to as:

    A. Self-help

    B. Delegation of IT

    C. Policy violation

    D. Shadow IT

97. Benoit, the company CISO, is researching high-security systems that authenticate everything attempting connections to the corporate network. Such an architecture is called:

    A. Zed trust

    B. No trust

    C. Zero trust

    D. Null trust

98. The following type of security learning yields a credential such as a certificate or a degree:

    A. Awareness

    B. Education

    C. Training

    D. Birds of a feather (BOAF) sessions

99. For most organizations, which is the most important asset when a firm enters into BCP or DRP mode?

    A. People

    B. Network

    C. Server room

    D. Cash

100. Eugenie is the production manager at *FAUX Widgets*, and the lights went out for the entire building. Which action does she execute *FIRST*?

    A. Contact the electric company.

    B. Check the fuse box.

    C. Follow the DRP plan.

    D. Follow the BCP plan.

Quick answer key

1. C	16. C	31. B	46. A	61. B	76. C	91. B
2. D	17. A	32. B	47. C	62. A	77. B	92. A
3. A	18. D	33. A	48. D	63. C	78. B	93. C
4. C	19. B	34. B	49. B	64. D	79. D	94. A
5. A	20. C	35. D	50. B	65. B	80. B	95. D
6. D	21. A	36. C	51. D	66. A	81. C	96. D
7. C	22. A	37. A	52. A	67. B	82. B	97. C
8. D	23. D	38. B	53. C	68. C	83. C	98. B
9. A	24. B	39. A	54. A	69. A	84. B	99. A
10. D	25. B	40. D	55. B	70. D	85. A	100. D
11. B	26. D	41. C	56. B	71. D	86. A	
12. B	27. A	42. B	57. C	72. B	87. A	
13. A	28. C	43. C	58. A	73. C	88. C	
14. C	29. D	44. D	59. C	74. D	89. D	
15.A	30. C	45. A	60. B	75. A	90. D	

Answers with explanations

1. **Answer: C** Dorian conducting nightly backups provides him availability in case his smartphone is lost or stolen. There is no mention of encryption or password protection, so confidentiality is not a possibility, and there is no discussion of hashing, so integrity is not a possibility. Finally, there is no mention of personal security to Dorian, so safety is not an option.

2. **Answer: D** Aisha's primary concern per the (ISC)² *Code of Ethics* is *the safety and welfare of society and the common good.* The preamble finally states: *strict adherence to this Code is a condition of certification.* Since option D, humanity, includes all of the other options, answer D is correct.

3. **Answer: A** PII refers to data that can be used to help identify an individual. A facial photo, MAC address, and IP address can be used to identify Ian, but not a password. Learn more here: `https://nvlpubs.nist.gov/nistpubs/Legacy/SP/ nistspecialpublication800-122.pdf`.

    Reference: *Guide to Protecting the Confidentiality of Personally Identifiable Information (PII)*, NIST Special Publication 800-122, McCallister, Grance, Scarfone, Apr 2010.

4. **Answer: C** Gwendolyn's job, in this case, is the data custodian because her role is to manage data for the data owners, which are her subscribers. Data subjects are the individuals referred to within the PII data. Data processors keep the PII content up to date.

5. **Answer: A** Usain's next best step is to recover credentials from the dark web. Most websites were not using **HyperText Transfer Protocol Secure** (**HTTPS**) during that period, so it is likely hackers stole PII from *Verbal Co.*, which likely contains clear passwords. If this fails, he can try contacting technical support again. Most corporate policies require data over 3 to 7 years old to be destroyed. Also, if the tapes are recovered, it is likely there are no passwords. Technical support firms are required to follow policies of not providing credentials, and recovery resets will not work because he no longer has access to the email account.

6. **Answer: D** Quinonez must report such incidents in writing. Although additional sponsors would boost the validity of the complaint, this is not required. Electronic submissions are not acceptable.

7. **Answer: C** Installing firewalls is a sign of due care. Exercising due care, such as setting up rules to block traffic and tracking the number of false positives, is due diligence. Due process is fair treatment of citizens in the judicial system. The question does not imply that Elimu's firm is required to follow specific regulations.

8. **Answer: D** Guidelines are non-mandatory, advisory recommendations. Policies are put together by management and are required to be followed across the organization. Procedures are detailed step-by-step instructions to achieve a given goal or mandate. Standards form metrics to help measure the success of procedures and policies.

9. **Answer: A** Wade would use ITIL, which provides best practices for delivering IT services. COSO is an internal framework for risk assessments. The ISO *27001* specification provides the framework for ISM systems. COBIT defines a framework for IT management and governance.

10. **Answer: D** Montrie is complying with her PCI-DSS contract to protect PII in credit cards. NIST provides a cybersecurity framework similar to ISO for ISM. ITIL provides best practices for delivering IT services. COSO is an internal framework for risk assessments.

11. **Answer: B** A KPI is a metric that quantifies the current state of reaching a goal, generally in dollars, quality, efficiency, or satisfaction. A KGI is a metric that monitors the evolution of efforts and helps to plan the next course of action, usually shown as a percentage of the goal. KPIs look to the future to see if corrections need to be made, but KGIs look at the past to see if plans are working.

12. **Answer: B** Phillip will use ISO *27002*, which focuses on security controls being put in place. ISO *27001* focuses more on security policy. ISO *27003* provides suggestions and guidance on the proper implementation of controls, and ISO *27004* focuses on the validation of controls after implementation.

13. **Answer: A** Since Nina is a forensic accountant, common accounting practices would have been validated, so this leaves collusion as the only possibility.

14. **Answer: C** Nina's next best step is to implement job rotation, which best mitigates collusion. Job rotation is a type of countermeasure because it offsets the threat, but job rotation is more specific. Business continuity means being able to operate after a disaster, and DLP would be an issue if corporate plans or finances were being leaked to the public.

15. **Answer: A** The TCO includes all costs for the entire life cycle of an asset. ROI is the value returned on an investment less the cost of the investment, divided by the cost of the investment. The RPO is the last point in time where data is in a usable format. The RTO is how long systems can be down without causing significant damage—for example, the business has to shut down. Learn more here: `https://ithandbook.ffiec.gov/it-booklets/business-continuity-management/iii-risk-management/iiia-business-impact-analysis/iiia3-impact-of-disruption.aspx`.

16. **Answer: C** The prudent person principle is a standard of care that a *reasonably prudent person* would follow in certain situations. This principle, borrowed from the law and insurance industries, is also followed in cybersecurity if it is outside a NIST, PCI-DSS, **Center for Internet Security** (**CIS**), or another standard. Due care is the effort made to avoid harm to others, such as putting mitigating controls in place. Due diligence is the practice of due care—for example, making sure the mitigating controls work. Measuring negligence helps to determine if an organization acted prudently.

17. **Answer: A** Scoop will use the CAC. This is the best authentication type to combine *something-that-you-know* authentication with. Since your password, mother's maiden name, and birthday are all *something you know*, these combined with a PIN would simply be **single-factor authentication** (**SFA**).

18. **Answer: D** Randi must always follow the corporate policy. Getting customer feedback is good, and rewarding inside information can be beneficial, but following management policy is always the most important. Transferring Percy exposes the client to the threat of an immediate bad hire; for example, the new hire may get searched by the **Federal Bureau of Investigation** (**FBI**).

19. **Answer: B** If Greg provides a written contract, Dito will have a signed document stating what was expected. If the opportunity fell through, Dito could ask for alternatives by enforcing the contract. An NDA states that Dito keeps corporate secrets private. An AUP states Dito will use the product in an acceptable manner. **Intellectual property (IP)** is works or inventions that have value to an organization.

20. **Answer: C** Yaza needs to consider the GDPR because she wants to sell masks to EU clients, and in order to do that, she must abide by GDPR law. (A key tenet of GDPR is the data subject's *right to be forgotten*, which is not a part of most other privacy acts). The FTC focuses on US trade and consumer protections. HIPAA affects hospitals and other medical providers. SOX makes corporate fraud a criminal act.

21. **Answer: A** Trevor would consider CSA STAR certification, which demonstrates the **cloud service provider's (CSP's)** adherence to privacy and security best practices, and the only option that is vendor-neutral. Azure certification is a Microsoft-only standard. AWS is an Amazon-only standard. RH cloud certification is a Red Hat-only standard.

22. **Answer: A** PCI-DSS is a contractual standard between stores and credit card providers. Vendors agree to provide minimal security measures to protect customer PII. Results from poor audits risk the shop owner losing the ability to accept credit cards. Federal and legal standards may include fines and even prison time, but PCI-DSS is a contractual standard. PCI-DSS is not an industry standard, and there is no credit card license. Industry standards are non-contractual agreements—for example, automotive manufacturers deciding to put steering wheels on the right if selling to Japan.

23. **Answer: D** Pat would use an SLA to monitor the effectiveness of the service provider. KRIs, KGIs, and KPIs are part of SLAs.

24. **Answer: B** This is an excellent example of ransomware. Once Tara pays the attacker, there is a good chance she will have access to her data. Ransomware is a type of malware that asks for a ransom payment. This is a type of DoS attack, but DoS attacks are, in general, considered availability attacks over a network. MitM attacks in general are network attacks design to sniff packets.

25. **Answer: B** Karthik was attacked with a sextortion scam. Most of these are fake, and the victim should not send money. Ransomware is distinguished by locking the victim's data. Although this is unwanted email like spam, sextortion demands a monetary threat. Most social engineering attacks come with a degree of spoofing, where the sender pretends to be someone they are not.

26. **Answer: D** Alexis' next best step would be to implement security hardening standards, which includes disabling Telnet and FTP services, installing the latest security updates and patches, and removing default logins and passwords.

27. **Answer: A** Of the four options, the only administrative option is having staff sign the NDA. Zosimo can further layer security with technical controls (for example, DLP and proxy servers) as well as physical controls (for example, security guards).

28. **Answer: C** The key point to this question is *on a budget*. Dummy cameras are deterrent-type controls that reduce the likelihood of an attack and are very inexpensive. RFID is a detective-type control that is not that expensive but requires a lot of labor expense to add the RFID tags to the books. Security cameras are detective and deterrent control types and are expensive to purchase, install, and monitor. Security guards are an expensive detective type of control as well.

29. **Answer: D** Coop has some of the plain text that goes with the encrypted message, so this is a known plaintext attack.

30. **Answer: C** Guard dogs are detective control types that recognize attacks and other negative activities. PPs, ToS, and signage are all directive control types.

31. **Answer: B** Ysaline is performing risk transference since *AXQO Corp* will now manage the day-to-day IT functions. Risk mitigation is what happens if she continues to operate as is. Risk avoidance would not work for her because it would mean not having any IT equipment at all to manage. Risk acceptance is the amount of acceptable risk after mitigations are put in place.

32. **Answer: B** AV = $2,000; EF = 50%

    SLE = AV * EF = $2,000 * 50% = $1,000

    ARO = 5

    ALE = SLE * ARO = $1,000 * 5 = $5,000

33. **Answer: A** Quantitative risk analysis takes more time than qualitative risk analysis because participants need all of the data to proceed. This can be time-consuming. Qualitative risk analysis is much quicker because it relies on *educated* guesses. It is important that the people who understand the areas of risk to their departments are in the room. Likelihood and impact are used in risk analysis to prioritize asset protection.

34. **Answer: B** Security directors advise on security matters, draft security policy, and contribute to the Configuration Management Board. Senior management includes positions such as CEO, CFO, CIO, and so on, and mandates policies, determines strategic goals, and determines which security frameworks to use. Security personnel follow the security processes of the organization. System administrators manage day-to-day IT operations, including helpdesks.

35. **Answer: D** Bianca's next best step is to submit a DCMA takedown request to the DMCA designated agent of the hosting company, with a list of the copyrights and location on the website. Legal action generally follows this step if the copyrighted material is not removed. Legal action is a much longer process, and it will take much longer to have her material removed. Free publicity and watermarking do not help her get her images removed.

36. **Answer: C** A BEC contains characteristics of spear phishing, but the domain name is very similar, and the email appears to be from internal management. Finally, large sums of money are directed outside of the company. Sometimes, funds can be recovered by working with the federal police.

37. **Answer: A** An EAC is when a hacker uses phishing, spear phishing, whaling, password attacks, malware, and so on to compromise a C-level executive's email account for the purpose of tricking targets to send funds.

38. **Answer: B** Updates of firewalls, SpamAssassin, and proxies can help reduce the volume of attacks, but none of these systems is perfect. Continuous training programs via live training, videos, podcasts, and so on are the best way to safeguard the organization.

39. **Answer: A** The RPO represents the acceptable amount of data loss in time— for example, snapshots might be taken every 15 minutes, so 15 minutes is the RPO. The RTO is the period to bring all systems back online after a disaster. WRT is the time needed to verify systems and data integrity. MTD is the maximum amount of downtime before going out of business and is generally the sum of WRT and RTO.

40. **Answer: D** BIA includes prioritization of risks based on impact, likelihood, and exposure. Risk analysis can be qualitative or quantitative. BIA is part of BCP, which defines how to continue business operations after a disaster. DRP details how to recover business operations after a disaster. IRPs are executed when legal authorities must be involved—for example, when PII or financial records are stolen over the internet.

Reference: *Contingency Planning Guide for Federal Information Systems, NIST Special Publication 800-34 Revision 1, Swanson et al., May 2010.*

41. **Answer: C** Dumpster diving, phishing, baiting, and piggybacking are all non-high-technical methods to engage the victim. MitM attacks use high-tech tools to download conversations of the victim. DoS is a network attack where data floods the device. Doxxing is searching and publishing private information about individuals.

42. **Answer: B** Mandatory vacations are designed to expose any fraud that might be occurring. If Coco is involved in fraud, she needs to be at work to be monitored for fraudulent activity. Healthy worker vacations are planned and expected. Phishing email issues are better resolved with training than with vacation. Staff need to be on-site for DR simulations so that they know their part in a disaster.

43. **Answer: C** Risk is the product of vulnerability and a possible threat.

44. **Answer: D** Cold sites are empty rooms and designed for low-priority data that can take several weeks or months for recovery. Warm sites have some computer equipment but no current backup tapes. Hot sites have recent backups for fast recovery within minutes to hours. Mirrored sites have the most current information in case of failure.

45. **Answer: A** Although D might be true, the strategy is called DiD, or a layered approach.

46. **Answer: A** Preventative functionality implements incident avoidance—for example, locks or mantraps. Detective functionality detects or alerts an incident—for example, motion detectors and job rotations. Deterrents diminish threats by reducing the confidence of the intruder—for example, fences and fake cameras. Recovery brings organizations back to normal operations.

47. **Answer: C** The CSO is an advisor to the organization, seeking ways to implement operations and enable business functions within an acceptable risk level. Option A is wrong because there is no such thing as zero risks, and B is wrong because CMOs are not in charge of security.

48. **Answer: D** SP *800-53* is the *Security and Privacy Controls for Federal Information Systems and Organizations* document. The document outlines various administrative, technical, and physical security controls to protect organizations.

49. **Answer: B** Script kiddies are in general non-sophisticated and new to hacking. APTs generally work as a group, carefully study the target, and are patient enough to wait for the right time to exploit a vulnerability. Ethical hackers are generally paid to attack organizations to find vulnerabilities but do not harm. Bud could almost be an internal threat since he is a student at the school, but he does not work for the school.

50. **Answer: B** The Wassenaar Arrangement applies export controls and rules for computers, electronics, encryption, and more.

51. **Answer: D** Criminal law is invoked when a person violates governmental laws, whereas civil law depends on the preponderance of the evidence. Administrative law is handled internally within organizations, similarly to internal affairs for police. Contract law is handled between the parties of a working agreement and can be disputed in court or through a mediator.

52. **Answer: A** Copyrights and software patents require the algorithm to be published, making it easy for a competitor to reverse-engineer. Trademarks are used to protect an organization's logo or brand.

53. **Answer: C** Shareware, commercial, and academic licenses come with a EULA, which states how software can be used. Linux's EULA is a call to the **GNU General Public License (GNU GPL)**, giving freedom to users to distribute software as long as they give credit to the authors.

54. **Answer: A** The Digital Millennium Copyright Act helps to reduce software piracy by criminalizing the dissemination of stolen software. The EULA limits what users can do with software they purchase—for example, only allow 10 users. The BSA promotes the enforcement of software copyrights. The Privacy Act helps to protect user PII.

55. **Answer: B** Fritz is working with procedures because they provide explicit directions on performing specific operations. Policies are documents with concepts developed by management and must be followed. Guidelines are strong recommendations from management but do not have to be followed. Standards are metrics and are meant for use as a type of scoring system.

56. **Answer: B** Naomi will need support costs, maintenance costs, and asset costs to calculate the TCO, but not replacement costs.

57. **Answer: C** Viktor needs the exposure factor, which defines the percentage of loss of an asset if a threat is realized. Safeguards add controls to mitigate risks, such as locks or firewalls. Vulnerabilities are weaknesses or flaws in a system, and risk is the probability of an attack or negative event.

58. **Answer: A** Management controls develop policies. Logical and technical controls support technology such as firewalls, switches, and so on. Operational and physical controls support day-to-day activities such as security guards, grounds security, and so on.

59. **Answer: C** Guidelines are informal recommendations that do not have to be followed. Policies are generated by management and are mandatory. Procedures are step-by-step instructions, and standards detail metrics that should be met.

60. **Answer: B** Since Kei's team has decided not to locate their business in a dangerous area, they are avoiding the risk. Mitigation would be building the business and then adding 8-**foot** (**ft**)-tall barbed wire fences around the building. When they purchase insurance on the building, they will be transferring that risk to the insurance company. Any leftover risk, they will accept.

61. **Answer: B** The security life cycle for products and software starts with idea planning, then putting together the requirements, designing an item based on the requirements, and then developing the item based on the design. Testing ensures that the item functions correctly. Now that the item has passed testing, it can be moved into production. Once the item reaches the **end of life** (**EOL**), it is disposed of securely.

62. **Answer: A** PCI-DSS requires firewalls, encryption, antivirus software, physical restrictions, regular testing, and more to protect cardholder data.

63. **Answer: C** The REP signed by employees waives their privacy rights at the organization. Employee monitoring has to be work-related—that is, only work-related conversations can be monitored, not personal conversations. Monitoring must also be consistent (all staff, not just Vania).

64. **Answer: D** PHI is details about an individual's medical records. HIPAA makes healthcare providers use due care for patients' PHI. HITECH states that if healthcare providers properly protect PHI, they do not have to report breaches to HHS.

65. **Answer: B** Credit card issues are managed under PCI-DSS merchant contract agreements. RMS Foods may launch an internal investigation to fire and file criminal charges for the staff that conducted the theft, but the CEO does not face criminal charges for such incidents. NIST, ISO, and GDPR do not direct credit card merchant agreements.

66. **Answer: A** Boris is transferring the risk when asking for assistance from a contractor or other third party. The relationship with the contractor will be finalized with a working agreement. Risk acceptance is when Boris accepts the risk of the project not being completed on time. Risk division is not a proper risk response. Risk avoidance is if Boris decided not to continue with the project.

67. **Answer: B** Trade-secret lawyers help their clients protect trade secrets with licensing agreements, NDAs, and NCAs. Unlike patents, copyrights, and trademarks, trade secrets are not registered with governments.

68. **Answer: C** Since Bjorn heard evidence of the threat through a third party, this is considered hearsay and is normally inconclusive and inadmissible in court. The best evidence rule holds that an original document is the best evidence, not a copy, assuming the original is accessible.

69. **Answer: A** Auditors make sure security policies are followed. Audit reports go to senior management. The CISO sets policy and assigns responsibilities. Managers generally design and implement policy. Data owners make certain security classification levels are properly set.

70. **Answer: D** A SIEM system and an IDS can collect plenty of records regarding an incident, but these can be compromised. Evidence handling is also very important in the case of court prosecution or insurance investigations, but the policy is the most important because it explains how the teams should respond to an incident and which procedures should be followed.

71. **Answer: D** With the checklist test, groups review checklists on their own and follow up with changes later. A tabletop test is a *walkthrough* where no live changes are made to any systems. A parallel test interrupts the DR environment, but primary systems remain untouched. A full interruption *interrupts* the primary site to test the backup site. A full interruption event can cause a real disaster event but is the most thorough test.

72. **Answer: B** Since Simona is in the military, she will use top-secret, secret, confidential, and unclassified. Most corporate environments use confidential, private, sensitive, and public. Classified is generally considered any data that is not unclassified, including top-secret or secret.

73. **Answer: C** In this case, Andre is the data subject, or who the data is about. A data owner is a party liable for the protection of the data—in this case, Pyramid Grocer. A data custodian is responsible for protecting the data—for example, Azure or Amazon Cloud. A data auditor verifies that security policies are being followed on any PII.

74. **Answer: D** An NDA is the only administrative control listed here. Security guards and fencing help prevent data leaks but are physical controls. A DLP mitigates data leaks, but this is a technical control.

75. **Answer: A** Fuzz-testing applications load tons of random input into fields—for example, the name, address, phone number, and so on. Input validation mitigates fuzz testing, throwing away invalid input. Malware is software installed on a system to harm functionality. DoS is an attack on the network or memory to make a system unusable.

76. **Answer: C** Privilege creep occurs as individuals move from department to department and administrators neglect to remove their old privileges. Least privilege occurs when privileges are removed, leaving the user with the *least privileges needed to do their jobs*. Collusion is when two or more people work together and commit fraud against an organization, mitigating SoD.

77. **Answer: B** Usernames are for identification purposes only, combined with a password for authentication. A retinal scanner, palm vein scanner, and a CAC are used for both identification and authentication.

78. **Answer: B** Billie performs risk mitigation to take proper steps before negative events occur. A risk assessment identifies potential events and prioritization of assets. Risk acceptance is risk allowed after mitigations are in place. Risk avoidance is deciding not to take on an activity or purchase an asset.

79. **Answer: D** An AUP states practice users must agree to access the organization's network or internet. For best security, all users must accept the AUP.

80. **Answer: B** Alpha and beta services are for testing new customer features that users might enjoy, but could go away if enough users don't like them. Financial credits, covered services, and SLOs are all part of SLAs.

81. **Answer: C** Non-repudiation is a method whereby the sender of an email cannot dispute their authorship. Hashing and encryption are used as part of this process but alone are not non-repudiation. A fingerprint might help on a physical document, depending on the process.

82. **Answer: B** Everyone within an organization needs security education. Threats such as malware come through computers, and anyone can leave a door open that allows an attacker to enter the building.

83. **Answer: C** The employment candidate-screening process or policy includes conducting background checks, drug screenings, lie-detector screening, interviewing of neighbors, fingerprinting, and so on, depending on the job.

84. **Answer: B** NCAs are legal agreements, but in most cases are unenforceable because workers need to earn an income on what they have been trained in.

85. **Answer: A** HR understands the policies best for proper provisioning and deprovisioning of staff, and can handle it with the lowest risk of litigation. Other departments may be involved to provide data for the termination, but HR is in charge.

86. **Answer: A** Since Daniil worked the last week, he does not have to return the paycheck. All of the other items are corporate-owned and must be returned.

87. **Answer: A** Sunk costs are expenditures that cannot be recovered. An item the organization has purchased—for example, a computer—is an asset, but not an expense. Trademarks and other intellectual property are also assets, even though they are intangible. Staff are also assets.

88. **Answer: C** Risk is the likelihood a threat will exploit a vulnerability and cause harm to some asset. Safeguards protect assets from threats. Exposure is the degree of asset loss endangerment due to threats. A breach occurs when security has been compromised.

89. **Answer: D** The biggest threat to organizations is internal threats that develop from disgruntled employees. All of the others are threats and can cause a lot of damage and expensive recoveries, but because internal threats have white-box knowledge of the organization, they are the biggest threat.

90. **Answer: D** Do not use firms that bring risk to zero because they are working with firms that do no business, as there is no such thing as zero risks. Risk assessment and analysis involve determining scope, categorizing assets, and bringing risks to acceptable levels.

91. **Answer: B** The following values get used in quantitative risk analysis. SLE = AV * EF. The ARO is the frequency a risk occurs in a year. The ALE = the ARO * SLE.

92. **Answer: A** Qualitative risk analysis depends less on hard calculations such as quantitative risk, and more on rankings and judgment.

93. **Answer: C** The NIST SP *800-37* provides guidance on using the RMF for federal systems. The steps include categorizing the asset, selecting controls, implementing controls, assessing controls, authorizing assets, and monitoring controls.

94. **Answer: A** Once risk reaches an acceptable level, no other mitigations need to be applied.

95. **Answer: D** According to Thycotic Engineering, the remembering and changing of passwords is the number 1 source of cyber fatigue. To ease this fatigue, implement 2FA, autofill, and simpler password rules. Learn more here: `https://www.cisco.com/c/en/us/products/security/ciso-benchmark-report-2020.html`.

96. **Answer: D** Although all of the others are true, working around the central IT department is referred to as shadow IT.

97. **Answer: C** A **zero trust architecture** (**ZTA**) trusts no one, verifying inside and outside traffic before connecting to the network or any of the systems.

98. **Answer: B** Education leads to some type of a degree such as a Bachelor or Master. Training is target-focused on specific knowledge or a specific job. Awareness is a minimal understanding of security issues. BOAF sessions generally occur at conferences where people with similar backgrounds exchange knowledge and ideas.

99. **Answer: A** The military is one exception where secret data could be more important than people. Others might argue the Star Trek defense, where *the many (lives) outweigh the few.*

100. **Answer: D** A DRP is only executed if at first, the BCP fails. Checking the fuse box or contacting the electric company might be the first steps of the BCP, but always follow the plan first.

2
Asset Security Domain 2 Practice Questions

Questions from the following topics are included in this domain:

- Identifying and classifying assets
- Provisioning resources securely
- Managing the data lifecycle
- Security controls and compliance
- Asset management
- Data protection methods

To pass the CISSP exam, you have to score high in the Asset Security domain. Domain two has a 10 percent weighting in the exam and requires you to understand asset management, data classification, asset classification, and to look at the big picture when it comes to data security and compliance. Keeping assets and data secure is of great importance.

Proper classification and implementation of assets assures they get the level of protection required. This is especially important when dealing with customer and user privacy.

Understanding asset handling and defensible destruction is also important for domain two. Knowing this domain puts you in the driver's seat, and a step closer to passing the exam.

Questions

1. Filip installs and integrates a nondiscretionary system. Which access control policy gets enforced?

    A. Physical

    B. Mandatory

    C. Role-based

    D. Rule-based

2. Anett has decided to use a passphrase instead of a dictionary-word password for better security. Her new password converts into _____?

    A. The strongest password

    B. A virtual password

    C. An unusual password

    D. A username

3. Hubert desires the best and most expensive security protection for his firm. Which of the following does he select?

    A. Passwords

    B. Smart cards

    C. Palm vein scanner

    D. Fingerprint reader

4. A control category that reacts after an incident is called:

    A. Corrective

    B. Directive

    C. Preventative

    D. Deterrent

5. Alison is a security manager charged with investigating a recent breach into the corporate network. What control category does this fall under?

    A. Retroactive

    B. Investigatory

    C. Preventative

    D. Detective

6. Reilly is performing a security audit for a customer and finds several cases where users gained access to data without a formal access approval procedure. Reilly recommends a formal access approval process to fix the issue. Which role should he list that approves policies for users to gain access to data?

    A. Data processor

    B. Data custodian

    C. Data subject

    D. Data owner

7. Yulia is setting up an IDS that is rule-based. A rule-based IDS does/contains which of the following?

    A. Recognizes new types of attacks

    B. Can recognize patterns and multiple activities

    C. IF statements

    D. Protocol recognition outside normal settings

8. Passive entities that subjects access are called what? (Choose the *BEST* answer)

    A. Objects

    B. Computers

    C. Processes

    D. Files

9. When it comes to providing a user with access to resources, the step that follows authentication is called?

    A. Identification

    B. Authorization

    C. Accounting

    D. Credentialization

10. Marin is the manager of the quality department and uses his RFID card to access the building, and later uses the same card to access his office. This would be considered which type of control?

    A. Physical

    B. Technical

    C. Operational

    D. Management

11. Karolina needs to add 2FA to her social networking account so that she can chat with her friends and keep them up to date on what she is doing. Adding 2FA would require her to combine her password with what?

    A. Smartphone authenticator

    B. Birthday

    C. Mother's maiden name

    D. PIN

12. David, a writer for *RMS Publishing*, read his emails and opened an attachment to help him find a lost package. Later that week, he discovered his bank account no longer had money, and he was locked out of several social networking accounts. What *MOST LIKELY* occurred?

    A. Phishing attack

    B. Cross-site scripting attack

    C. Cross-site request forgery attack

    D. Malware in the attachment downloaded passwords from his password manager

13. Dayana is a CISO putting together the password policy for her organization and wants to assure users follow the policy, and don't find workarounds. Which of the following is her *MOST SECURE* choice?

    A. Minimum 12-character password with uppercase, lowercase, numbers, and special characters

    B. Minimum 16-character passphrases

    C. Minimum 8-character password

    D. 4-digit PIN

14. Identity management systems maintain user authentication information. Which of the following are two types of identity management systems? (Choose two)

    A. LDAP

    B. AD

    C. DC

    D. DN

15. An SSO system is characterized by which of the following options?

    A. Provides multiple usernames and passwords to access resources

    B. Provides a single username with various passwords to access resources

    C. Provides a single username and password to access each system

    D. Provides a single username and password to access the entire network

16. When an employee or contractor leaves the company, which of the following steps is the least important?

    A. Return the corporate phone to the organization

    B. Return their corporate identification card to the organization

    C. Return desk nameplate to the organization

    D. Deprovision their username and password from all systems

17. Albert logs into an airline website to purchase a plane ticket for a cross-country flight. The site offers him the ability to also rent a car from a separate company without having to provide a new login name and password. What is this process called?

    A. Identity management

    B. Provisioning

    C. Single sign-on

    D. Federation

18. What do the best performing biometric authentication systems have?

    A. Low crossover error rate

    B. The greatest type I error rate

    C. The least type II error rate

    D. High crossover error rate

19. After a user's thumbprint has been enrolled for future authentication, what does their print get stored as?

    A. Image of their thumbprint

    B. Hash

    C. Password

    D. Electronic image

20. Which of the following options is a non-technical method to obtain a user's password?

    A. Eavesdropping

    B. Dumpster diving

    C. Social engineering

    D. Impersonating tech support

21. Nadia is a security administrator tasked with finding users with weak passwords. Which attack would she attempt *FIRST* as part of this security audit?

    A. Rainbow tables

    B. Birthday

    C. Dictionary

    D. Brute force

22. Lorenzo has been transferred from the marketing department to sales. Six months earlier he worked in the finance department. Which risk should be *MOST* considered?

    A. Non-disclosure agreement

    B. Non-compete agreement

    C. Need to know

    D. Authorization creep

23. Which SSO system uses secret keys, principals, and tickets?

    A. Kerberos

    B. SESAME

    C. LDAP

    D. NDS

24. Sam, a security manager, is considering Kerberos as his single sign-on system for the organization. He knows the system is very secure but wants to also learn its weaknesses. Which of the following is he *NOT* concerned with?

    A. Brute-force attacks against the keys

    B. Keys temporarily sit on users' computers, which are prone to attack

    C. Asymmetric keys are vulnerable to attackers

    D. If the KDC goes down, users will not have access

25. Diskless computers with lots of memory and fast CPUs that obtain their operating system and data from a centralized server are called what?

    A. Thick clients

    B. Distributed computing

    C. Backup servers

    D. Thin clients

26. Qiang is a systems administrator charged with implementing security containers on her systems. These will be divided into top-secret, secret, confidential, and unclassified. Which type of system is she implementing?

    A. DAC

    B. MAC

    C. Rule-BAC

    D. NDAC

27. Which of the following is *NOT* an SSO system?

    A. CIRCUMFERENCE

    B. RADIUS

    C. DIAMETER

    D. Kerberos

28. Ekaterina is an air force captain and has top-secret access to all objects, including submarines. A review shows that since she is not in the Navy, she does not need access to ship and submarine details. What is this enforcing?

    A. Least privilege

    B. Need to know

    C. Single sign-on

    D. Federation

29. Donna learned on Linux systems that passwords are stored in a file called /etc/shadow. She uses the sudo command to view the contents of the file, and although she sees her username, she does not see her password. This is because?

    A. Passwords are kept within the /etc/passwd file

    B. A hash representation of her password is displayed

    C. Passwords are kept within the /etc/password file

    D. Passwords are kept within the SAM file

30. Miomir needs to tighten security access into the server room and wants to add three-factor authentication. Which two should he combine along with a swipe card to enter the room? (Choose two)

    A. Authenticator

    B. OTP

    C. Retina scan

    D. PIN

31. Which of the following access control models prioritizes availability over confidentiality and integrity, so that owners of their files determine the authorizations of their objects?

    A. Rule-BAC

    B. Role-BAC

    C. MAC

    D. DAC

32. Jordan adds the following to a file:

    ```
    Allow MAC Address 35:35:43:ab:ac:1b
    Deny All
    ```

    This is an example of what?

    A. Rule-based access control

    B. Role-based access control

    C. Non-discretionary access control

    D. Discretionary access control

33. Svetlana's security manager asks her to provide data as to whether they should stay on their RADIUS AAA server or move to TACACS. What are two differences between TACACS and RADIUS? (Choose two)

    A. TACACS encrypts all the data. RADIUS encrypts the password only.

    B. TACACS encrypts all the data. RADIUS encrypts the username and password only.

    C. TACACS transmits data via TCP, and RADIUS transmits data via UDP.

    D. TACACS transmits data via UDP, and RADIUS transmits data via TCP.

34. Which of the following is *NOT* a physical access control type?

    A. 8-foot fencing

    B. Data backups

    C. Security-awareness training

    D. Network segregation

35. Which of the following are examples of deterrent control functions? (Choose two)

    A. Fake security cameras

    B. Secure hiring practices

    C. Guard dogs

    D. Security cameras

36. Which of the following are examples of recovery control functions? (Choose two)

    A. Separation of duties

    B. Data backup tapes

    C. Offsite facility

    D. Locks

37. Which of the following are examples of administrative controls? (Choose two)

    A. Non-disclosure agreement

    B. Dress code policy

    C. Firewall rules

    D. Painted parking lot lines

38. Aljaz, a security engineer, is tasked with finding and installing a device that monitors network activities. Which of the following does he recommend?

    A. Intrusion detection system

    B. Intrusion prevention system

    C. Data loss prevention

    D. Proxy server

39. Magda, a security engineer, has been tasked with lowering the threshold of monitoring activities as part of her seeking to discover an external threat. What is one of the *FIRST* things she notices?

    A. The threat made itself visible

    B. The system performance reduces

    C. The logging tables take longer to fill up

    D. False positives decrease

40. Which of the following are examples of technical control types? (Choose two)

    A. Change control

    B. Motion alarm

    C. Antivirus

    D. Encryption

41. Feliciano, a security engineer, is given the task of assuring log files cannot be scrubbed by attackers. Which of the following is the *BEST* solution to mitigate data loss from log files?

    A. Save logging data in the cloud

    B. Save logging data to backup tapes

    C. Save logging data to WORM media

    D. Save logging data to hard drives

42. Barbara is a junior administrator given privileges to manage printers and hard drives. She is not given the privilege to manage networks and users. This is an example of enforcing which practice?

    A. Mandatory access control

    B. Need to know

    C. Separation of duties

    D. Least privilege

43. Tommy is a senior system administrator looking to mitigate external threats against his Unix and Linux systems. What is the *BEST* feature to implement to mitigate brute-force attacks?

    A. Encrypt the hard drive

    B. Hash passwords using SHA-256

    C. Implement stronger password policies

    D. Change the root login name to `roto-root3r`

44. A USB drive is found lying on the floor near a user's desk who only has access to unclassified documents. By default, we should assume this drive to have what clearance?

    A. Top secret

    B. Secret

    C. Classified

    D. Unclassified

45. Tempest equipment is used to mitigate which of the following?

    A. Ship damage due to storms

    B. Building damage due to storms

    C. Electromagnetic emissions

    D. Electronic fires

46. Some switches have an extra port for a NIDS called the switch port analyzer or SPAN port. This allows the NIDS to monitor the traffic on the network using mirrored data, also known as which mode?

    A. Monitor

    B. Promiscuous

    C. Audit

    D. Accounting

47. This type of IDS learns what is normal for the environment, and triggers events when outside of these profiles. What is this *BEST* described as?

    A. Rule-based IDS

    B. Stateful IDS

    C. Signature-based IDS

    D. Anomaly-based IDS

48. Which of the following is a good example of a tablet's antivirus?

    A. HIPS

    B. HIDS

    C. NIDS

    D. NIPS

49. Saisai's supervisor, the security manager, has asked her to install a device to attract hackers so that they can analyze current and upcoming attacks. Saisai recommends installing which of the following devices?

    A. Honeypot

    B. Bastion host

    C. DMZ

    D. Website

50. Lucas is a hacker at a coffee shop who uses a network sniffing device called Pineapple to monitor network traffic, copy password hashes, and download session IDs. This would *BEST* be known as what type of attack?

    A. Phishing

    B. Spoofing

    C. MITM

    D. Sniffing

51. Shuai is an attacker monitoring the network traffic of users accessing their bank accounts. She sniffs for passwords, and will use them as part of which type of attack?

    A. Social engineering

    B. Rainbow attack

    C. Replay attack

    D. Brute-force attack

52. Which statement is true about federated identity management (FIM)?

    A. A transportable ID obtained when connected with dialup access

    B. A transportable ID used to access different services within an organization

    C. A transportable ID used across different organizations' computer systems

    D. A transportable ID used to keep domain identities consistent

53. DLP is the securing and protection of data that does which of the following?

    A. Enters the organization from users

    B. Could be leaked from the organization

    C. Could be inserted by hackers

    D. Is entering the organization from managers

54. The compilation and derivation of data from databases is called which of the following?

    A. Aggregation and inference

    B. Compilation and derivation

    C. Compiling and deriving

    D. Certification and accreditation

55. Marton is the CEO of *Generic Smartphones* and is holding an emergency meeting with the CISO because their new unpublished phone designs were just published on the internet. He asks the CISO what more can be done since they already have an EDLP solution?

    A. Upgrade and enhance the EDLP solution

    B. Encrypt all hard drives

    C. Encrypt all network traffic

    D. Deploy an NDLP solution

56. Veronika has completed the business year balance sheets, and the financial records are no longer needed since the taxes were recently filed. What should she do with the records next?

    A. Archive the records

    B. Destroy the records

    C. Use the records for the next business year

    D. Share the records with the tax preparer

57. Which of the following is considered defensible destruction of data? (Choose two)

    A. Clearing

    B. Curie destruction

    C. SSD Cypto erase

    D. Wiping and encryption

58. Steven, a user with classified access, finds a thumb drive left on a table in the break room. What is his next step?

    A. Connect it to a sandboxed, air-gapped computer for analysis

    B. Announce the lost thumb drive as lost on the corporate social networking site

    C. Take it to the security team for evaluation

    D. Immediately destroy the thumb drive

59. Jelena, a security administrator, alerts her manager to unencrypted data that's accessible to their customers and prospects. Why does her manager request she leave it unencrypted?

    A. The data is labeled sensitive

    B. The data is labeled confidential

    C. The data is labeled public

    D. The data is labeled top secret

60. Krishnan is a junior systems administrator hired to protect user data. His manager states he is allowed to perform data backups on the west systems, but not the east systems. Which of the following is the *MOST LIKELY* reason for this?

    A. He is new to the job and needs more experience

    B. The east systems are top secret, and his access is only classified

    C. This is a cost-cutting measure, and allows the company to save money

    D. It is not necessary to back up systems labeled sensitive but unclassified

61. David-Michael runs the *RMS hospital* in Cleveland. Randigreg is the owner/operator of *SGI Medical Billing*, a supplier to the *RMS hospital*. *SGI Medical Billing* was attacked by overseas hackers, and the *RMS hospital's* records were stolen. Which organization is legally accountable for the data breach?

    A. SGI Medical Billing because they are the data owners

    B. The RMS hospital because they are the data custodians

    C. SGI Medical Billing because they are the data custodians

    D. The RMS hospital because they are data owners

62. Which of the following would an organization hire to be responsible for policies around PII and PHI?

    A. Chief security officer

    B. Chief information security officer

    C. Chief executive officer

    D. Chief privacy officer

63. Which of the following members of the staff are responsible for the implementation of security controls?

    A. Security administrator

    B. Systems administrator

    C. Chief security officer

    D. Chief information security officer

64. Pablo is hired every few months to verify and validate that security controls are in place and functioning as they should. Which of the following is likely to be his job title?

    A. Analyst

    B. Auditor

    C. Quality control

    D. Quality assurance

65. Shivani finds web traffic log files over 20 years old. The retention policy is to defensibly destroy web traffic log data over 7 years old. Which is her *BEST* strategy?

    A. Save the data for best security

    B. Overwrite the 20+-year-old data with zeros

    C. Mechanically shred and melt the hard drives with the 20+-year-old data

    D. Overwrite the 20+-year-old data with zeros three times and encrypt

66. Data that resides on a hard drive, solid-state drive, optical disk, or magnetic tape, is also known as what?

    A. Data in use

    B. Data in motion

    C. Data at rest

    D. Data on disk

67. Kristina is securing the internet of staff working from home by installing VPNs for the users. What would this protect and secure?

    A. Data in motion

    B. Data at rest

    C. Data in use

    D. Data in a network

68. A social engineering attack where the hacker gains PII from garbage is known as?

    A. Garbage dumpster

    B. Dumpster diving

    C. Garbage picking

    D. Dumpster pull

69. Virtual private networks connected from home to office have an extra layer of protection that encrypts the internet address headers, as well as the messages. What is this type of encryption called?

    A. Header encryption

    B. Meta encryption

    C. End-to-end encryption

    D. Link encryption

70. Jeremy is a systems administrator that secures data by backing it up to magnetic tapes. After backing up the data, he labels the tapes and stores them in a room with restricted access. What is the *BEST* next step he should take to secure the data?

    A. Encrypt the data on the backup tapes

    B. Verify the data on the backup tapes

    C. Make duplicate backups on WORM drives

    D. Make a duplicate backup to cloud-based servers

71. What is the *BEST* way for an organization to protect corporate mobile devices such as smartphones, tablets, and laptop computers?

    A. Password protection

    B. MDM policy

    C. Disable location for photos

    D. Encrypt all data

72. Marie is finished with her development project. After backing up the important data, her drive will be wiped for reuse on another project. Which mode of data erasure will she use?

    A. Erasing

    B. Purging

    C. Clearing

    D. Destruction

73. Backup media should avoid which of these environments? (Choose two)

    A. Basement

    B. Office space

    C. Magnetics

    D. High temperature

74. Polona, a systems administrator is investigating performance issues and verified that log files exist to help resolve slowness issues. What is her next step?

    A. Validation

    B. Verification

    C. Processing

    D. Testing

75. Dominik, a security manager, creates a naming system for various data depending on security needs. What is this process called?

    A. Categorization

    B. Classification

    C. Prioritization

    D. Enumeration

76. Frances is following up on several Data Subject Requests (DSRs) and is charged with updating the records for these customers. What is his data role?

    A. Data subject

    B. Data controller

    C. Data owner

    D. Data steward

77. Ankita is president of *SUN Mail Order Services* and is a vendor to firms that need bulk letters sent to their clients. According to GDPR, what is *SUN Mail Order Services BEST* considered as?

    A. Data custodian

    B. Data processor

    C. Data controller

    D. Data steward

78. Large United States companies that do not offer data subjects the *right to be forgotten* may not do which of the following?

    A. Operate anywhere in the world due to OECD

    B. Conduct business with European clientele due to GDPR

    C. Operate in the USA due to OECD

    D. Operate in the UAE

79. The Organization of Economic Cooperation and Development has classified _____ principles to ensure PII is secured?

    A. 6

    B. 7

    C. 8

    D. 9

80. Fiona, a security manager, is putting together a minimum level of requirements for specific levels of classifications. These are also known as what?

    A. References

    B. Maximum requirements

    C. Baselines

    D. Minimum requirements

81. The NIST Risk Management Framework is also known as?

    A. SP 800-37

    B. SP 800-53

    C. SP 800-60

    D. SP 800-94

82. Alize, a security engineer is setting up Wi-Fi hotspots across her organization. These are older devices that provided WEP. After a security firmware upgrade, which level of security should these be set up with?

    A. WEP

    B. WPA

    C. WPA2

    D. WPA3

83. Corentin, a systems administrator, received notification that several systems he supports will reach EOL in 12 months. What is the biggest risk to his organization?

    A. Insider threats

    B. Newer systems may not support the applications

    C. Exposure on the network

    D. No more security firmware upgrades

84. Iga needs an asset inventory system to help track hardware and software assets, as well as system updates and upgrades. Which of the following systems would assist her *BEST*?

    A. SYSLOG

    B. CMDB

    C. SIEM

    D. NESSUS

85. A company that provides cloud security features such as defining and monitoring cloud risks and security is known as what?

    A. Cloud provider

    B. CASB

    C. SAAS

    D. Private cloud

86. Agent-based CASBs inspect which of the following data?

    A. Organizational data only

    B. Personal data only

    C. Both organizational and personal data

    D. Lower-privileged data only

87. Which of the following is *NOT* a trait of DRM?

    A. Product keys

    B. Watermarking

    C. Automatic failover

    D. Copy restriction

88. Many social networking sites such as WhatsApp protect communications with _____ to secure conversations from hackers.

   A. End-to-end encryption

   B. Link encryption

   C. Data in motion

   D. Data in use

89. The Center for Strategic and International Studies (CSIS) has defined 20 critical security controls. Which of the following options is *NOT* included in the top 5?

   A. Offense informs defense

   B. Boundary defense

   C. Metrics

   D. Automation

90. Which of the following is *NOT* one of the Generally Accepted Security Principles?

   A. Prevent, detect, respond, recover

   B. External systems are assumed to be insecure

   C. Auditability and accountability

   D. HSM for every computer

91. Juan, a security manager, decides to use the United States Government Configuration Baseline system, but needs to remove some of the options because they do not fit with his environment. This is also known as what?

   A. Tailoring

   B. Scoping

   C. Fine-tuning

   D. Baselining

92. Which OECD principle states that user data may not be shared with outside companies?

   A. Collection limitation principle

   B. Use limitation principle

   C. Individual participation principle

   D. Accountability principle

93. Which role is responsible for documenting data, such as ownership and protection policies, and how it will be secured?

    A. Data custodian

    B. Data steward

    C. Data owner

    D. Data subject

94. What must be done after an asset is identified and classified?

    A. Archived

    B. Monitored

    C. Secured

    D. Recovered

95. Which of the following is *NOT* an asset?

    A. Bot

    B. Trademark

    C. Copyright

    D. Staff

96. Ricardas has completed the asset inventory for his department and has assigned owners to the assets. What is his *BEST* next step?

    A. Handle assets based on classification

    B. Classify the assets based on value

    C. Protect assets based on classification

    D. Review and assess assets

97. Amos, a security manager is notified that sketches of new car designs have made their way onto the internet and have been posted online. His worksite has no computers or other technology. What is his *BEST* next step?

    A. Enable encryption

    B. Deploy a firewall

    C. Install dummy cameras

    D. Implement a clean desk policy

98. Some safes have the capability of detecting heat changes, for example, from the tools used to break in. What is this feature known as?

    A. Passive relocking

    B. Thermal relocking

    C. Glass relocking

    D. Fire safe

99. The Guidelines for Media Sanitization, which describe the best practices to thwart data remanence, are also known as what?

    A. NIST SP 800-53

    B. NIST SP 800-88

    C. NIST SP 800-122

    D. NIST SP 800-137

100. Caroline needs to destroy sensitive data from her printed emails. What is the *BEST* way for her to defensibly destroy it?

    A. Standard shredder

    B. Crosscut shred

    C. Crosscut shred and burn

    D. Discard into the trash

Quick Answer Key

1. C	16. C	31. D	46. B	61. D	76. D	91. B
2. B	17. D	32. A	47. D	62. D	77. B	92. B
3. C	18. A	33. AC	48. A	63. A	78. B	93. C
4. A	19. B	34. C	49. A	64. B	79. C	94. C
5. D	20. C	35. AD	50. C	65. C	80. C	95. A
6. D	21. C	36. BC	51. C	66. C	81. A	96. B
7. C	22. D	37. AB	52. C	67. A	82. B	97. D
8. A	23. A	38. A	53. B	68. B	83. D	98. B
9. B	24. C	39. B	54. A	69. D	84. B	99. B
10. B	25. D	40. CD	55. D	70. B	85. B	100. C
11. A	26. B	41. C	56. A	71. B	86. C	
12. D	27. A	42. D	57. BC	72. C	87. C	
13. B	28. B	43. D	58. C	73. CD	88. A	
14. AB	29. B	44. A	59. C	74. A	89. B	
15. D	30. CD	45. C	60. B	75. B	90. D	

Answers with explanations

1. **Answer: C** Role-based models are created implicitly by **Non-Discretionary Access Control** (**NDAC**) systems, in that the users inherit their privileges from within the role. Mandatory access control puts data into containers, for example, *Top Secret*, *Secret*, and so on. Rule-based access control is defined by specific rules such as denying an IP address or allowing a MAC address. *Physical* is a control type, not a policy.

2. **Answer: B** Most systems today convert the password (or biometric) into a hash or some *representation* of a password so that if the system gets hacked, the attacker only has password hashes (garble) instead of actual passwords. The hash acts as a virtual password because its value authenticates the user, not the password itself. Reference: https://www.semanticscholar.org/paper/A-Virtual-Password-Scheme-to-Protect-Passwords-Lei-Xiao/341eead2eb9c56c61918dd2446018e071711e4f5

3. **Answer: C** Vascular scanners observe and capture vein patterns of palms and fingers. The biometric scan gets converted into a hash. Passwords are the least expensive, and not as secure as vascular systems. Fingerprint readers are not as secure, and not as expensive as vascular systems. Smart cards are not as secure as vascular scanners.

4. **Answer: A** Directives such as signs, deterrent controls such as fake cameras, or preventatives such as fences are designed to stop an incident, but once an incident occurs, such as a fire, a corrective control will attempt to mitigate the effects after the incident; for example, releasing water sprinklers to stop the fire.

5. **Answer: D** Preventative controls react to stop an incident. Since there was a breach, these have failed where detective controls activate. Retroactive and investigatory are not control categories.

6. **Answer: D** Data owners are responsible for allowing access to data they own. Data owners approve access policies, and then operations implement them. Data subjects are individuals whose privacy information is being saved. Data custodians maintain and protect data, and data processors process the data in use with mailing lists or email blasts.

7. **Answer: C** A rules-based **Intrusion Detection System (IDS)** uses rules to evaluate whether packets are allowed or denied. For example, if MAC address `33:44:11:aa:bb:cc` is permitted to access the network, those packets will be allowed. Pattern recognition, attack recognition, and protocol recognition are characteristics of signature-based or anomaly-based systems.

8. **Answer: A** Computers, processes, files, hard drives, printers, and so on, are different types of objects that can be accessed by subjects. Subjects include people and processes.

9. **Answer: B** The process of providing resources to users is when the user provides their credentials. This includes identification and authentication. After the user has access, they are provided with enough authorization to do their job. Finally, accounting is used to monitor and log user activity for debugging purposes.

10. **Answer: B** Although Marin is accessing the physical building, and physical office, he is using a technical or logical control to authenticate. Physical controls are items such as fences and emergency water sprinklers. Operational and management controls include contracts and policies, such as non-disclosure agreements.

11. **Answer: A Two-factor authentication (2FA)** asks for two different types of verification. Verification types include something you know, such as a password or PIN, something you have, such as a swipe card or one-time password token, or something you are (biometric), such as a fingerprint or iris scan. Combining a password with a birthday, maiden name, or PIN is only one type of authentication (something you know), so thereby does not qualify as 2FA.

12. **Answer: D** Although what initiated the attack was a phishing email, the attached malware downloaded David's password manager. Cross-site scripting and cross-site request forgery could both steal session keys from the user if currently logged into his bank account, but the question does not state he was currently logged in, added to the fact that other accounts were tampered with.

13. **Answer: B** For best password security, passwords must first be long, then complex because most brute-force tools start with shorter passwords, and then slowly get longer. Passphrases are easily accepted by users because they allow sentences they will remember and include the special character *space*. The policy can be made stronger by adding a numeral requirement. Once the CISO defines the policy, this is enforced administratively via the employee agreement, and technologically with systems such as **Pluggable Authentication Modules (PAMs)**, or **Active Directory (AD)** group policies. References: `https://www.sans.org/security-awareness-training/ouch-newsletter/2017/passphrases`

    `https://www.grc.com/haystack.htm`

    `https://www.nist.gov/blogs/taking-measure/easy-ways-build-better-p5w0rd`

14. **Answer: A, B Lightweight Directory Access Protocol (LDAP)** is open source **Identity Management (IdM)**, and **Active Directory (AD)** is a Microsoft-only IdM tool. Part of AD is a **Domain Controller (DC)**, which contains the identity database. **Distinguished Names (DNs)** are a way that entities are defined within LDAP, such as first name, last name, phone, and so on.

15. **Answer: D** A **Single Sign-On (SSO)** system allows a user to access network resources with one login name and password, easing usability. Using a single username and password to access each system requires the user to log in and log out of one system and into another to access new resources. SSO does not require leaving one resource, such as email, to access another, such as a shared file server.

16. **Answer: C** The desk nameplate displays the user's name and often job title, but is not a means of access to the firm, because guards are required to see a corporate ID card to grant access, not a desk nameplate. For best security during the exit interview, the organization must collect the corporate phone, laptop, identification card, and desk nameplate from the exiting staff because this could be used in a social engineering attack, but it is the *least* important of these. System administrators must remove their account(s) from the network.

17. **Answer: D** When the user's authentication credentials are transferred seamlessly to another company, this is called federation. SSO allows a user to access multiple resources or objects on their organization's network. Provisioning is the process of setting up a new user's corporate credentials. Identity management is a general term that includes SSO, provisioning, deprovisioning, and federation.

18. **Answer: A** Crossover error rate is defined where type I errors and type II errors are equal. The lowest crossover error rate device currently is a retinal scan.

19. **Answer: B** Biometric images are converted to hashes so that if a hacker exploits the passwords, they will only obtain representations of the biometrics and not the real images.

20. **Answer: C** Eavesdropping (listening to conversations), dumpster diving (digging through physical trash for information), and impersonation are all social engineering attacks that can be used to reveal a user's password.

21. **Answer: C** The weakest passwords that users implement, and the simplest for hackers to exploit, come from the dictionary. The birthday attack uses probability and statistics to narrow down passwords from a list of possible passwords. Rainbow tables are lists of hashes and their passwords. Brute-force attacks would be the final attack option, as they check for every possible pattern.

22. **Answer: D** The **Non-Disclosure Agreement** (**NDA**) is signed when Lorenzo joins the company. The non-compete is signed when Lorenzo leaves the company. Need to know provides Lorenzo with only the authorizations necessary to do his job. Authorization creep occurs as Lorenzo moves from department to department, and the rights and privileges from previous departments are not removed.

23. **Answer: A** Kerberos uses a **key-distribution center** (**KDC**) to grant tickets to users for services to use, such as email or file sharing. The system's security comes from not passing passwords over networks, making them harder to attack. **SESAME** is a SSO service that uses asymmetric keys and certificates to authenticate users into the network. LDAP and NDS are both directory services that keep track of users' identities, such as phone numbers, addresses, and emails.

24. **Answer: C** Kerberos only uses symmetric keys called session keys and secret keys as part of the system. Provide redundancy with the KDC to mitigate it being a single point of failure. Make certain to use long keys to resist brute-force attacks. Protect the network from hackers by assuring security patches are installed as needed.

25. **Answer: D** Thick clients and backup servers have hard drives. Thin clients can be used for distributed computing, but the question asked is what type of computer this is, not what can it be used for.

26. **Answer: B Mandatory Access Control** (**MAC**) allows users with specific clearances, such as secret, to access files in containers marked secret, confidential, and unclassified. **Discretionary Access Control** (**DAC**) allows users to set authorizations of files they own, as desired. **Role-based Access Control** (**RBAC**) is used within firewalls. NDAC is the same as role-based access control, where authorizations are defined by a user's job or position in the organization.

27. **Answer: A** SSO allows a user access and authorizations for all of the resources on the network with a single username and password. SSO systems include RADIUS, DIAMETER, Kerberos, TACACS, TACACS+, and more.

28. **Answer: B** Need to know is similar to least privilege but contains the user's rights based on their role. SSO grants a user access to the network with a single username and password. Federation grants a user additional services based on relationships with the primary vendor, that is, the user logs into the bank, and then the user's credentials are federated to the check printing company without having to enter them again.

29. **Answer: B** Usernames and user IDs are part of the /etc/passwd file on Linux systems, and within the SAM file on a Microsoft Windows system. There is no such file as the /etc/password file.

30. **Answer: C, D** For three-factor authentication, Miomir needs to provide something you have, with something you know, and something you are type authentications. Smartphone authenticators and **One-Time Passwords** (**OTP**) are both something-you-have type devices and would not qualify. Retina scans and PINs finalize the authentication with something you are, and something you know, respectively.

31. **Answer: D Discretionary Access Control** (**DAC**) allows users to set authorizations on their data at their discretion; usually used within corporate environments where access to information is prioritized. **Mandatory Access Control** (**MAC**) prioritizes confidentiality over availability and integrity so that once files are stored in the *Top Secret* bin, only those with that clearance can access the file. Role-BAC is defined by the user's job title, and rule-BAC is used within firewalls and routers.

32. **Answer: A** Rules such as allowing a MAC address or denying an IP address are found in firewalls, routers, and switches where access is allowed or denied with single-line entries. Role-based access control (RBAC) and NDAC are the same in that group, for example, junior administrators have rights to add hard drives, but not to configure networks. DAC allows users to set rights per their discretion.

33. **Answer: A, C** TACACS is an improvement over the older RADIUS, which even offers dial-in access. TACACS can separate authentication, authorization, and accounting, whereas RADIUS combines authentication and authorization.

34. **Answer: C** Training is an administrative control. Examples of technical access controls include network access rules, encryption, system logging, and monitoring.

35. **Answer: A, D** Security cameras are both a deterrent, discouraging attacks, and detective control functions, which help to identify attacks. Other control functions include compensating, which provides an alternative backup control, such as an online, replicated backup system, and directive control functions, which inform, for example, a "beware of the dog" sign.

36. **Answer: B, C** Recovery control functions attempt to bring systems back to normal operations. Locks and separation of duties are examples of preventative control functions, which help to stop an incident from occurring. Another control function is corrective, which fixes issues after an incident, such as antivirus protection.

37. **Answer: A, B** Policies and agreements are administrative controls because they are developed by management. Firewall rules are an example of technical controls. Painted parking lines are an example of a physical control.

38. **Answer: A** An **intrusion detection system (IDS)** is a detective access control type device that identifies activities. An **Intrusion Prevention System (IPS)** and **Data Loss Prevention (DLP)** are preventative access control type devices that block incidents. IPS blocks incoming traffic, and DLP blocks outgoing traffic, usually from insider threats desiring to leak corporate secrets. A proxy server is simply a go-between for message passing, often designed to hide original IP addresses or help with traffic management.

39. **Answer: B** Lowering the threshold for monitoring increases the alerts, so false positives will increase (that is, false alarms), and logging tables will fill up more quickly. The increased monitoring might eventually uncover the threat, but that will take more time.

40. **Answer: C, D** Change control is an administrative control type, which is the process for evaluating and the prioritization of change within an organization, answering, for example, whether the word processing software should be updated, or should a new badging process be implemented. A motion alarm is a physical control.

41. **Answer: C** Write-once, read-many media mitigates loss or alteration of data saved to it. Other forms such as cloud, hard drives, and tape can be modified.

42. **Answer: D** In this example, Barbara is given only the privileges she needs to do her job. The separation-of-duties policy does not come into play here because she installs and tests the printers and hard drives and does not leave that to another party. Need to know has to do with rights to view documents, and mandatory access control contains levels of top-secret, secret, and confidential access to documents.

43. **Answer: D** Changing the root user's name to some unknown name makes it harder for attackers to break into Linux or UNIX systems because attackers know that the administrator account is named `root`. When the account is renamed, attackers are attempting their brute-force attack on `root`, an account that no longer exists. The other options harden the system but will not mitigate brute-force attacks.

44. **Answer: A** When a user finds unmarked media, it is assumed to be top secret.

45. **Answer: C** Electromagnetic emissions can be converted back to data and must be blocked at the source to maintain confidentiality.

46. **Answer: B** Tools such as Wireshark monitor network activity on a computer. Wireshark requires mirrored traffic, and this is done using a packet capture utility, or PCAP. Some systems for Windows and Linux include `libpcap`, `WinPcap`, and `Npcap`.

47. **Answer: D** Signature-based and rule-based IDS cannot identify new attacks or *zero days* like an anomaly-based IDS because either their signature or rules need to be updated. Anomaly-based IDS can also compare protocols outside what is normally used or identify unusual network activity patterns.

48. **Answer: A** Since a tablet is an endpoint device, antivirus is a host-based intrusion prevention system, preventing known viruses from being installed onto the system. Antivirus on a firewall would be network-based intrusion prevention. Detection devices only report, and do not block.

49. **Answer: A** A honeypot is designed to attract and distract hackers. Be careful not to harm a hacker's system with this device because *hackback* is against the law. A bastion host is a computer stripped of all utility so that it can perform one job, such as a firewall, mail server, and so on. A demilitarized zone separates a corporate website from the organization's internal network.

50. **Answer: C** This is best known as a **man-in-the-middle** attack since he is technically in between the users and the services they are connecting to. He is using sniffing to conduct this attack. Spoofing would mean that he is attempting to imitate one of the servers that the user is connecting to. Phishing is a spoofed email, usually containing a link or attachment with a payload.

51. **Answer: C** Shuai is collecting and saving passwords for later abuse of the users' accounts by entering their passwords or password hashes. Mitigations include encryption and session IDs. Brute-force attacks would attempt to use every password. Rainbow attacks would attempt to authenticate with various password hashes. Social engineering is a non-technical attack, tricking user's into giving their passwords.

52. **Answer: C** Federation is used in systems to make customer experiences smoother, allowing users to authenticate with their bank, for example, and then automatically *federate* their identity to the check printing company, making it unnecessary to re-authenticate. A system that uses identities within dial-up is called RADIUS. Kerberos uses tickets to access different services within an organization, and domains are used within Microsoft Windows systems.

53. **Answer: B** Data loss prevention (data leak prevention) are tools and controls put in place to prevent confidential information from leaving the organization. For example, many government accounts do not allow the use of thumb drives and will disable USB ports to reduce the risk of attackers *leaking* data onto their thumb drives and taking it home.

54. **Answer: A** When there are large pools of data, such as big data, the compilation of the information is known as aggregation. Deriving private information from the data pool is inference; for example, being able to narrow down the suspect of a crime because his relatives provided DNA to researchers. Certification is verifying that a product will function in an organization. Accreditation is management approval to use the product.

55. **Answer: D** Upgrading and enhancing the **Endpoint Data Leak Prevention** (**EDLP**) system could help, but they already have a solution in place. The next best step is to deploy **Network Data Leak Prevention** (**NDLP**). Encryption will not help as much with data leaks because these are the result of insider attacks.

56. **Answer: A** Financial records can only be used for the business year in which they occur, and the tax preparer already has a copy of the records since they were filed. Destruction of the records would harm the organization if there was an audit, so it is best that she archives the records. Once the records exceed a compliance period, for example, 7 years, they can be destroyed.

57. **Answer: B, C** Clearing, wiping, and encryption can recover data with advanced techniques. Curie destruction melts a hard drive at the Curie temperature. Crypto-erase is a NIST-approved standard for the defensible destruction of SSD drives.

58. **Answer: C** Since the thumb drive is not labeled, Steven must assume the highest level of data security, which in this case is top secret.

59. **Answer: C** Public data, or what military organizations deem as unclassified, is the least protected data in the enterprise. Top-secret data receives the highest level of protection, encrypting the data using AES, for example.

60. **Answer: B** When taking the CISSP exam, seek answers that point to security-related issues. In this case, users that do not have the proper clearance are not allowed to protect data outside of their level of clearance. Data marked sensitive but unclassified must be backed up.

61. **Answer: D** When there is a data breach, the data owner is accountable for any legal issues due to the breach. The data owner could sue their suppliers as needed, but to the data subjects of the **Personal Health Information** (**PHI**), the owner is accountable. In this case, SGI Medical Billing is the data custodian.

62. **Answer: D** **Personal Identifiable Information** (**PII**), and **Personal Health Information** (**PHI**), and risks around those are managed by the **Chief Privacy Officer** (**CPO**). The Chief Security Officer creates policy around the types of mechanisms to use to maintain security. The CISO focuses on controls around information (data) security. The CEO's main concerns are sales and marketing.

63. **Answer: A** The security administrator handles the implementation and maintenance of security controls. The systems administrator manages computer uptime and access control. The **Chief Security Officer (CSO)** and **Chief Information Security Officer (CISO)** create policies that security administrators and systems administrators must follow.

64. **Answer: B** An auditor assures the firm meets its policies and complies with laws and regulations. Analysts function to review data and run statistical comparisons. Quality assurance validates that manufactured items meet specifications, and quality control verifies that manufactured items function normally when in the customers' hands.

65. **Answer: C** Defensible destruction assures there is no way to recover the information. Data that resides after its retention policy puts organizations at risk if there is a legal discovery request for this information. Sometimes having the data could make the organization liable in certain prosecutorial situations.

66. **Answer: C** Data on disk is the incorrect terminology for data states. Data in motion is traveling through a network. Data in use is data being processed on the central processing unit, or on the computer screen.

67. **Answer: A** Data in a network is incorrect terminology for data states. Virtual private networks encrypt traffic and headers from home to office, allowing workers to work remotely in a secure manner. Data at rest sits on a hard drive, and data in use is being processed on a CPU and RAM.

68. **Answer: B** Garbage dumpster, garbage picking, and dumpster pull are all distractors.

69. **Answer: D** End-to-end encryption encrypts messages only, but not the headers. Header and meta encryption are both distractors.

70. **Answer: B** If the backup tapes are blank, encrypting, duplicating, or relocating backups with nothing saved will be useless when restoring data after a disaster. Remember, availability is a security component of **CIA (confidentiality, integrity, and availability)**. **Write Once, Read Many (WORM)** media includes CD-ROM and DVD-ROM drives. Also, encryption occurs *during* the backup process, so the next **best** step is to verify the backup is complete.

71. **Answer: B** A mobile-device management policy requires staff to implement encryption, add passwords, disable the location feature on photos, never leave the device unattended, use cable locks for laptops, use hardening with malware protection, and more.

72. **Answer: C** Clearing is done for the reuse of hard drives within the organization. Purging, which includes degaussing, or a minimum of seven overwrites allows a drive to be reused when selling or donating equipment. Destruction destroys the media, such as with use from hard drive shredding or melting. Erasing is a type of clearing, and clearing is the proper terminology.

73. **Answer: C, D** Magnetics, high temperatures, and high humidity can harm backup tapes. Basements and office space are fine as long as they are secure and maintain proper temperature and humidity.

74. **Answer: A** Polona seeing that the log files exist is verification. Assuring that the log files contain data to resolve the performance issues is validation. Processing already occurred as the log files contain the recorded information of the events. Testing occurs after analysis and resolutions are made to the system.

75. **Answer: B** Classification names data groups or classes, such as top secret, secret, confidential, and so on. Categorization sorts the data into these security classes. Prioritization is the process of defining which is most important to accomplish in project management. Enumeration follows information gathering and reconnaissance steps of penetration testing where targets are named.

76. **Answer: D** The data steward is responsible for the data content. The subject is the user that the **personally identifiable information** (**PII**) is about. The data owner (the organization) is legally accountable for any data loss, and the controller (an individual) works directly for the organization.

77. **Answer: B** The data processor utilizes the data for the data owner or data controller. The data steward is responsible for the internal data integrity, and the data custodian is responsible for data backups.

78. **Answer: B General Data Protection Regulation** (**GDPR**) is similar to the **Organization for Economic Cooperation and Development** (**OECD**), except they also add the right to be forgotten. The USA and UAE do not follow the GDPR principles but do follow the OECD when working with private data.

79. **Answer: C** The principles include collection limitation, data quality, purpose specification, use limitation, security safeguards, openness, individual participation, and accountability.

80. **Answer: C** Baselines are minimum levels of protection used as a reference to evaluate security effectiveness.

81. **Answer: A** The other NIST standards posed in the question are:

    NIST Special Publication 800-53 – Security and Privacy Controls for Federal Information Systems and Organizations

    NIST SP 800-60 – Guide to Mapping Types of Information and Information Systems to Security Categories

    NIST SP 800-94 – Guide to Intrusion Detection and Prevention Systems

82. **Answer: B** Older systems that supported WEP can only be updated to WPA with a firmware update because they both use the symmetric RC4 encryption algorithm. WPA2 and WPA3 use AES symmetric encryption.

83. **Answer: D** The biggest security risk is the lack of security updates. The other risks will be there whether or not security updates are applied, but the lack of security support is the worst in this case.

84. **Answer: B** A **Configuration Management Database** (**CMDB**) tracks inventory and modifications for the entire organization. **Security Information and Event Management** (**SIEM**) tracks syslogs and accounting data for the entire organization's network. Nessus is a vulnerability management scanning tool.

85. **Answer: B** A CASB is placed between the organization and the cloud provider to enforce security policies, and comply with legal, contractual, and regulatory requirements. A cloud provider that provides the application is offering a **Software as a Service** (**SaaS**) implementation. If the service is only for that client, they will be on a private cloud.

86. **Answer: C** An Agentless CASB inspects organizational data only, and not personal data. An API-only CASB manages security with APIs. Multi-mode CASBs offer management and security.

87. **Answer: C** Other **Digital Rights Management** (**DRM**) traits include limited install activations, persistent online authentication, encryption, anti-tampering, and regional lockout. Automatic failover is unrelated to DRM but is a server feature so that when one computer fails, another boots up automatically to take its place.

88. **Answer: A** End-to-end encryption does not encrypt IP address headers like link encryption, so metadata on conversations is not protected. Data in motion and data in use is not secured by default; encryption still needs to be applied to secure it.

89. **Answer: B** Also, in the top 5 are prioritization and continuous monitoring. Boundary defense, data protection, and data recovery capability are all parts of the top 20.

90. **Answer: D Hardware Security Modules (HSMs)** save and maintain encryption keys on computers. Although this is important, this would be a procedure and not a principle. The other principles include information system security objectives, protection of information while being processed, in transit, and in storage, and resilience for critical information systems.

91. **Answer: B** Scoping is removing security considerations that do not apply to the environment. Tailoring is adding considerations that are specific to the environment. Baselines are the security starting point, and fine-tuning a specification includes both tailoring and scoping.

92. **Answer: B** Collection limitation states a firm collects the minimum PII required. Individual participation states a data subject can get a report of their PII. The accountability principle means the data controller is accountable for any data breach issues.

93. **Answer: C** The data owner also documents compliance requirements, intellectual property rights, and protection policies of the data. The data subject is who the PII is about, such as their address, phone number, and/or IP address. The data steward is responsible for day-to-day data quality. The data custodian is responsible for the safe transport and storage of data.

94. **Answer: C** The data lifecycle steps are identify and classify, secure, monitor, recover, disposition, archive, and defensible destruction.

95. **Answer: A** A bot is a compromised computer used as part of **Distributed Denial of Service (DDoS)**. The others are all assets. An asset can be tangible or intangible.

96. **Answer: B** The asset classification process starts with inventory, then assigning ownership, classifying based on value, protecting and handling based on classification, and finally assessing and reviewing.

97. **Answer: D** Since the area has no technology, encryption and firewalls will not help the data leak. Dummy cameras might discourage visitors from taking pictures of drawings, but drawings put away at night or when not being used is the best mitigation in this case.

98. **Answer: B** Glass relocking is a type of passive relocking that engages another bolt within the safe so that it cannot open if an attacker is tampering with it. A fire safe protects items within the safe in the event of a fire.

99. **Answer: B** The other NIST standards have the following meanings:

    NIST 800-53: Security and Privacy Controls for Federal Information Systems and Organizations

    NIST 800-122: Guide to Protecting the Confidentiality of PII

    NIST 800-137: **Information Security Continuous Monitoring (ISCM)** for Federal Information Systems and Organizations

100. **Answer: C** Crosscut shredding and burning the printed documents is the best way to mitigate dumpster diving..

3
Security Architecture and Engineering Domain 3 Practice Questions

Questions from the following topics are included in this domain:

- Research and manage secure design principles
- Understand fundamental security models
- Select and determine cryptographic solutions
- Understand cryptanalytic attacks
- Apply security principles to the facility
- Design facility security controls

To pass the CISSP exam, you have to score high in the Security Architecture and Engineering domain. Domain 3 has a 13% weighting on the exam and requires you to understand the engineering and design of servers, databases, embedded devices, and the **Internet of Things** (**IoT**), and know how to mitigate risks on such devices and systems.

Practice questions for domain 3 include understanding security models such as **Biba**, **Bell-LaPadula**, and **Clark-Wilson**. Also, important concepts covered on the exam include privacy by design, zero-trust, and defense in depth.

After studying these practice questions, you will be prepared to pass the Security Architecture and Engineering section of the exam, including the important scenarios on cryptography, encryption, and facility design and security.

Questions

1. The architecture for a secure network has several stakeholders. These include who?

   A. Company suppliers

   B. System operators

   C. Software developers

   D. Anyone concerned with the functionality or usability of the system

2. Computers add multiple CPUs to improve performance. These systems are called what?

   A. Multiprocessing computers

   B. Multi-CPU computers

   C. Multithreaded computers

   D. Multiheaded computers

3. After powering on a computer, it eventually boots the Linux operating system. Which of the following loads the kernel?

   A. BIOS

   B. MBR

   C. UEFI

   D. USER

4. A device that resides on computer motherboards to manage cryptographic keys and passwords is called what?

    A. MBR

    B. HSM

    C. TCG

    D. TPM

5. The primary difference between RAM and ROM is what?

    A. RAM data cannot be altered; ROM data can be altered.

    B. RAM loses data when powered off; ROM retains data when powered off.

    C. RAM has stored programs pre-loaded onto it; ROM comes stripped of programs.

    D. RAM retains data when powered off; ROM loses data when powered off.

6. Cameron, a software developer, creates an application in the C language allowing users to enter their name and address. Which of the following is his primary concern?

    A. Potential for buffer overflow attacks.

    B. Potential of users having malware.

    C. Users spelling their names incorrectly.

    D. Software will be used on systems without C compilers.

7. Jill, a software developer, creates software using the C language, and has entries for users to enter their phone number and email address. What is her *BEST* mitigation for buffer overflow attacks?

    A. Malware protection

    B. Input validation

    C. Host-based firewall

    D. Optimizing the compiler

8. Which computer security technique randomly and continuously repositions an application's data in memory to mitigate buffer overflows?

   A. EPROM

   B. SRAM

   C. DRAM

   D. ASLR

9. Laslo, a software developer, implements the garbage collector service to resolve which of the following?

   A. Dumpster diving

   B. Memory leaks

   C. Spam emails

   D. Data deduplication

10. Shelby and Stefano, system administrators, are changing passwords for multiple users at the same time. What facilitates this process so that the system does not deadlock attempting to access the same configuration file at the same time?

    A. Hard drive driver

    B. Operating system

    C. Central processing unit

    D. Random access memory

11. Heather, a systems technician, is examining two systems. SystemA has four CPUs and SystemB has one CPU with four cores. Which one has the MOST CPUs?

    A. SystemA.

    B. SystemB.

    C. SystemB has more CPUs, but only by 1.

    D. They both have the same number of CPUs.

12. A computer is running a process that starts to use all of the available RAM on the system. Once the RAM fills up with data, the system will do what? (Choose 2)

    A. Page some of the data to the PAGEFILE.

    B. Perform a graceful shutdown.

    C. Page some of the data to swap space.

    D. Kill the offending program.

13. Gosia, a software developer, is creating a driving simulator. To make her job easier, she acquires a library of cars and trucks recommended to her by a newsgroup. A week later, an overseas hacker is detected on her computer. What *MOST LIKELY* happened?

    A. The DLL or shared object had a back door.

    B. The malware protection was not updated.

    C. The system was air gapped.

    D. The application is written in the C language.

14. Heather, a systems administrator, following PCI-DSS requirements encrypts all credit card information on the hard drive. A breach of the system is discovered, and over 10,000 customer credit card details are stolen. What is the *MOST LIKELY* cause?

    A. The hacker downloaded the credit card information from the hard drive.

    B. The hacker downloaded the credit card details while processing in RAM.

    C. The hacker downloaded the credit card details while traveling across the internet.

    D. The hacker tricked the customers into providing their credit card numbers.

15. Jannik, a senior engineer, runs a lab, and several hard drives were stolen. The drives were swap space drives. What is Jannik's primary concern?

    A. Whether they can be replaced with the exact same model.

    B. Whether the backup tapes were validated.

    C. The hard drives were expensive.

    D. Data that resides in swap space is unencrypted.

16. When viewing the protection rings of a computer system, which two are true?

    A. Applications run at ring 2.

    B. Applications run at ring 3.

    C. The kernel is at ring 1.

    D. The kernel is at ring 0.

17. Danielle is a software developer porting her app to a new watch that measures blood pressure using the API provided by the watch manufacturer. A few weeks later, the support line at her company is bombarded with calls stating that the app is tracking locations. What *MOST LIKELY* is the problem?

    A. The API is programmed with built-in spyware.

    B. The customers' watches are buggy.

    C. The customers did not disable location tracking.

    D. The complaining customers' blood pressure is outside the range of the watch.

18. Software running at which level has full access to hardware and other system resources?

    A. Application

    B. Kernel

    C. User

    D. Driver

19. Which of the following is not an advantage of virtual machines?

    A. Multiple operating systems can exist on the same computer.

    B. Isolation from other virtual machines.

    C. Snapshot capability.

    D. Networking is only available in bridged mode.

20. Jiri, a systems administrator, upgraded the containers for his software developers. The developers complain that their code now runs much slower. What is Jiri's *BEST* next step?

    A. Upgrade the compiler.

    B. Roll back to the previous state.

    C. Apply the tested patches.

    D. Open the application's port on the firewall.

21. Bud is a black hat hacker seeking to corrupt several virtual machines on a public cloud model. Which is the *BEST* technical attack for him to run?

    A. Cloudburst

    B. Phishing

    C. Cross-site scripting

    D. SQL injection

22. Jiri has confidential-level access to documents on the system. When he attempts to access files with secret access, he is denied. Which model does this *BEST* represent?

    A. DAC

    B. MAC

    C. RBAC

    D. NDAC

23. Computer system features such as unified extensible firmware interface, GUID partition table, UUID, SELinux, and trusted platform module are a part of which security feature?

    A. BIOS

    B. EFI

    C. MBR

    D. TCB

24. The control that enforces policy over a subject's (user or process) ability to interact with objects (files or systems) is known as the what?

    A. Referee

    B. Reference monitor

    C. Biba

    D. Access control system

25. Anna is an internal threat that works for *SNU Corp* seeking to exfiltrate drawings and designs of their upcoming computers. She uses an encrypted tunnel over port 80. What type of attack is this?

    A. Covert channel

    B. Encrypted tunnel

    C. SSH-over-HTTP

    D. Telnet-over-HTTP

26. Which security model is also known as the Chinese Wall and monitors conflicts of interests?

    A. Graham-Denning

    B. Brewer-Nash

    C. Clark-Wilson

    D. Harrison-Ruzzo-Ullman

27. Which of the following systems requires strict identity verification for every subject accessing resources over a network?

    A. Identity management

    B. Identity and access management

    C. Castle-and-moat

    D. Zero-trust architecture

28. Joao is a security engineer that just successfully completed the certification process for firewalls he has reviewed. What step should he take next?

    A. Schedule installation of firewalls.

    B. Submit the device for accreditation.

    C. Install a few firewalls as part of a beta test.

    D. Immediately install all of the firewalls for best security.

29. Jessica is a security auditor that receives her email online from a cloud provider and uses social media to communicate with her supervisor. Which cloud model is she *MOST LIKELY* using?

    A. SaaS

    B. PaaS

    C. IaaS

    D. NaaS

30. What type of attack could occur when implementing shared folders in a virtual machine environment?

    A. Data leak

    B. Data loss

    C. Virtual machine escape

    D. Cloudburst

31. What is the framework that uses seven evaluation assurance levels to help evaluate the security of technology devices?

    A. Evaluation Assurance

    B. United Labs

    C. Common Criteria

    D. Functional Testing

32. Databases use four transaction properties to guarantee data validity. Which of the following is *NOT* one of these data validity properties?

    A. Aggregation

    B. Consistency

    C. Isolation

    D. Durability

33. A firewall self-detects that it is faulty. Based on the programming, the device "decides" to shut down, and allow no traffic. This is an example of which type of failure mode?

    A. Fail up

    B. Fail secure

    C. Fail open

    D. Fail down

34. Websites generally reside in the corporation's demilitarized zone (DMZ), which does not offer the same level of security as the corporate local area network (LAN). What additional component can be added to better secure the website?

    A. WPA2 encryption

    B. Database

    C. Screened subnet

    D. WAF

35. Bernarda is a chief information security officer and is working with the board of directors on securing the business from possible issues with employee smartphones. What is her *FIRST* step?

    A. Enable the location setting on smartphones in case an emergency wipe is needed.

    B. Develop and release an employee smartphone policy.

    C. Install malware protection on all employee smartphones.

    D. Require all employees to put passwords on their phones.

36. Which of the following security models is designed with confidentiality as its priority?

A. Bell-LaPadula

B. Clark-Wilson

C. Graham-Denning

D. Biba

37. Computer components that are signed, consistently monitor integrity and confidentiality, and consist of *rings of protection* are called what?

A. Memory protection

B. Trusted components

C. Hard drive encryption

D. Process encapsulation

38. What is the strong-star property rule that is part of the Bell-LaPadula security model?

A. An object with the same clearance as the subject can read and write to the subject.

B. A subject with the same clearance as an object cannot modify or read the object.

C. A subject with the same clearance as an object can only read the object.

D. A subject with the same clearance as an object can read and write to the object.

39. Patricia is a security manager investigating the best models to use for their next automated teller machine (ATM) design. Which of the following would be her *BEST* choice?

A. Graham-Denning

B. Biba

C. Clark-Wilson

D. Bell-LaPadula

40. Rosemary, a security manager, has log files in her home directory that her team needs immediate access to. She sets the privilege so that her team can read the files. What access model does this *BEST* represent?

    A. DAC

    B. MAC

    C. ABAC

    D. RBAC

41. Vasek is a hacker looking to pass a message discreetly to a system he has attacked. The *BEST* way for him to accomplish this is with which channel?

    A. Override channel

    B. Timing channel

    C. Supra channel

    D. Secret channel

42. Roger is the president of Action Shots and shoots photos at sporting events. He sells his pictures for hundreds of dollars. After installing a new fish tank, his company is hacked, and all of the photos are stolen. What *MOST LIKELY* happened?

    A. The fish tank thermometer is connected to the corporate network.

    B. The fish tank thermometer is not encrypted.

    C. There is no authentication on the fish tank thermometer.

    D. Poor IoT security practices.

43. Judy encrypts the message GOLD HERE for Carolyn. Carolyn receives MWLI CMOM, which is an example of what?

    A. Plaintext

    B. Ciphertext

    C. Asymmetric

    D. Diffusion

44. Erving creates a cipher where every *A* is the letter *G*, *B* is the letter *J*, *C* is the letter *B*, and so on. This is also known as what? (Choose 2)

    A. Encryption

    B. Key

    C. Cryptovariable

    D. Decryption

45. Mikael is a hacker that desires to launch an attack with the least technology possible. Which is the *MOST* likely attack that he performs?

    A. Social engineering

    B. Spam

    C. Trojan horse

    D. Phishing

46. Of the following encryption methods, which system is the *MOST DIFFICULT* to crack?

    A. Caesar

    B. One-time pad

    C. Vigenère

    D. Null cipher

47. Which encryption standard is vulnerable to a meet-in-the-middle attack?

    A. 0DES

    B. 1DES

    C. 2DES

    D. 3DES

48. Royal, a security manager, considers what would be the best setup for biometric controls. Which is he likely *NOT* to choose?

    A. Retinal scan

    B. Height and weight

    C. Fingerprint

    D. Voice

49. Thomas, a security engineer, is passing values from one system to another, but only after the data has been XORed. What result does he get by XORing the following two values? *11001110* and *10111010*

    A. 11111110

    B. 01110100

    C. 10001011

    D. 10001010

50. Nicole, a systems administrator and data custodian, seeks the best option to store backup tapes. Which of the following does she choose?

    A. Fireproof safe within the SOC

    B. Lower level of the SOC facility

    C. Offsite facility that is climate controlled

    D. A cool, dry location

51. Edward is a software developer creating applications for Windows, Linux, and Apple. Which cloud model will he *MOST LIKELY* use for programming projects?

    A. SaaS

    B. PaaS

    C. IaaS

    D. NaaS

52. Cheryl is a junior systems administrator given rights that standard users do not have, such as the ability to add and remove printers and hard drives. Senior systems administrators can also add and remove networks, which Cheryl is not allowed to do. What model does this *BEST* represent?

    A. RBAC

    B. MAC

    C. DAC

    D. NDAC

53. Cheng is a security controls buyer seeking products that perform method testing and design. Which assurance level is he selecting?

    A. EAL7

    B. EAL4

    C. EAL2

    D. EAL1

54. Pierre is a detective with the police department and has collected DNA data of an incident but cannot find a match in any police database. He decides to use a worldwide DNA database and is able to narrow down suspects because of 70% matches. Which two processes did he use?

    A. Durability

    B. Inference

    C. Consistency

    D. Aggregation

55. Radu, a security engineer, sends a secret, encrypted message to another security engineer named Katerina. Katerina will decrypt the message using which key?

    A. Radu's private key

    B. Her private key

    C. Her public key

    D. Radu's public key

56. Biniyam is a black hat hacker with access to password hashes. He runs a *collision attack* for which purpose?

    A. To attempt to find a value that creates the same hash

    B. To uncover the private key

    C. To determine the user's exact passwords

    D. To break the hash into multiple parts

57. Leon, a systems administrator, just completed backing up several servers for the organization. Which is the *BEST* way for him to verify the entire backups?

   A. Restore a few test files.

   B. Conduct full restores.

   C. Read the first 100 bytes of the tapes.

   D. Perform a tape retention.

58. Su-Wei, the chief security officer, seeks ideas to protect her facilities from cars accidentally running into them. Which of the following is the *BEST* for her to choose?

   A. Parking block

   B. Polycarbonate glass

   C. Fencing

   D. Bollards

59. Federico, a security administrator, is designing the message system for six users in his environment. What makes him decide to use symmetric key cryptography over asymmetric?

   A. Public key features

   B. Ease of scaling

   C. Speed

   D. Key strength

60. Ajla is a hacker desiring to forge email messages and make it appear that messages are signed by a trusted person. Why will this fail for her?

   A. Copying valid digital signatures to another document results in a different hash.

   B. The symmetric key must be identical.

   C. The public key must be identical.

   D. A script kiddie would have no trouble forging messages.

61. Kwon is the chief security officer of *BCN Corp.* and desires to further secure the physical perimeter. What is his *BEST* option for 24-hour monitoring of the building exterior?

    A. Intrusion detection system at the doors

    B. Cameras aimed at doors and the parking lot

    C. Four-foot fencing around the parking lot perimeter

    D. Flooding the parking lot with magnesium lighting

62. What is the difference between the DSA and RSA algorithms?

    A. DSA is used for hashing, RSA for signing.

    B. DSA is used for signing, RSA for hashing.

    C. DSA is used for encryption only; RSA is for signing and encryption.

    D. DSA is used for signing only; RSA is for signing and encryption.

63. Alison, a security engineer, investigates multiple hashing algorithms to manage the integrity of millions of her documents. What does she finally decide?

    A. MD5SUM results in fewer collisions than 3DES.

    B. SHA256 results in fewer collisions than MD5SUM.

    C. DES results in fewer collisions than MD5SUM.

    D. MD5SUM results in fewer collisions than SHA256.

64. Egor is an administrator at *VBC Corp.* and sends encrypted messages to his boss. Which keys are distributed?

    A. Public

    B. Private

    C. Passwords

    D. Encrypted

65. Several computers are running very slowly on the network. An investigation shows that the problem is malware. The malware is removed, and all systems have returned to normal operations. What is the next step in the incident management process?

    A. Response

    B. Reporting

    C. Remediation

    D. Lessons learned

66. Which antenna is commonly used for long-range and two-way connections?

    A. Multi-bay reflective

    B. Omnidirectional

    C. Dipole

    D. Yagi

67. Laura is a black hat hacker that has a stolen `shadow` file from a Linux system. What can she do with this?

    A. Attempt to unencrypt the `shadow` file.

    B. Attempt to crack the password hashes.

    C. Use the user IDs and clear passwords to attack the Linux system.

    D. Convert the `shadow` file into the `passwd` file.

68. A digital signature must have which qualities? (Choose 2)

    A. Be unique

    B. Contain letters, numbers, and special characters

    C. Be readable and legible

    D. Be easy to remember

69. Which of the following attacks can be used against an asymmetric system?

    A. Ciphertext only

    B. Known plaintext

    C. Chosen ciphertext

    D. Chosen plaintext

70. Which asymmetric system calculates keys using large prime numbers and modulo math?

    A. HMAC

    B. RC4

    C. RSA

    D. MD5

71. Mohamed emails Danielle a wedding proposal, and Danielle responds with "yes, I want to marry you." Later that day they meet, and Mohamed denies ever sending the email. How can Danielle prove that Mohamed sent the email?

    A. Non-repudiation

    B. Confidentiality

    C. Availability attack

    D. Integrity checking

72. Which hashing algorithm produces a 160-bit digest from a message with the maximum length of *(264 – 1)*?

    A. MD5

    B. SHA-1

    C. SHA-2

    D. SHA-3

73. What advantages do demilitarized zones provide?

    A. The location to build out the honeynet

    B. Allows employees to reach their home-office network

    C. Allows customers to reach the website and corporate network

    D. Allow customers to reach the website but denies them access to the corporate network

74. Encryption algorithms such as IKE, SSL, and PGP are all families of what type of cryptography?

    A. Private key

    B. Public key

    C. Personal key

    D. Pearson key

75. Arantxa, a systems administrator, seeks to start the computer management console on her Windows 10 system. Which command does she use?

    A. `compmgmt.msc`

    B. `eventvwr.msc`

    C. `perfmon.msc`

    D. `regedit.exe`

76. Aria, a data analyst, notices that Camilla's computer catches fire. Which fire extinguisher does she grab to put the fire out?

    A. Class D

    B. Class C

    C. Class B

    D. Class A

77. Mikhail is a worldwide traveler. What is his *BEST* protection for his top-secret documents carried on his first-generation smartphone in case it is lost or stolen?

    A. Eight-number PIN

    B. Swipe password

    C. Bootup password

    D. FDE

78. Lauren, a systems administrator, finds that several systems are displaying the message *Your files are encrypted. Pay us $1,000 to decrypt them.* Which is her *BEST* solution?

    A. Pay the ransom.

    B. Apply antivirus.

    C. Restore from backup tapes.

    D. Calculate the decryption key and restore data.

79. Gianluca, a security manager, follows his employees into the building without scanning his common access card. This is an example of what type of attack?

    A. Piggybacking

    B. Phishing

    C. Vishing

    D. Social engineering

80. When comparing encryption systems, asymmetric systems have which feature that is *NOT* available in symmetric systems?

    A. Encryption algorithm

    B. Non-repudiation

    C. Key

    D. Decryption algorithm

81. 3DES (triple DES) has four modes. Which mode uses three keys: two for encryption and one for decryption?

    A. DES-EDE0

    B. DES-EDE1

    C. DES-EDE2

    D. DES-EDE3

82. Thiago, a security engineer, is researching encryption algorithms for his "Wi-Fi" system. One requirement is that he uses a stream cipher. Which of the following does he select?

    A. RC6

    B. RC5

    C. RC4

    D. RC3

83. Sara, a security administrator, seeks an encryption algorithm that can be used to pass a shared key securely. Which option does she choose?

    A. Diffie-Hellman

    B. RC4

    C. MD5

    D. Blowfish

84. Which of the following asymmetric algorithms encrypts and decrypts files based on calculating logarithms?

    A. RSA

    B. ElGamal

    C. RC6

    D. AES

85. MD5 hashing is more vulnerable than SHA-1 to which attack because it has a shorter message digest?

    A. Collision

    B. Correlation

    C. Happy

    D. Birthday

86. Tim is a security administrator that manages expired encryption keys. Where will he put these expired keys?

    A. Secure key disposal

    B. Key escrow

    C. Key layaway

    D. Keychain

87. Public key certificates are defined by the X.509 standard format. Which of the following is *NOT* part of the standard?

    A. Public key

    B. Time zone

    C. Expiration date

    D. Username

88. Kristyna, a systems administrator, maintains a list of digital certificates that were revoked because they expired or were compromised before their expiration date. This list is called which of the following?

    A. PKI

    B. CA

    C. CRL

    D. RA

89. Attila, a systems administrator, enables a technique to strengthen passwords, making them harder to crack. Which feature does he engage?

    A. Injection

    B. Input validation

    C. Salting

    D. Scripting

90. Willard, an insider threat, emails top-secret, next-generation smartphone drawings hidden inside of regular-looking photos to vloggers. What technique is he using?

    A. Steganography

    B. Encryption

    C. Hashing

    D. Confusion and diffusion

91. Winter is a facility manager considering backup methods for stopping fires in the systems operation center (SOC). After selecting the proper gas system, which would be the *BEST* backup liquid system?

    A. Deluge

    B. Pre-action

    C. Wet pipe

    D. Dry pipe

92. River is a data custodian planning the backup and recovery strategy for laboratory systems. Which of the following will he consider the *LEAST* from a security perspective?

    A. Backup tape quality

    B. Restoration times

    C. Off-site storage distance

    D. Cost of the tape drive and backup tapes

93. Pedro is a system technician setting up devices to reduce noise and power spikes entering the data center. Which system provides the *BEST* filtering?

    A. Generator

    B. UPS

    C. Dual power feed

    D. PDU

94. Chantel is a network engineer assigned the task of installing wireless networks in the most secure way possible. Which of the following does she *AVOID*?

    A. Setting maximum signal strength

    B. Disabling SSID broadcast

    C. Setting WPA2 encryption

    D. Enabling MAC address filtering

95. Which of the following are true about a public key infrastructure's digital certificate? (Choose 2)

    A. Signed by the certificate issuer

    B. Contains the owner's public key

    C. Signed by the owner

    D. Contains the owner's private key

96. Larry, a marketing specialist, uses pretty good privacy (PGP) to aid in sending emails to friends. PGP contains all of the following features, *Except* for what?

    A. Encryption

    B. Signing

    C. Certificates

    D. Availability

97. Phillip creates a simple cipher where every *A* is the letter *Q*, every *B* is the letter *J*, and every *C* is the letter *W*. What type of cipher did he create?

    A. Asymmetric

    B. Diffusion

    C. Substitution

    D. Plaintext

98. The proper setup of IoTs that are refrigerators, smart speakers, televisions, alarm systems, cameras, and so on includes which of the following?

    A. Remove and replace the default login and password.

    B. Position the cameras properly and balance refrigerators properly on the floor.

    C. Make certain the devices are certified and accredited.

    D. Ensure the devices function properly (for example, TVs show TV shows and so on).

99. Within the Common Criteria, the phrase *security problem to be resolved* is also known as what?

    A. Security requirements

    B. Protection profile

    C. Evaluation assurance level

    D. Target of evaluation

100. When using the Biba security model, users not being able to write to a higher level of security is also known as what?

    A. Strong-simple integrity

    B. Simple integrity

    C. Strong-star integrity

    D. Star integrity

Quick answer key

1. D	16. B, D	31. C	46. B	61. B	76. B	91. B
2. A	17. A	32. A	47. C	62. D	77. D	92. D
3. B	18. B	33. B	48. B	63. B	78. C	93. B
4. D	19. D	34. D	49. B	64. A	79. A	94. A
5. B	20. C	35. B	50. C	65. D	80. B	95. A, B
6. A	21. A	36. A	51. B	66. D	81. D	96. D
7. B	22. B	37. B	52. A	67. B	82. C	97. C
8. D	23. D	38. D	53. B	68. A, B	83. A	98. A
9. B	24. B	39. C	54. B, D	69. C	84. B	99. B
10. B	25. A	40. A	55. B	70. C	85. D	100. D
11. D	26. B	41. B	56. A	71. A	86. B	
12. A, C	27. D	42. D	57. B	72. B	87. B	
13. A	28. B	43. B	58. D	73. D	88. C	
14. B	29. A	44. B, C	59. C	74. B	89. C	
15. D	30. C	45. A	60. A	75. A	90. A	

Answers with explanations

1. **Answer: D** Stakeholders are anyone concerned with the performance, security, and ultimate success of the system, including suppliers, developers, operators, users, and more.

2. **Answer: A** Multiprocessing systems have two, four, or more CPUs. Threading is the string of instructions from an application, and multiprocessors can improve the performance of an application by running multiple threads simultaneously. Multiheaded computers have more than one monitor.

3. **Answer: B** *Step 1.* The boot process after powering on a computer starts the BIOS, or on modern systems the UEFI, which is a *secure* BIOS that verifies drivers and devices. *Step 2.* The **master boot record** (**MBR**) is loaded from the first sector on the hard drive of legacy systems (modern systems load the GPT, or GUID Partition Table, a more secure version of the MBR). *Step 3.* The MBR selects a default Linux kernel from the bootloader, and it loads into memory. *Step 4.* The kernel calls daemon processes to start, such as an SSH server and/or web server, and a login prompt is displayed. Reference: `https://www.thegeekstuff.com/2011/02/linux-boot-process`.

4. **Answer: D** The **Trusted Platform Module** (**TPM**) is a specification developed by the **Trusted Computing Group** (**TCG**) to manage symmetric keys, digital signing, asymmetric keys, and encryption. The **hardware security module** (**HSM**) performs the functions of the TPM as a plugin device for legacy systems that are not configured with a TPM. The **master boot record** (**MBR**) contains a pointer to locate the kernel at boot time.

5. **Answer: B** Applications read and write data to **Random Access Memory** (**RAM**) as the computer operates, whereas **Read-Only Memory** (**ROM**) is write once, read many. ROM is generally used for firmware.

6. **Answer: A** Software development in the C language is prone to buffer overflow attacks when users are allowed to enter input. When an attacker successfully exploits a buffer overflow, they can download private files, or shut the system off. Malware is always a concern, but more so to the user or systems administrator. The software does not require a C compiler on the user's system, and misspelled names are a very minor concern that users can fix later.

7. **Answer: B** By validating input within the application before being processed, the program can drop suspected buffer overflow entries. Malware protection and host-based firewalls would be useful for the user or systems administrator, but not for buffer overflow attacks. Optimizing compilers would warn Jill that the application contains code prone to buffer overflows, but input validation must still be performed.

8. **Answer: D** **Address Space Layout Randomization** (**ASLR**) makes it very difficult for hackers to locate the address of the executable in memory. **Dynamic RAM** (**DRAM**), **static RAM** (**SRAM**), and **erasable programmable ROM** (**EPROM**) are types of memory where data must stay constantly refreshed, remains intact due to more transistors, and can be modifiable firmware, respectively.

9. **Answer: B** The garbage collection service searches and destroys memory leaks in RAM. Dumpster diving is a social engineering attack in which the hacker goes through trash seeking **personally identifiable information** (**PII**). Spam is unwanted email, and deduplication means *delete duplicate* files.

10. **Answer: B** Operating systems manage the time sharing and resource sharing of applications including access to the CPU, RAM, network, and hard drive. In this case, on Linux or Unix systems the file that is modified is called `/etc/shadow`, and on Windows systems, it is called `C:\WINDOWS\system32\config\SAM` (**Security Account Manager**).

11. **Answer: D** CPUs with four cores are the same as four CPUs.

12. **Answer: A and C** On Windows systems, the data will move from memory to `C:\PAGEFILE.SYS`, which is similar to swap space on a Linux system. If the PAGEFILE or swap start to fill up, the system will kill programs, usually starting with the application that is using the most memory.

13. **Answer: A** DLLs for Windows systems and shared objects for Linux/Unix systems must first be tested for security before they are used within applications. Malware protection will not uncover back doors and writing a program in the C language is fine if security protocols are followed. The system is connected to the internet and is not air gapped since the attack came from an overseas hacker.

14. **Answer: B** Data on the hard drive and network is encrypted, but data is rarely encrypted while residing on RAM or swap space. It is possible to trick over 10,000 users into providing their credit card information, but highly unlikely.

15. **Answer: D** Data in swap space is extended RAM, and is unencrypted as it is in RAM. Others may be concerns but the biggest security issue is data loss.

16. **Answer: B and D** For computer security, ring 0 represents the kernel, ring 1 is the operating system, ring 2 is where drivers operate, and ring 3 is for applications.

17. **Answer: A** Blood pressure watches do not have location tracking, so an internal threat at the supplier level added spyware within the **application programming interface** (**API**) that the developers use.

18. **Answer: B** In user mode, applications are isolated from each other as differing processes, and do not have direct access to the hardware. The kernel assists applications by monitoring and accessing RAM, disk, CPU, or the network as needed to support applications.

19. **Answer: D** Virtual machines have the ability to operate in bridged and **Network Address Translation** (**NAT**) modes. Snapshots allow system administrators to create a flash backup anytime they like, space permitting.

20. **Answer: C** Rolling back would take the developers back to a less secure state. Upgrading the compiler would still cause the code to run slowly and opening a firewall port would do nothing for this application. In this case, the new libraries have a bug that needs to be patched.

21. **Answer: A** The cloudburst attack works by having the guest machine run malicious code on the host machine that forms a communication tunnel between the two. The attacker can then control the host and other guest machines. Phishing is a non-technical attack that tricks the user into clicking a **cross-site scripting** (**XSS**) link in an email, sending the user to a vulnerable website. SQL injection is an attack on a database, usually from a web-based form.

22. **Answer: B Mandatory access control** (**MAC**) denies access to objects based on the classification level. **Discretionary access control** (**DAC**) allows individual users to set the rights to their files. **Role-based access control** (**RBAC**) sets privileges based on a person's role or position in the organization. **Non-discretionary access control** (**NDAC**) disallows users' rights to specific files and commands.

23. **Answer: D** The **trusted computing base** (**TCB**) enforces security policy using a system of hardware, software, and other controls. The BIOS has been replaced with the UEFI as a more secure boot method, for example, verifying the validity of the operating system at boot time. UEFI uses a `.EFI` file stored within the **EFI system partition** (**ESP**) for booting instructions. The **master boot record** (**MBR**) is replaced by the **GUID Partition Table** (**GPT**) allowing for drives larger than 2 terabytes.

24. **Answer: B** Biba is an access control system and type of reference monitor that enforces integrity. Referees judge contests such as sporting events, or whether research papers should be published in scholarly journals.

25. **Answer: A** Encrypted tunnels with tools such as SSH-over-HTTP and others create covert channels that allow attackers to leak data from organizations.

26. **Answer: B** Graham-Denning and Harrison-Ruzzo-Ullman are enhanced security models that monitor confidentiality, integrity, and availability. Clark-Wilson prevents unauthorized and authorized users from tampering with the system.

27. **Answer: D** Castle-and-moat assumes that users within the intranet are secure. Zero-trust requires mutual authentication from subjects and objects. These are both types of **identity management (idM)**, also known as **identity and access management (IAM)**.

28. **Answer: B** The firewalls must be accredited before they can be scheduled for installation. The change management process generally requires beta testing or piloting of new devices before they roll out into the production environment.

29. **Answer: A** The **Software as a Service (SaaS)** model allows individuals to use the service. No programming experience or knowledge of operating systems is required. **Platform as a Service (PaaS)** requires programming knowledge as the cloud provider only supports the hardware and operating system. **Infrastructure as a Service (IaaS)** requires the user to understand operating systems because the cloud provider only supports hardware. When the cloud provider supports network performance only, they are delivering **Network as a Service (NaaS)**.

30. **Answer: C** Cloudburst is another type of virtual machine escape that is an attack on system memory. Virtual machine escape can cause both data leak, where confidentiality of the data has been lost, and data loss, in which data is stolen and there is no idea where it is.

31. **Answer: C** United Labs is functional testing of electronics for home devices. The Common Criteria level EAL1 only performs functional testing. EAL7 is formally verified design and testing.

32. **Answer: A** To guarantee data validity, database transactions have ACID properties. Atomicity assures each transaction that is submitted succeeds or fails completely. Consistency ensures transactions remain valid from one state to the next. Isolation ensures transactions retain their state among the several other transactions. Durability states transactions stay committed, even if the system crashes.

33. **Answer: B** When a firewall fails open (also known as fail safe), all traffic is allowed through the firewall, including traffic from potential threats. This option is selected when uptime is of critical importance. Fail closed (also known as fail secure) blocks all traffic, leaving the environment secured but unusable until repaired. Fail up and fail down are both distractors. Reference: *Building Secure & Reliable Systems, Adkins, Beyer, Blankinship, Lewandowski, & Stubblefield, published by O'Reilly, p. 158, 2020.*

34. **Answer: D** A **web application firewall** (**WAF**) installed on a website can mitigate attacks on the website and protect the database from injection attacks, and protect the application from defacement attacks. A screened subnet is a firewall that protects the **local area network** (**LAN**) from the **wide area network** (**WAN**).

35. **Answer: B** Since Bernarda is a chief information security officer, she is mainly in charge of policy around smartphones, and not procedures such as security managers and technicians. Password policies, malware protection, and location settings will all be part of the smartphone policy.

36. **Answer: A** Biba prevents unauthorized users from tampering with the system. Clark-Wilson prevents unauthorized and authorized users from tampering with the system. Graham-Denning focuses on securely creating, deleting, and rights transfering to subjects and objects.

37. **Answer: B** Memory, hard drive, applications, security kernel, and so on make up all the pieces that are trusted components in a **trusted computing base** (**TCB**) environment.

38. **Answer: D** The simple property for Bell-LaPadula allows the subject to read data at their security level and below. The star property allows the subject to modify data that is visible at higher levels. Bell-LaPadula is designed primarily for confidentiality. Integrity and availability are at a lower priority.

39. **Answer: C** Clark-Wilson prevents tampering from both authorized and unauthorized users. Also, it maintains the consistency of transactions, such as a user can only withdraw money if they have it in their account.

40. **Answer: A Discretionary access control** (**DAC**) allows individual users to set the rights to their files. **Mandatory access control** (**MAC**) denies access to objects based on their classification level. **Role-based access control** (**RBAC**) sets privileges based on a person's role or position in the organization. **Attribute-based access control** (**ABAC**) looks at other attributes, such as user location, time, and temperature, to determine rights.

41. **Answer: B** Vasek will use a covert channel called the timing channel, which sends signals over an existing channel. The others listed here are not attack system types.

42. **Answer: D Internet of Things** (**IoT**) devices include any embedded systems that connect to the internet such as IP cameras, printers, refrigerators, and thermometers. Such devices should be secured by not using the default login and password, enable authentication, and place them on sub-networks that are not part of the production network.

43. **Answer: B** Asymmetric is an encryption algorithm that uses two keys, one public and the other private. Diffusion ciphers is a substitution type cipher where E is M one time, and another time E is R, and so on. Plaintext is the unencrypted message.

44. **Answer: B and C** Encryption and decryption are the processes of converting a plaintext message into ciphertext, and from ciphertext to plaintext, respectively; so, this only leaves **cryptovariable** as the possible answer, which is synonymous with our key ($A=G$, $B=J$, $C=B$, and so on). If someone receives the cipher BGJ, using the key or cryptovariable they can decrypt this to CAB. Reference: *85 Fundamentals of Cryptography and Encryption, R. Gove, 2007.*

45. **Answer: A** Social engineering uses tricks called spoofing where Mikael pretends to be technical support pretending to assist users but steals their passwords by simply asking for it. Spam is unwanted emails advertising both fake and legitimate goods. A trojan horse is attached to desirable software, such as a video game, but also executes malware. Phishing is emails containing deceptive links that lead to a website with malware.

46. **Answer: B** A one-time pad requires both sides to decode from the same source, for example, a book, and never encode from that sentence again. Caesar is a simple substitution cipher where A is N, B is O, and so on, and Vigenère strengthens the Caesar cipher by adding diffusion. The null cipher is hiding in plain sight, for example, "Harry is doing encryption" spells "Hide" using the first letter of each word.

47. **Answer: C Double DES (2DES)** is an improvement over DES, which was very easy to crack due to the small key size of 56 bits. But 2DES was broken soon due to the meet-in-the-middle attack where once half of the system was cracked, it was simple to crack the other half. **Triple DES (3DES)** uses three encryption steps and continues to be difficult to crack. 0DES and 1DES do not exist.

48. **Answer: B** Retinas, fingerprints, and voice patterns are unique for individuals. Height and weight vary too much and are not unique expressions of persons.

49. **Answer: B** *11111110* is the result of performing OR operations. *10001010* is the result of performing AND operations.

50. **Answer: C** Backups can be kept at the **systems operations center (SOC)** but for best security, keep a set far from the SOC in case of a disaster.

51. **Answer: B** The **Software as a Service (SaaS)** model allows individuals to use the service. No programming experience or knowledge of operating systems is required. **Platform as a Service (PaaS)** requires programming knowledge as the cloud provider only supports the hardware and operating system. **Infrastructure as a Service (IaaS)** systems are designed more so for system administrators that frequently modify and test multiple operating systems and applications, because the cloud provider only supports hardware. When the cloud provider supports network performance only, they are delivering **Network as a Service (NaaS)**. In this case, Edward purchases three PaaS systems: one Linux-based, one Windows-based, and one Apple-based. These are more economical than IaaS systems.

52. **Answer: A Role-based access control (RBAC)** sets privileges based on a person's role or position in the organization. **Mandatory access control (MAC)** denies access to objects based on the classification level. **Discretionary access control (DAC)** allows individual users to set the rights to their files. **Non-discretionary access control (NDAC)** disallows users' rights to specific files and commands.

53. **Answer: B** Under the Common Criteria framework, EAL1 is just a functional test. EAL2 is a structured test. EAL7 is the highest level of testing where the device is compared to mathematical models.

54. **Answer: B and D** Aggregation is the process of using multiple sources of data and learning content of higher value than found in either source, and inference is using the information; for example, in this case, Pierre can execute a search warrant.

55. **Answer: B** Since this is a secret message, the message is encrypted with Katerina's public key, and decrypted with her private key. If the message is an open message, it is encrypted with Radu's private key, and decrypted with his public key.

56. **Answer: A** Collisions occur when different values create the same result. Collision-resistant hashes include SHA256 and SHA512. MD5SUM is the weakest system and results in the most collisions.

57. **Answer: B** Tape retention is fast forwarding and rewinding *without* reading or writing any data. This is to make sure the tape is stabilized for a good recovery. A full restore actually recovers data and can be verified with hashing or by physical means.

58. **Answer: D** Bollards are posts that allow people to walk through, but not cars. Bulletproof glass, fencing, and parking stops might slow down cars, but are not as effective as bollards in protecting the building from being struck.

59. **Answer: C** Symmetric keys perform encryption and decryption operations hundreds of times faster than asymmetric algorithms. Asymmetric systems have stronger keys, scale better, and provide a public key and private key for each user.

60. **Answer: A** The hash of a message is encrypted with the sender's private key to confirm integrity. Digital signatures use asymmetric encryption, and are signed by the sender's private key, not public; nor is a symmetric key used. Script kiddies are beginner hackers and lack the sophistication to launch this attack.

61. **Answer: B Intrusion detection systems (IDSes)** are used to monitor network traffic, not foot traffic. Fencing and lighting help deter crime but are not monitoring systems.

62. **Answer: D** The **digital signature algorithm (DSA)** is for signing and verification only. **Rivest, Shamir, and Adleman (RSA)** is for signing, verification, message encryption, and decryption.

63. **Answer: B** Both DES and 3DES are symmetric encryption algorithms, not hashing algorithms. SHA256 results in fewer collisions, but processing time is about 10% slower than MD5SUM.

64. **Answer: A** Egor encrypts messages with the recipient's public key. Recipients decrypt the messages with their private key. It is not secure to send passwords by email, and the keys are not encrypted when sending an email, just the hash if it is a signed message.

65. **Answer: D** Response comes immediately after the Detection phase, and contacting the experts so the incident can be handled properly. Reporting is contacting the proper stakeholders, such as customer, vendors, and users. Remediation is determining the root cause of the incident, followed by Lessons Learned to grade how the incident was handled, and putting mitigations in place so it will not occur again.

66. **Answer: D** Yagi is a long-range antenna used for two-way communications. But the signal breaks down if there is any interference from a tree branch or too many clouds.

67. **Answer: B** The `/etc/shadow` file contains the hashed passwords for all users. The `/etc/passwd` file is simply the user database, containing the user IDs and the user's default shell, for example, the **Bourne Again** shell.

68. **Answer: A and B** Digital signatures created with **digital signature algorithm (DSA), Rivest, Shamir, and Adleman (RSA),** and others are numbers, letters, and special characters. Digital signatures are not GIFs, TIFFs, or JPGs of an individual's signature, but a piece of an algorithm used for digital signing and digital verification.

69. **Answer: C** With the chosen ciphertext attack, the hacker has some of the ciphertext and has access to the device that performs the decryption. With chosen plaintext, the hacker chooses the plaintext and has access to the device that performs the encryption. With known plaintext, the hacker has the plaintext and ciphertext to derive the key. With the ciphertext only attack, the hacker derives the key from only having the ciphertext only.

70. **Answer: C** RSA encryption is the only asymmetric form of encryption from the options listed. MD5 and HMAC are forms of hashing. RC4 is symmetric encryption (not asymmetric).

71. **Answer: A** Non-repudiation is the process of proving the sender sent the email by comparing the signature with the sender's public key.

72. **Answer: B** MD5 produces a 128-bit digest; because of this small size, MD5 is prone to collisions (two different inputs result in the same hash output). SHA-2 and SHA-3 produce digests from 224 bits to 512 bits.

73. **Answer: D** The **demilitarized zone (DMZ)** protects employees because they reside in a type of *employee-only* network, and customers are allowed to shop on the website store.

74. **Answer: B** Public key cryptography involves a public key that is available to anyone in the world, and a private key that is only available to that individual.

75. **Answer: A** EVENTVWR.MSC starts the log management system. PERFMON.MSC starts performance monitoring. REGEDIT.EXE starts the registry editor.

76. **Answer: B** Class C extinguishers are designed for electric-based fires. Class D extinguishers are designed for metallic fires, such as mercury. Class B extinguishers are designed for liquid fires, such as grease. Class A fires are designed for wood or paper fires.

77. **Answer: D** Since the smartphone is first-generation, secure options are minimal, such as eight-digit PINs, bootup passwords, or swiping passwords. **Full-disk encryption (FDE)** is the best option also because moving the hard drive to another phone makes it difficult to decrypt.

78. **Answer: C** Paying the ransom does not guarantee the data will be decrypted. Once decrypted, it does not guarantee that the attacker left behind malware, such as a back door. Calculating the decryption key could take years, and even if successful within an hour, there is no guarantee the attacker left malware on the systems.

79. **Answer: A** Although this is a social engineering attack, in a case such as this go with the more specific answer. Phishing attacks are spoofed links inside of emails. Vishing is spoofing tech support to trick a user into providing information.

80. **Answer: B** Symmetric systems use a single key for encryption and decryption. Asymmetric systems use a private key for decryption, and a public key for encryption. Asymmetric systems also provide signing and verification for non-repudiation.

81. **Answer: D** Options *A* and *B* do not exist, and are distractors. DES-EDE2 uses only two keys in total: one for encryption and one for decryption. DES-EEE3 uses three keys for encryption, such as encrypt with key 1, then encrypt the same packet with key 2, and encrypt the same packet again with key 3. DES-EEE2 uses two keys for encryption, that is, encrypt with key 1, then encrypt the same packet with key 2, then encrypt the same packet again with key 1.

82. **Answer: C** The other algorithms are block ciphers. RC4 is the only stream cipher.

83. **Answer: A** Key exchange is only done with asymmetric algorithms, of which Diffie-Hellman is the only one. RC4 and Blowfish are symmetric algorithms, and MD5 is a hashing algorithm used for validating file integrity.

84. **Answer: B** The RSA algorithm uses the factoring of large prime numbers for the encryption and decryption of documents. RC6 and AES are both symmetric algorithms.

85. **Answer: D** The result of a positive birthday attack is for a collision to occur even though the input values are different. Even though the value will correlate with the correct digest, there is no integrity because a different input value created the message digest. There is no known attack called happy.

86. **Answer: B** Disposing of the keys is not proper because there might be older data encrypted with those keys, so the keys go into escrow and are never used again to encrypt new data (so there is no such feature as key layaway). A keychain protects a user's passwords, and other keys in a database with a password.

87. **Answer: B** Each X.509 certificate contains many identifiers, including the name of the certificate issuer, the certificate version, and the algorithm used to sign the certificate.

88. **Answer: C** CRL is the **certificate revocation list**. The **registration authority** (**RA**) is the front-facing organization of the **certificate authority** (**CA**). The RA registers the website owners, collecting their name, address, and phone. The CA collects the website owner's public key, and signs it with the CA private key. **Public-key infrastructure** (**PKI**) defines this certification system, roles, and policies.

89. **Answer: C** When a user provides their password, a few characters get added to it, which are called *salts*. This is so that identical passwords return different hashes, making it tougher for hackers to determine the user's password.

90. **Answer: A** Steganography is hiding in plain sight, for example, hiding messages within other messages such as regular files, pictures, videos, and music.

91. **Answer: B** Pre-action systems delay water from being sprayed into the server room until certain conditions are met, for example, high temperatures. Water should only be released in the server room if absolutely necessary because it can damage computer components.

92. **Answer: D** The cost of tape drives and backup tapes is the least important security consideration.

93. **Answer: B** An uninterruptable power supply is the best device to use to clean power to the server room from the choices listed. The **power distribution unit** (**PDU**), dual power feed, and generator provide unclean power to systems.

94. **Answer: A** Setting maximum signal strength increases security risk because the wireless signal extends far beyond the building or service area. The others help to secure the wireless network.

95. **Answer: A and B** Digital certificates are signed by the certificate issuer. When someone shops at the owner's site, the signature is verified with the issuer's public key.

96. **Answer: D** Availability of messages is provided by networks and applications that operate normally. PGP also provides a web of trust and security quality.

97. **Answer: C** Asymmetric is an encryption algorithm that uses two keys, one public and the other private. Diffusion ciphers is a substitution type cipher where *A* is *Q* one time, another time *A* is *R*, and so on. Plaintext is the unencrypted message.

98. **Answer: A** Although the other options are important, remember that an exam such as the CISSP is looking for the most *secure* solution, always. So, the position of **internet of things** (**IoT**) devices is important, as well as devices within an organization being certified and accredited (approved by management). Finally, the devices must work, but securing the devices with a new login and password helps prevent theft of information such as **personally identifiable information** (**PII**).

99. **Answer: B** The protection profile defines the objectives and security requirements that the security control device should meet. The evaluation assurance level is used to show that the device met the protection profile. The target of evaluation is the security device being tested.

100. **Answer: D** Simple integrity prevents users from reading data at lower levels of security because the data may have inaccuracies.

4
Communication and Network Security Domain 4 Practice Questions

Questions from the following topics are included in this domain:

- Assess secure network design principles.

- Implement secure network design principles.

- Secure network components using network access control devices.

- Implement secure design communication channels.

- Understand data communications and virtualized networks.

Understanding security around network and communications design principles is critical to passing the CISSP exam, and you need to score well because there is a high 13% weighting on this topic.

Practice questions for domain 4 include understanding the OSI layers, the TCP/IP model, IPsec, the details of IPv4, and the basics of IPv6. The successful CISSP will know how to design, secure, and manage wired and wireless networks.

After studying these practice questions, you will be prepared to pass the communication and network security section of the exam, including the important scenarios on networking protocols, wireless networks, and content distribution networks.

Questions

1. James, a network engineer, considers using SCP for copying files from one computer to another. Which connection-oriented protocol will be used?

   A. PAP

   B. TCP

   C. UDP

   D. ICMP

2. Daria, a network engineer, seeks to set up a network that uses CSMA/CA. Which of the following should she select?

   A. Wi-Fi

   B. FDDI

   C. Ethernet

   D. Token Ring

3. Dennis, a systems engineer, is upgrading 10 fax machines. What process should he use to dispose of the old fax machines?

   A. Print the last fax, and then dump in a dumpster.

   B. Use secure destruction methods.

   C. Clear the memory buffer and then discard.

   D. Simply dump in a dumpster.

4. Melanie, a systems administrator, needs a secure, private connection from her home to the office. Which technology makes this possible for her?

   A. IPsec

   B. Encryption

C. Tunneling

D. VPN

5. Emil is a network administrator setting up systems so that when users use
    FQDN, they are converted to IP addresses. Which technology is he configuring?
    (Choose two.)

    A. HTTPD

    B. NAMED

    C. DHCPD

    D. BIND

6. Danka, a network engineer, desires to add routers that make routing decisions based
    on hop count only. Which protocol should she select?

    A. EIGRP

    B. RIP

    C. OSPF

    D. IGRP

7. Camila is a network engineer in charge of the placement of detection systems for
    her organization. What type of device does she install for this functionality?

    A. Firewall

    B. IDS

    C. IPS

    D. HIPS

8. Sugita is a network engineer installing Network Intrusion Prevention Systems
    (NIPS) in his organization. What are the two methods he should employ to detect
    incidents and attacks? (Choose two.)

    A. Host

    B. Network

    C. Heuristic

    D. Pattern matching

9. Uchiyama is a network engineer tasked with explaining to management the differences between fraggle and smurf attacks. Which of the following is his *BEST* explanation?

    A. A fraggle attack is the same as a smurf attack but sends UDP packets instead of ICMP packets.

    B. A fraggle attack is the same as a smurf attack but sends ICMP packets instead of UDP packets.

    C. A fraggle attack is the same as a smurf attack but sends TCP packets instead of UDP packets.

    D. A fraggle attack is the same as a smurf attack but sends half-open packets instead of ICMP packets.

10. Darcey, a network administrator, needs to set up a web server that allows customer access. To do this, the device sits outside of the corporate firewall. In which area should she deploy this system?

    A. Intranet

    B. DMZ

    C. Internet

    D. Honeypot

11. IPv4 allows for about 4.3 billion IP addresses to be used on computers, tablets, smartphones, cameras, thermometers, and so on. Since the world ran out of IP addresses, IPv6 is one solution that extends the address space to more than 300 trillion trillion trillion IP addresses. What other systems increase IP address utilization? (Choose two.)

    A. DAT

    B. FAT

    C. NAT

    D. PAT

12. Kirlyam is a security administrator seeking the best way to defend her organization's network against sniffing. What is the *BEST* way for her to accomplish this?

    A. Enable DHCP.

    B. Encryption.

    C. Monitor for rogue access points.

    D. Heuristic firewall.

13. Aya is a network engineer looking to implement a security protocol that operates on the OSI application layer. Which of the following does she select?

    A. S/MIME

    B. RIP

    C. SSL

    D. TLS

14. Which of the following is an attack on web applications that injects client-side scripts into a web page?

    A. XSRF

    B. XSS

    C. SQL injection

    D. Input validation

15. Yamir, a network administrator, is asked to install a router to separate two networks within his LAN where there are no web or email services, instead of a firewall. After asking "Why not a firewall?", how does his network manager respond?

    A. Firewalls are less expensive.

    B. Routers are less expensive.

    C. Routers are stateful by default.

    D. Routers are stateless by default.

16. Which VPN protocol operates at layer 2 of the OSI model using 256-bit encryption?

    A. PPTP

    B. L2TP

    C. PPP

    D. IPsec

17. Chelsea is a security engineer completing setups for a single-sign-on system. Which system should she set up for the *MOST* secure authentication?

    A. EAP

    B. PAP

    C. MD5

    D. AES

18. A full-mesh network of four nodes requires how many connections?

    A. 7

    B. 6

    C. 5

    D. 4

19. Evelin is a network engineer tasked with architecting the network connection from headquarters to a field office 50 miles away. Which solution should she choose for *BEST* security and performance?

    A. 802.11n

    B. CAT5 cable

    C. Coaxial cable

    D. Fiber optic media

20. Brett is a network manager architecting a wired network through *KloutCo*. Part of the cabling will run above drop ceilings and through raised floors. Which of the following is his *BEST* recommendation?

    A. Use standard-grade cables because it is the least expensive.

    B. Use plenum-grade cables because in the case of a fire, standard-grade cables emit deadly gas.

    C. Use standard-grade cables because they are fireproof.

    D. Use plenum-grade cables because of their encryption features.

21. Daya, a network engineer, desires to configure a network using a star-type topology. Which of the following should she select?

    A. Partial mesh

    B. Wi-Fi

    C. Token ring

    D. Bus

22. Which of the following *BEST* describes the Media Access Control (MAC) address burned into a Network Interface Card (NIC)?

    A. A MAC address is 24 bits, and the whole thing is a manufacturer code.

    B. A MAC address is 24 bits, and the whole thing defines a unique address.

C. A MAC address is 48 bits, and 24 bits define the manufacturer.

D. A MAC address is 96 bits, and 48 bits define the manufacturer.

23. Cassia is an ethical hacker who cannot penetrate the network due to an advanced firewall. Which of the following should be her next step?

A. Conclude the test and inform the client that their security levels will stop all attacks.

B. Conduct reconnaissance.

C. Attempt war dialing.

D. Collect data using OSINT.

24. What is the primary purpose of an attacker launching an ARP poisoning attack?

A. As a man-in-the-middle exploit

B. To change the network's ARP table

C. To modify IP addresses

D. To decrease the acceptable resource pool

25. Jason, an ethical hacker, is working with *Jefferson Bank* to perform a penetration test. Which of the following is the *MOST* important step for him to complete?

A. Reconnaissance.

B. Confirm management buy-in by having them sign the working agreement.

C. Network mapping and scanning for open ports and other vulnerabilities.

D. Running the exploit.

26. Wireless access points and wireless systems use which technology?

A. CSMA/CD

B. Polling controls

C. Token passing

D. CSMA/CA

27. Which of these is *NOT* an attribute of a packet filter firewall?

A. Makes use of access control lists

B. Runs at the application layer

C. Is a first-generation firewall type

D. Inspects the source and destination addresses

28. TACACS and TACACS+ systems have which of the following two features? (Choose two.)

    A. Allows password changes

    B. Communicates via UDP protocols

    C. Encrypts passwords but not data

    D. Two-factor authentication

29. Which of the following *BEST* describes UTP cables?

    A. UTP cables have two conductors in concentric circles.

    B. UTP cables have two insulated twisted wires.

    C. UTP cables transfer data using laser signals.

    D. UTP cables have a range of 1 km before data signal loss.

30. Alexei is a marketing representative for *GL Food Bars* and maintains a mailing list for 5,000 customers. His ISP alerts him that his email server is sending spam to millions of users at 100 messages per minute. What is *MOST LIKELY* the problem?

    A. The most recent update to the email server was buggy.

    B. Millions of new clients have signed up for GL Food Bars information

    C. Hackers have compromised his email list.

    D. He has an open relay SMTP server.

31. Loren runs the networking department and desires to architect a system for her website customers that will simplify scalability, improve security, and ease implementation on various devices, such as smartphones, smartwatches, and laptops. Which model should she select?

    A. Demilitarized zone

    B. N-tier architecture

    C. Split DNS

    D. Split tunneling

32. Benvele is a hacker launching attacks on smartphones to gain access and download photos and contacts. What type of attack is this?

    A. Bluesnarfing

    B. Bluejacking

C. Bluebugging

D. BlueBorne

33. Kyle is a secretary working fast to get work done for his boss. During a short break, he visits social media and clicks a link for cheap Ray-Ban glasses. Unbeknownst to Kyle, a hacker has downloaded his browser's cookies. What is the name of this attack?

A. XSRF

B. XSS

C. Cookie stealing

D. Cookie monster

34. Fernando is a salesperson visiting one of his corporate field locations. He has the Wi-Fi password but still cannot access the internet because his browser requests another username and password. What is *MOST LIKELY* to be the trouble?

A. The RADIUS server is not granting him a ticket.

B. The SAML system has an incorrect password.

C. Improper user ID for extensible authentication protocol.

D. Port authentication is required through 802.1x.

35. Two popular networking models include OSI and TCP/IP. The TCP/IP application layer represents which layer(s) of the OSI model?

A. Transport, session, presentation, application

B. Session, presentation, application

C. Presentation, application

D. Application

36. Graphical imagery, whether it is JPEG, TIFF, or GIF, is generally processed in which layer of the OSI model?

A. Application

B. Presentation

C. Session

D. Transport

37. Mikoopst is a hacker seeking vulnerabilities to attack a bank and steal money electronically. Which network device is likely to be the weakest vulnerability?

    A. The bank website

    B. The firewall

    C. Fish tank thermometer

    D. The internal corporate website

38. Which protocol uses sequence and acknowledgment numbers to keep track of communications?

    A. ICMP

    B. UDP

    C. TCP

    D. IP

39. Sandor is a hacker attacking a user's online banking experience. While the user is logged in to their banking account, the user clicks an enticing email for free check-printing from their bank and allows the attacker to transfer money from the user's bank account. Which of the following *BEST* describes this attack?

    A. TCP hijacking

    B. XSRF

    C. XSS

    D. SQL injection

40. Which of the following is an example of protocols that would operate at the session layer of the OSI model?

    A. RPC and FTP

    B. PAP and PPTP

    C. TCP and UDP

    D. ICMP and RIP

41. Aleksandra is an ethical hacker manipulating TTL values to determine where firewalls are located. What technique is she using?

    A. Ping-of-death

    B. TTL trace

C. Tracerouting

D. Firewalking

42. The networking system designed to guarantee good performance of data flow and prioritize applications is known as what?

A. Prioritization

B. QoS

C. Service quality

D. Guaranflo

43. Jorge is starting a new CBD business and desires to set up his online shopping cart. He wants users to trust his store, so he registers a digital certificate with which role for the PKI?

A. RA

B. CA

C. CRL

D. Root

44. What is the primary difference between baseband and broadband technologies?

A. Baseband is for cable TV only.

B. Baseband transmits over a single channel, and broadband over multiple channels simultaneously.

C. Broadband is for cable TV only.

D. Broadband transmits over a single channel, and baseband over multiple channels simultaneously.

45. Anfisa, a network engineer is asked to inspect a network and determine whether it should be upgraded to fiber optic. Building-to-building connections are connected using coaxial cables, and privacy information is showing up on PASTEBIN. What is her recommendation for *BEST* security?

A. Save money and make no changes because fiber optic cable is expensive.

B. Save money and enable encryption for business-to-business communications.

C. Upgrade the network to fiber because it is less expensive than STP.

D. Upgrade the network to fiber because EMI transmissions are being intercepted.

46. Philyuk is a sales manager who is ready to get to work. He opens his laptop, connects to the Wi-Fi, but cannot access the internet. He notices that he has an IP address of `169.254.3.4` but still cannot access his online bank. What is *MOST LIKELY* to be the problem?

    A. The internet is down.

    B. The DHCP server is down.

    C. The bank's web server is down.

    D. His network card is disabled.

47. Azan is part of the network security team and they are setting up a Wi-Fi system that allows any member of the company to connect to the network when at the office. Which feature should he recommend to help secure access to the network?

    A. DHCP snooping

    B. Flood guards

    C. Integrity checking

    D. Encryption

48. Marcgerm is an overseas hacker conducting reconnaissance on the victim's network at *EB Inc*. What safeguards can the security team put in place to mitigate the attack?

    A. Install an NIDS to block network threats.

    B. Close ports 161 and 162 on the firewall and enable SNMPv3.

    C. Upgrade the network from SNMPv1 to SNMPv2.

    D. Attacks using SNMP are impossible to mitigate.

49. Nicole, a systems administrator, is seeking methods to defend her public DNS server from hackers. Which of these is her *BEST* solution?

    A. Enable encryption.

    B. Deny access to everyone except staff.

    C. Install an HIDS.

    D. Enable DNSSEC.

50. Matt is a salesperson for *Wilco* and plans to use the Wi-Fi offered at his local restaurant. He enters the Wi-Fi password but cannot access the internet like others there. The computer works fine at home on the VPN and at work. What is *MOST LIKELY* to be the problem?

    A. He cannot access the DHCP server in the restaurant.

    B. He has a static IP address set.

    C. The DHCP server is down within the restaurant.

    D. A hacker is altering the restaurant's network.

51. Luis is a systems administrator at *East School*, and the board is requesting a network that allows students to reach Google but disallows access to X-rated websites. Which system is *BEST* for him to install?

    A. Switch

    B. Proxy

    C. Repeater

    D. Router

52. Which of the following is a difference between an application-level firewall over a circuit-level firewall?

    A. Circuit-level firewalls are, in general, slower than application-level firewalls.

    B. Application-level firewalls do not require a proxy for each protocol monitored.

    C. An application-level firewall can perform deep packet inspection.

    D. A circuit-level firewall performs deep packet inspection.

53. What are the port numbers for these services, respectively?

    HTTP, FTP, SSH, SMTP, IMAP

    A. 443, 21, 23, 25, 123

    B. 80, 21, 23, 53, 143

    C. 80, 21, 22, 25, 143

    D. 443, 20, 22, 25, 110

54. Molly is a network engineer tasked with reducing interference on VoIP phones within the network. Which of the following is her *BEST* solution?

    A. Place all SIP- and RTP-related traffic into a separate VLAN.

    B. Place VoIP phones onto their own switch within the subnet.

    C. Reduce the thresholds on the NIDS devices.

    D. Develop corporate policies to limit phone use.

55. Alla, a network engineer, needs to extend a network so that computers 100 meters away from each other are on the same subnet. Which technology should she use to extend the network?

    A. Router

    B. Bridge

    C. Gateway

    D. Firewall

56. RIP is a distance-vector routing protocol. Distance-vector routing protocols make routing decisions based on what?

    A. Physical distance measured in centimeters and kilometers if preferred

    B. A combination of physical distance and number of hops

    C. Number of hops, network load, and packet size

    D. Minimum number of hops to reach the destination

57. Narkyia is an email administrator and her email server is being used to send forged emails. What technology can she install to mitigate this issue?

    A. SSL

    B. SPF

    C. SASL

    D. SMTP

58. Difata is new to hacking and has discovered a new attack. The instructions state that to best breach the victim server, you should launch the attack on IP address 127.0.0.1. What type of individual is Difata?

    A. Script kiddie

    B. Skilled hacker

    C. Ethical hacker

    D. White hat hacker

59. Olulowo is a network engineer asked to install an internal DNS server for staff and a separate DNS server on the internet for the public. He decides to install which type of setup?

    A. Split-network

    B. Split-DNS

    C. Split-VPN

    D. Split-IP

60. Alice is a network engineer being consulted as to why network transmissions have slowly degraded over time. The small company has grown and installed microwave ovens in the break rooms, and the 100 new staff are using cell phones. What is her recommendation?

    A. Create new policies not allowing the use of cell phones at work, and remove the microwave ovens.

    B. After researching the environment, there is really nothing more that can be done.

    C. Upgrade the STP cabling to UTP cabling.

    D. Upgrade the UTP cabling to STP cabling.

61. Technologies such as Fiber Channel over Ethernet, Multiprotocol Label Switching, VoIP, and Internet Small Computer System Interface are examples of which protocol?

    A. Fiber optics

    B. IP convergence

    C. Ethernet

    D. Storage

62. Translating a set of public addresses to private addresses is accomplished with what method?

    A. NAT

    B. TCP

    C. RFC

    D. Teredo

63. Mattrich uses a VPN to work from his Apple computer. While connected, he clicks a link from his personal email account. Days later, corporate offices are down because of a massive ransomware attack. What *MOST LIKELY* occurred?

    A. Mattrich infected the company because he read his personal email.

    B. Mattrich infected the company because he was using VPN split tunneling.

    C. Mattrich infected the company because he disabled VPN encryption.

    D. Mattrich infected the company because they mostly use Microsoft computers.

64. Josh, a networking intern, is connecting two computers in a LAN. System A has IP address 192.168.4.7/24, and system B has IP address 192.168.5.8/24. He tests the connections using ping but gets the error message host unreachable. They are both properly plugged in to the switch. What is *MOST LIKELY* the problem?

    A. One of the cables is broken.

    B. The systems are improperly connected.

    C. Josh needs to use a hub instead of a switch.

    D. The systems are on separate subnets.

65. Which ports are considered the *MOST* well-known ports?

    A. 1-1024

    B. 0-1023

    C. 0-1024

    D. 1-1023

66. In the OSI model, which layer converts voltages to bits?

    A. Bitwise

    B. Physical

    C. V2Bit

    D. Data link

67. Carolina is a network engineer and notices that network traffic has degraded to 50% of normal. After investigating, she discovers the problem. What did she determine?

    A. A new employee was streaming online music.

    B. The firewall was blocking the ports to access the web server.

    C. The manufacturer of the routers reported several zero-days that affected performance.

    D. Degradation only occurs in the evening when the users shut down their computers.

68. Noon, a network engineer, has been tasked with setting up a Wi-Fi network by upgrading the firmware of older-generation WAPs currently using WEP security. She is asked to improve the security without replacing the WAPs. Which level of security should she choose?

    A. Open authentication

    B. WEP

    C. WPA

    D. WPA2

69. This technology logically groups networked computers by function or department and enhances security by segregating data traffic, for example, by separating VoIP traffic. What is this technology called?

    A. VLAN

    B. VPN

    C. DNS

    D. DMZ

70. The TCP and UDP protocols are common in that they transfer data. What is the key difference between the two protocols?

   A. TCP is unreliable and transmits data faster than UDP.

   B. UDP is connectionless and has greater potential for data loss.

   C. UDP utilizes a three-way handshake.

   D. TCP is great for digital video and audio applications.

71. VPNs have which of these characteristics? (Choose two.)

   A. VPN connections occur through software applications only.

   B. VPN connections can occur through hardware or software utilities.

   C. VPN connections must utilize IPsec.

   D. VPN implementations can be accomplished through certificate or key exchange.

72. Peter is a security analyst reviewing network logs and notices that from 10 PM-4 AM, the server reports attempted connections on ports 0, 1, 2, 3..., and 1023 from an unknown system on the internet. What type of attack is occurring?

   A. NMAP

   B. Port scanning

   C. HPING

   D. DDOS

73. Serena is a hacker, exfiltrating corporate files to her partner, Janine. What is the BEST way for Serena to launch the upload without getting caught?

   A. Janine builds an SSH server so that Serena can launch a covert channel and tunnel HTTP over SSH.

   B. Janine builds an SSH server so that Serena can launch a covert channel using SSH.

   C. Janine builds an FTP server so that Serena can launch a covert channel using FTP.

   D. Janine builds a Telnet server so that Serena can launch a covert channel using Telnet.

74. Simone-Jeannelle is a chemical engineer transferring work-from-home data to her office. As she transfers files from her house, she notices the transfer is taking much longer than expected. The network administrator states the network is functioning normally. What is the *MOST LIKELY* issue?

    A. She needs to upgrade her home-based SDSL modem to ADSL.

    B. Her home-based ADSL modem downloads faster than it uploads.

    C. The office firewall is doing deep packet inspection.

    D. The office server is under a DOS attack.

75. Which of these are characteristics of a bridged network? (Choose two.)

    A. Layer 3 network device

    B. Connects two disparate networks

    C. Layer 2 network device

    D. Extends the current network

76. Bryce is a network engineer reviewing an RFP that states they require systems that work with CSMA/CD technologies. Which solution should he suggest?

    A. Wireless access points throughout the environment

    B. Ethernet connections because of the cabling

    C. Fiber optics because of its performance

    D. DVD/CD technology because it will work with CDs

77. Lai is a security engineer working with the networking department. During an audit, she notices the use of several old hubs in secure, networked environments. What is *MOST LIKELY* to be her recommendation?

    A. Replace the hubs with switches.

    B. Update the firmware on the hubs.

    C. Upgrade the hubs to the latest hub technology.

    D. Divide hubs with eight connections to make two hubs with four connections each.

78. Barry is a network engineer seeking to directly network two nearby buildings. Which option should he choose since the empty land between the two buildings is owned by his competitor?

    A. Connect the buildings via fiber channels.

    B. Install a Yagi antenna.

    C. Connect the buildings using CAT5 ethernet.

    D. Install building-to-building Bluetooth.

79. Avril is a systems administrator setting up email for her users. They are able to send email but not receive it. What is the *MOST LIKELY* problem?

    A. No email client is installed.

    B. No email server is installed.

    C. Port 25 needs to be opened on the firewall.

    D. Port 110 needs to be opened in the firewall.

80. Which protocols operate at the application, presentation, network, and data link layers, respectively?

    A. Pretty Good Privacy, routing information protocol, address resolution protocol, IPsec

    B. Routing information protocol, Pretty Good Privacy, IPsec, address resolution protocol

    C. Address resolution protocol, IPsec, Pretty Good Privacy, routing information protocol

    D. IPsec, Pretty Good Privacy, routing information protocol, address resolution protocol

81. Huisha is a security engineer deploying several honeypots. Her manager suggests that once a hacker is identified, the system should automatically attack the hacker's system and wipe the hacker's hard drive. Why does she tell the manager this is not recommended?

    A. It is technically impossible to launch a counter-attack.

    B. Hackback is against the law.

    C. There are not enough staff to conduct the remote hard-drive wipes.

    D. Hackback is too difficult to automate.

82. Of the following options, which provides the least protection to data in motion?

    A. WEP

    B. WPA

    C. L2TP

    D. PPTP

83. Which of these is a type of prevention system that performs IOC pattern matching, such as comparing instruction sequences of known malware or correlating known file hashes?

    A. Heuristic-based

    B. Network-based

    C. Signature-based

    D. IDS

84. What is another term for a pharming attack where victims get diverted to an attacker's fake website?

    A. DNS poisoning

    B. Flooding

    C. IP forwarding

    D. Phishing

85. Which setting does traceroute manipulate in the TCP/IP model?

    A. UDP

    B. TTL

    C. Data link

    D. Frame header

86. Hackers look for soft, vulnerable targets to attack, as they make it easier to upload exploits. Security engineers harden these systems by disabling which features? (Choose two.)

    A. FTP

    B. SSH

    C. HTTPS

    D. Telnet

87. Justin is a senior security officer asked for his opinion on installing wireless access points in a secure area. What does he recommend as security levels for the implementation?

    A. WPA

    B. WPA2

    C. WEP

    D. Open system

88. Of the following, which two are *NOT* VPN protocols? (Choose two)

    A. RADIUS

    B. Kerberos

    C. L2TP

    D. PPTP

89. Aziza is a network administrator setting up a private network with non-routable IP addresses. Which network block should she use?

    A. 169.254.0.0/16

    B. 192.168.0.0/8

    C. 127.0.0.0/8

    D. 192.16.0.0/8

90. Louis, a security engineer, is testing methods to defeat the firewall. Which method would he find *MOST* effective?

    A. Fragmentation

    B. Firewalking

    C. Changing static IP address

    D. Encryption

91. Alan is a network engineer tasked with writing firewall rules that allow SYN-ACK-SYN communications. Which protocol should he set to permit?

    A. UDP

    B. TCP

    C. ICMP

    D. IP

92. What are the *BEST* examples of IPv6 addresses here? (Choose two.)

    A. `::1`

    B. `a:b:c:d:d:c:b:a`

    C. `:::1`

    D. `a:b:c:d:e:f:g:h`

93. A system that encrypts a symmetric key so that two users can use this key for secret messages is known as what?

    A. DSS

    B. Diffie-Hellman

    C. AES

    D. MD5

94. At which layer does IPsec operate within the OSI model?

    A. Application

    B. Physical

    C. Data Link

    D. Network

95. Devar is a systems administrator who manages 1,000 users and their email usage. What is his number one security issue with email?

    A. Poor passwords

    B. Phishing attacks

    C. Use of Thunderbird and other open source email clients

    D. Disk space utilization

96. The network interface layer of the TCP/IP model is equivalent to which layer of the OSI model?

    A. Application

    B. Data link

    C. Session

    D. Network

97. Which device operates at the data link layer of the OSI model?

    A. Firewall

    B. Hub

    C. Switch

    D. Router

98. Which of these protocols operate at the transport layer of the OSI model?
    (Choose two.)

    A. TCP

    B. ICMP

    C. UDP

    D. RARP

99. The ARP command (address resolution protocol) notifies the user of which MAC
    address a computer uses by providing the IP address of that system. ARP collects
    data from which layers of the OSI model?

    A. Network and data link

    B. Physical and data link

    C. Network and transport

    D. Presentation and application

100. Irina, a systems engineer, is in the process of installing fax machines on a corporate
     network. Where is the *BEST* place for her to install these for the best security?

    A. Break room

    B. SOC

    C. Computer room

    D. Utility closet

Quick Answer Key

1. B	16. B	31. B	46. B	61. B	76. B	91. B
2. A	17. A	32. A	47. A	62. A	77. A	92. A, B
3. B	18. B	33. B	48. B	63. B	78. B	93. B
4. D	19. D	34. D	49. D	64. D	79. D	94. D
5. B, D	20. B	35. B	50. B	65. A	80. B	95. B
6. B	21. B	36. B	51. B	66. B	81. B	96. B
7. B	22. C	37. C	52. C	67. C	82. C	97. C
8. C, D	23. C	38. C	53. C	68. C	83. C	98. A, C
9. A	24. A	39. B	54. A	69. A	84. A	99. A
10. B	25. B	40. B	55. B	70. B	85. B	100. B
11. C, D	26. D	41. D	56. D	71. B, D	86. A, D	
12. B	27. B	42. B	57. B	72. B	87. B	
13. A	28. A, D	43. A	58. A	73. A	88. A, B	
14. B	29. B	44. B	59. B	74. B	89. B	
15. D	30. D	45. D	60. D	75. C, D	90. D	

Answers with explanations

1. **Answer: B Password Authentication Protocol** (**PAP**) is an authentication system used for verifying users. SCP does not use PAP because it does not encrypt like **Extensible Authentication Protocol** (**EAP**) will. The **Transmission Control Protocol** (**TCP**) verifies that each packet has reached its destination. The **User Datagram Protocol** (**UDP**) does not verify that a packet has reached its destination. The **Internet Control Message Protocol** (**ICMP**) is a protocol that sends error messages based on whether a packet can reach a router or node.

2. **Answer: A** FDDI and Token Ring networks use tokens to pass messages from one node (computer) to another. Ethernet uses **Carrier Sense Multiple Access with Collision Detection** (**CSMA/CD**), where systems listen for the absence of data transmission before sending packets. **Carrier Sense Multiple Access with Collision Avoidance** (**CSMA/CA**) includes systems that transmit a ready-to-send signal to determine whether it is okay to send data.

3. **Answer: B** Secure destruction means removing and destroying the hard drive because it contains records of fax messages sent and received. The other options can leak users' private records.

4. **Answer: D Virtual Private Networks (VPNs)** use tunneling protocols, including IPsec and encryption, to allow private, secure networks from home to office or office to office.

5. **Answer: B and D** On Linux systems, the **Domain Name Service (DNS)** feature is either called NAMED or BIND, which resolves frequently used domain names (FQDNs) to IP addresses. HTTPD is used to run a web server on the computer. DHCPD allows the computer to run as a DHCP server and supply IP addresses to new clients that join the network.

6. **Answer: B Routing Information Protocol (RIP)** is a distance routing protocol that uses hop count metrics to transfer packets from a client to a server. **Open Shortest Path First (OSPF)** uses link states such as congestion or lag to determine the best path for packets. **Enhanced Interior Gateway Routing Protocol (EIGRP)** is an upgrade of **Interior Gateway Routing Protocol (IGRP)**, which relearns the best paths for packets, always using the better-performing paths for packets to travel by.

7. **Answer: B** An **Intrusion Detection System (IDS)** will report and log, but not block, an incident. Firewalls, **Intrusion Prevention Systems (IPSes)**, and **Host-Based Intrusion Prevention Systems (HIPSes)** all report and block the exploit.

8. **Answer: C and D** Heuristic prevention systems look for anomalies outside of a baseline to detect attacks. Pattern-matching systems look for signatures of known attacks, leaving them vulnerable to zero-day attacks since there is no known solution. **Host-Based Intrusion Detection Systems (HIDSes)** and **Network-Based Intrusion Prevention Systems (NIPS)** are programmed to employ pattern matching and heuristics to detect attacks.

9. **Answer: A** A fraggle attack sends UDP packets to the local broadcast address and spoofs the source address, which is the target server the attacker wants to disrupt with a **Denial of Service (DOS)** attack. Smurf and fraggle attacks can be mitigated by disabling echo requests. Half-open packets are TCP packets that do not respond to ACK requests, thereby not completing the handshake.

10. **Answer: B** The **Demilitarized Zone (DMZ)** allows organizations to provide customer access to servers and still provide some level of security. The intranet is a protected area for employees only. A honeypot is a system designed to distract hackers so that researchers can gain intelligence on new attacks.

11. **Answer: C and D Digital Audio Tape** (**DAT**) is used to record audio, video, and data. **File Allocation Table** (**FAT**) is a Windows-based filesystem. Network address translation and port address translation allow organizations to use a common set of internal addresses behind some unique internet address.

12. **Answer: B** Sniffing allows an attacker to monitor a network and collect information such as login names, passwords, emails, files, and more. The best mitigation is encryption. The other options do nothing to protect data on the network.

13. **Answer: A** RIP is an application layer protocol but contains no security features. The Secure Sockets Layer and Transport Layer Security provide encryption at the presentation layer.

14. **Answer: B** Input validation is one of the mitigations of **Cross-Site Scripting** (**XSS**) and SQL injection. XSRF is an attack that forces an end user to execute unwanted actions on a web application in which they're currently authenticated. SQL injection is an attack where an attacker injects SQL commands via a web application to extract unauthorized information from a backend database. Reference: `https://owasp.org/www-community/attacks/csrf`

    `https://owasp.org/www-community/attacks/SQL_Injection`.

15. **Answer: D** Since the users are operating within LANs that have no web or email services, there is no requirement for stateful services, so a stateless system is most desired in this case.

16. **Answer: B Layer 2 Tunneling Protocol** (**L2TP**) does not encrypt by default, so combined with IPsec, it provides better security compared to PPTP because of the higher-grade encryption but runs slower. PPP and IPsec are not VPN protocols.

17. **Answer: A** PAP sends login and password information in clear text, making it insecure. MD5 is a hashing algorithm, and AES an encryption algorithm. EAP not only encrypts authentication but also can manage certificates, tokens, and other authentication devices.

18. **Answer: B** The formula used to determine the number of connections in a full-mesh network is *N(N-1)/2*. In this case, *N=4*. Substituting the value into the formula *4(4-1)/2* equals *4x3/2*, which becomes *12/2*, and the result of that is *6*. So, six total connections for a four-node full-mesh network.

19. **Answer: D** The key point in this question has to do with range, where fiber optic media can travel around 200 kilometers before significant signal loss. Coaxial cable can travel about 500 meters before significant signal loss. The range for CAT5 is about 100 meters, and `802.11n` Wi-Fi gets about 30 meters before significant signal loss.

20. **Answer: B** Plenum-grade cables are coated with fire retardant so that they emit less smoke when they ignite. Plenum is used for **Heating, Ventilation, and Air Conditioning (HVAC)** systems and for circulating oxygen throughout entire buildings. The high oxygen content increases fire risk, so the cabling choice is critical for human safety.

21. **Answer: B** A partial-mesh topology connects all systems together. For example, if there are four nodes, there will be six connections, whereas if the star type was used, the four nodes would connect to a single switch. For a Token Ring topology, the four systems would be connected in a ring, and a token would move counterclockwise and receive and transmit data for that node. A bus network would simply daisy chain the four nodes, and resistors would be installed at each end to signal the end of the bus.

22. **Answer: C** The MAC address burned into a NIC is 48 bits, where the first 24 bits define the manufacturer and the last 24 bits are the card's unique identifier. Ideally, there will be no duplicate MAC addresses in the entire world.

23. **Answer: C Open Source Intelligence (OSINT)** is a reconnaissance technique to learn more about the victim using Google, Netcraft, and other public sources. After scanning for network vulnerabilities, hackers test for modems using war dialing because these are not often forgotten when securing the environment. *Answer A is wrong because there is no such thing as perfect security.*

24. **Answer: A** The key part of this question is the *primary purpose*. Changing the ARP table is how the attack is exploited, but the *purpose* of the attack is to listen to packets passing through the network, so *A* is the better answer here. Options *C* and *D* are false answers.

25. **Answer: B** An important key in understanding the CISSP exam is that it is more of a management exam than a technical exam. More often, the candidate should choose the management answer over technical answers because they define how and what technologies to use.

26. **Answer: D** Wireless technologies use **Carrier Sense Multiple Access/Collision Avoidance (CSMA/CA)** instead of **CSMA/Collision Detection (CSMA/CD)**. Token Ring networks use token passing to send and receive messages. Polling networks are used within SCADA technologies.

27. **Answer: B** Packet filtering firewalls work at the network and transport layers. Also, these firewalls are stateless, which means internal requests must be approved by an administrator. The network administrator will create a rule in the firewall to allow the user to communicate with the specific remote site.

28. **Answer: A and D** TACACS (pronounced "takaks") and TACACS+ (pronounced "tak plus") communicate via TCP for better reliability and encrypt all packets. RADIUS communicates via UDP and encrypts passwords only as a AAA (authentication, authorization, and accounting) server.

29. **Answer: B Unshielded Twisted Pair (UTP)** has a range of about 100 meters before signal loss, whereas fiber optics can run about 1 kilometer before data loss. Conductors in concentric circles form a coaxial cable.

30. **Answer: D** Most likely, Alexei is running an unsecured SMTP server. Recent updates to the server are not under the control of Alexei and are tested by the cloud provider. Hackers are sending spam to millions of accounts, not his 5,000 users, so the email list is of no concern to the hackers.

31. **Answer: B** An N-tier architecture decouples services into multiple tiers, the most common being the three-tier model. The presentation layer resides at the top and displays differently depending on the device. Below that sits the logic area, where coding is done, for example, HTML. The bottom layer is data where images, videos, customer information, and so on are stored. Split DNS provides a DNS server for the intranet and internet. Split tunneling allows an employee to use a VPN for work resources and not use the VPN for non-work activities. A DMZ is where the public-facing website resides.

32. **Answer: A** Bluejacking allows an attacker to send spam to the victim's phone. Bluebugging allows hackers to eavesdrop on phone calls. When the hacker infects the victim's device with malware and then takes control, this is considered a BlueBorne attack.

33. **Answer: B** CSRF is an attack that forces an end user to execute unwanted actions on a web application in which they're currently authenticated. XSS attacks occur when an attacker uses a web application to send a malicious script to a different end user that can access any cookies, session tokens, or other sensitive information and can even rewrite the content of an HTML page. Cookie stealing and cookie monster are false answers. Learn more here: `https://owasp.org/www-community/attacks/csrf`

    `https://owasp.org/www-community/attacks/xss/`

34. **Answer: D** Kerberos authenticates with tickets, not RADIUS. SAML is used to authenticate a user to another service provider, for example, a bank partnered with check printers, which is not happening here. EAP is a communication protocol, not an authentication protocol.

35. **Answer: B** The OSI transport layer matches the TCP/IP host-to-host layer, and the OSI network layer matches the TCP/IP internet layer, and the OSI data link and physical layers match the TCP/IP network access layer.

36. **Answer: B** The application layer is where programs reside. The presentation layer processes data on how it should appear or sound to the user. The session layer manages communications between applications. The transport layer manages communications between nodes (such as computers, laptops, and smartphones).

37. **Answer: C Internet of Things (IoT)** devices are attacked more frequently because security is often overlooked for these devices. This also includes thermometers, IP cameras, refrigerators, televisions, multi-function printers, and others (the question states they are all *network devices*).

38. **Answer: C** TCP provides a guaranteed connection from host to host. To do this, it tracks data receipts through acknowledgment numbers. UDP is connectionless and makes the greatest effort to ensure that data reaches its destination. If a packet is lost, it does not know. The IP header tracks data fragments, and ICMP is used to verify nodes exist and are running.

39. **Answer: B** The attacker uses the session information to strengthen the spoofing details of the victim and performs session hijacking using the victim's already-approved credentials with the bank. The user thinks they were simply disconnected. XSS allows the attacker to run a script on the user's computer. SQL injection is an attack on a web server to send SQL commands and download credit card numbers and so on. Learn more here: `https://owasp.org/www-project-web-security-testing-guide/latest/4-Web_Application_Security_Testing/06-Session_Management_Testing/05-Testing_for_Cross_Site_Request_Forgery`

40. **Answer: B** Although RPC operates at the session layer, FTP operates at the application layer. TCP and UDP operate at the transport layer, and ICMP operates at the network layer. RIP operates at the application layer.

41. **Answer: D** Firewalking uses traceroute and TTL values to find firewalls, determine which services the firewall allows, and map networks. Ping-of-death is a DOS attack that spoofs the source address, and all requests head to the victim machine.

42. **Answer: B Quality of Service (QoS)** prioritizes applications such as VoIP systems to guarantee a level of quality. The other options are false answers.

43. **Answer: A** The **Registration Authority** (**RA**) verifies and validates the user. The **Certificate Authority** (**CA**) signs the certificate and returns it to the user (Jorge, in this case). The **Certificate Revocation List** (**CRL**) is a list of expired and revoked certificates. The root CA maintains all of the certificates it has signed; this system is very secure; for example, it is air-gapped.

44. **Answer: B** Baseband is usually used for Ethernet networks over coaxial, fiber optic, or twisted pair. Broadband can transmit data, audio, and video at the same time as radio waves, coaxial, or fiber optic.

45. **Answer: D** Encryption can be broken, so the best option is fiber optic cable because it emits no **Electro-Magnetic Interference** (**EMI**). Shielded twisted pair is much lower in cost than fiber optic.

46. **Answer: B.** IP addresses in the form of 169.254.xxx.xxx have autoconfiguration enabled, which provides a system with an IP address until the DHCP server recovers. Use is very limited, and the user will not be able to access the internet with this IP address.

47. **Answer: A** DHCP snooping assigns IP addresses only to systems assigned by network administrators. Flood guards would help with DOS attacks. Integrity checking and encryption would not secure the network connections.

48. **Answer: B** An NIDS will only report threats, not block them. An NIPS would be more appropriate. Only SNMPv3 encrypts community strings, which carry passwords to routers and switches.

49. **Answer: D** Since this is a *public* **Domain Name Service** (**DNS**) server, restricting traffic to staff would make it useless to the public, and the encryption of zone information would make it useless as well. An HIDS would not protect the server, nor would **Domain Name System Security Extensions** (**DNSSEC**), which ensures that zone transfers are authenticated and robust.

50. **Answer: B** Since other customers are not complaining, the DHCP server is functioning fine, and a hacker would kick everyone off the network, not only Matt.

51. **Answer: B** Basic routers are not designed to block internal website requests, but advanced multi-layer routers can. Proxies are designed to protect the LAN and can be configured to block websites users are attempting to access.

52. **Answer: C** Application-level firewalls not only consider ports, IP addresses, sources, and destinations but can perform deep packet inspection. This further inspection hurts performance as compared to other firewalls, and encryption can mitigate the useful purpose of an application-level firewall.

53. **Answer: C** HTTPS = 443, FTP-DATA=20, FTP-AUTHENTICATION=21, Telnet=23, DNS=53, POP3=110, NTP=123

54. **Answer: A** SIP is used to initiate phone calls on VoIP systems, and **Real-Time Transport Protocol (RTP)** carries the conversation. Placing VoIP phones within their own VLAN assures that only VoIP traffic is allowed in this subnet.

55. **Answer: B** Routers and gateways can extend a network, but computers will reside on different subnets. A firewall is an NIPS designed to block threats from attackers.

56. **Answer: D** Link-state routing protocols are more accurate than distance-vector protocols such as RIP, because they look at the number of hops, network load, packet size, and more to determine the best routes for packets. OSPF is a link-state routing protocol.

57. **Answer: B Sender Policy Framework (SPF)** verifies that emails are coming from where they say they are coming from. **Simple Authentication and Security Layer (SASL)** is used to authenticate users so they can read their emails. **Secure Sockets Layer (SSL)** protects communications through encryption; TLS replaced SSL because of its vulnerabilities. SMTP manages sending email to people.

58. **Answer: A** Script kiddies are new to hacking and therefore very unskilled. In this case, the hacker has launched the attack on himself because 127.0.0.1 is the localhost address of his computer (and every computer). A white-hat hacker and ethical hacker are the same, and they are paid to audit the security of a business.

59. **Answer: B** Split-DNS provides a secured internal DNS server for internal requests, and the internet-based DNS server provides basic DNS servers for the public, and some access to corporate sites, such as other websites and mail servers.

60. **Answer: D Unshielded Twisted Pair (UTP)** cables can be vulnerable to crosstalk. **Shielded Twisted Pair (STP)** greatly reduces issues related to crosstalk and other interference.

61. **Answer: B** IP convergence entails utilizing internet protocols to provide other services not initially intended, such as phone services with VoIP or data transfers to storage devices with iSCSI.

62. **Answer: A Network Address Translation (NAT)** maps external addresses, such as 1.2.3.4, to internal addresses, such as 10.0.0.4. **Transmission Control Protocol (TCP)** provides connection-oriented communications. **Request for Comment (RFC)** is a set of standards provided by the Internet Engineering Task Force. Teredo provides IPv6 functionality within IPv4 networks.

63. **Answer: B** VPN split tunneling allows a user to connect with a secured corporate network for work-related activities and an unsecured public tunnel for personal work. In cases like this, it is possible for malware to transfer from the public to the private network. For best security, disable split tunneling.

64. **Answer: D** System A is on the 192.168.4.0 subnet, and system B is on the 192.168.5.0 subnet. One way to fix this is to switch system B's address to 192.168.4.8. Replacing cables and checking connections would result in the same issue. Hubs are inherently insecure because all traffic can be monitored.

65. **Answer: B** Well-known ports include FTP (port 21), SSH (port 22), HTTP (port 80), and others. Ports 1024-49151 are called the *registered ports*, which vendors specify for their proprietary applications. The *dynamic ports* start at 49152-65535 and are available as needed for applications.

66. **Answer: B** Bitwise and V2Bit are false answers because they are not layers in the OSI model. The data link layer converts bits into frames.

67. **Answer: C** The impact of digital music would introduce negligible performance issues, and if a firewall is blocking ports to a web server, degradation would be 100% for just that service only, not the entire network. Shutting down computers reduces network load, so the most likely cause is malware on the network routers.

68. **Answer: C** Open authentication provides no security at all because no password is required to access the network. WEP is relatively easy to crack. WPA2 would be the very best to use, but older-generation devices do not have that capability. WPA is much more difficult to crack than WEP.

69. **Answer: A Virtual LANs (VLANs)** allow administrators to group systems together based on function or need. VPNs allow direct connections from a single machine to home or office. DNS performs IP address lookups when a user provides a domain name. The DMZ is where companies position customer-accessible websites just outside of their LAN on the internet.

70. **Answer: B** UDP is connectionless, so is better for digital video and audio applications because it does not require packet-receipt verification, like TCP, because TCP utilizes a three-way handshake.

71. **Answer: B and D** VPN connections can encrypt data in other manners, not with IPsec only; but IPsec is supported worldwide.

72. **Answer: B** NMAP and HPING are utilities that can perform port scans, searching for vulnerabilities on the server. A **Distributed Denial of Service (DDOS)** attack would harm server performance and come from several multiple IP addresses.

73. **Answer: A** Telnet is used for remote logins, not remote file transfers, so Serena would get caught and not transfer any files. Serena is likely to get caught using FTP because it does not encrypt. SSH is used for remote logins. To transfer files, she would need to use **Secure Copy (SCP)**. Using HTTP services appears normal, so it would not alert system administrators.

74. **Answer: B Asymmetric Digital Subscriber Line** (ADSL) modems generally download eight times faster than they upload. Since she's transferring data to the office, it's uploading from home, at a much slower rate. **Symmetric Digital Subscriber Line (SDSL)** would be an upgrade for her from ADSL, giving her much faster upload speeds from home. C and D are not correct because the network administrator states the network is running fine.

75. **Answer: C and D** Routers operate at layer 3 and connect two disparate networks.

76. **Answer: B** CSMA/CD works in Ethernet bus networks only, which are half-duplex, so a message can only be sent when the network is clear. Full-duplex allows traffic to be sent without delay, such as in fiber networks. Wireless networks use **Carrier Sense Multiple Access/Collision Avoidance (CSMA/CA)**.

77. **Answer: A** Hubs, in general, are insecure because users can observe all traffic passing through the hubs, even data not intended for them. Switches allow traffic to connect directly to targets, making it more difficult for attackers to eavesdrop.

78. **Answer: B** Bluetooth is short-range, extending to about 10 meters, and fiber and Ethernet would require permission from the landowner between the two buildings. Yagi is best for site-to-site connections with ranges of up to several miles, as long as there is no interference.

79. **Answer: D** Since users are able to send emails, an email client and server are installed and running. Since users are able to send emails, SMTP is working fine on port 25.

80. **Answer: B** Yep, RIP is a layer 7 protocol. Encryption and decryption are generally done at layer 6 but can also occur at other layers, including layer 3, depending on the protocol. MAC addresses are utilized at layer 2. Reference: https://www.geeksforgeeks.org/routing-information-protocol-rip/.

81. **Answer: B** Many technologies exist to perform hackback, but it is against the law.

82. **Answer: C** The **Layer 2 Tunneling Protocol (L2TP)** provides no encryption. **Wired Equivalent Privacy (WEP)** is the weakest wireless standard. **Wi-Fi Protected Access (WPA)** provides even stronger security to wireless networks using TKIP to strengthen initialization vectors, which provides more variance to encryption keys. **Point-to-Point Tunneling Protocol (PPTP)** is a tunneling protocol to secure VPNs.

83. **Answer: C Indicators of Compromise (IOCs)** that match patterns are used in signature-based detection and prevention systems. Since the question specifically mentioned a prevention system, an IDS would be an incorrect answer. These systems can either be host- or network-based, and heuristic IOCs are measured against some baseline. When the IOC is outside of that baseline, it is flagged as malware.

84. **Answer: A** Phishing attacks use spoofed emails to gain the victim's trust, and usually contain links that forward users to fake websites when they click them. IP forwarding is used to re-route packets to an alternate network, for example, from the WAN to the LAN. Flooding is used as an availability attack on a website, sending noise so that others cannot access the site.

85. **Answer: B** The **Time-to-Live (TTL)** field decrements a counter for each router hop it takes for a packet to reach its destination. If the counter reaches zero before reaching the destination, the packet drops.

86. **Answer: A and D** Among other issues, Telnet and FTP both transmit data in clear text, allowing man-in-the-middle attackers to view entire conversations, including login names and passwords. SSH and HTTPS encrypt entire conversations, making it very difficult for hackers to run their exploits.

87. **Answer: B** An open system provides no security at all, allowing users to access a wireless access point without a password. WEP offers authentication, but it is very easy for even a script kiddie to attack. WPA is very strong, but WPA2 is the strongest and best solution for a secure area when using wireless access points.

88. **Answer: A and B** RADIUS and Kerberos are single-sign-on systems allowing users to access a network of systems with a single login and password. L2TP is the recommended VPN protocol over PPTP because it uses IPsec for encryption.

89. **Answer: B** The 127.0.0.0/8 network range is the localhost. Every computer has a localhost address, and it points to itself. 169.254.0.0/16 is the APIPA address suite, where a temporary IP address is provided for LAN usage, but not the internet. A DHCP server will provide an address for internet use once the server is up and running. 192.16.0.0/8 is an example of a public IP address.

90. **Answer: D** Encryption will also encrypt malware signatures that a firewall will not recognize. Firewalking is a method used to detect firewalls. Data fragments are mitigated by most firewalls to recognize malware signatures. After an IP address change, data still flows through the system.

91. **Answer: B** UDP, IP, and ICMP do not use SYN or ACK to confirm a connection.

92. **Answer: A and B** IPv6 address consist of 8 hextets using hexadecimal math where values go from 0 through *F*. A full IPv6 address looks like `1234:0000:4321:abcd:deef:feed:4321:9090`, but the system allows shortcuts. `0000:0000:0000:0000:0000:0000:0000:0001` or `::1` is the localhost address that every node has (equivalent to IPv4's `127.0.0.1`). `A:B:C:D:D:C:B:A` is the shortcut for `000A:000B:000C:000D:000D:000C:000B:000A`.

93. **Answer: B** The **Digital Signature Standard** (**DSS**) is an asymmetric encryption standard for signing and verification only. AES is a symmetric encryption standard for securing Wi-Fi connections. MD5 is a hashing algorithm for integrity checking.

94. **Answer: D** IPsec operates in two modes, transport and tunnel. Transport mode encrypts the data only, whereas tunnel mode encrypts the data and the message headers, providing additional location secrecy.

95. **Answer: B** Running out of disk space reduces availability, but in most cases this is easily fixed by increasing disk space or removing files. Change management systems will not allow the use of corporate-mandated email clients. Poor passwords are mitigated through policy and password validation tools. Phishing attacks can lead to network-wide ransomware, putting the organization at risk of going out of business.

96. **Answer: B** Layer 1 (physical), and layer 2 (data link) of the OSI model are equivalent to the network layer of the TCP/IP model. The TCP/IP model is four layers: layer one is the network interface, layer two is internetworking, layer three is transport, and layer 4 is the application.

97. **Answer: C** The seven layers of the OSI model are physical, where hubs operate; data link, where switches operate; network, where routers and some firewalls operate; transport; session, where stateful firewalls operate; presentation; and application, where application firewalls operate.

98. **Answer: A and C** ICMP operates at the network layer of the OSI model, and **Reverse Address Resolution Protocol** (**RARP**) resolves MAC addresses into IP addresses and operates between the data link and network layers.

99. **Answer: A** ARP collects the MAC address information from the data link layer and the **Internet Protocol** (**IP**) address information from the network layer.

100. **Answer: B** The **Security Operations Center** (**SOC**) monitors user ingress and egress as well as user activities on fax machines and other computers in the SOC. The SOC has integrity and transmission security controls in place as well.

5
Identity and Access Management Domain 5 Practice Questions

Questions from the following topics are included in this domain:

- Controlling physical and logical access to assets
- Managing authentication of people and devices
- Implementing and managing federation, and other authorization mechanisms
- Managing the provisioning and deprovisioning life cycle
- Implementing and managing authentication systems

Understanding **identity and access management** (**IAM**) via federation and other methods is critical to passing the **Certified Information Systems Security Professional** (**CISSP**) exam, requiring the candidate to score well here because there is a high 13% weighting on this topic.

Practice questions for *Domain 5* include understanding authentication into buildings and computers and the systems that make authentication work. The successful CISSP will know popular **single sign-on** (**SSO**) systems and the accounting processes that go with them.

After studying these practice questions, the candidate will be prepared to pass the IAM section of the exam, including the important scenarios on **multi-factor authentication** (**MFA**), **just-in-time** (**JIT**) authentication, and **mandatory access control** (**MAC**).

Questions

1. Candace suspects the Harvard diploma from the new employee is fake. What is her *BEST* next step to verify their background?

    A. Inspect the paper type of the diploma.

    B. Run a credit check.

    C. Contact the college verification department.

    D. Contact the employee's references.

2. Technical controls are a type of access control for organizations. What are two other access-control types?

    A. Physical

    B. Turnstile

    C. Firewall

    D. Administrative

3. Which of the following is considered the strongest form of authentication?

    A. Fingerprint scan

    B. Retinal scan

    C. Iris scan

    D. Password

4. Annie is a security engineer seeking to improve authentication from using just a password, to a password and a smartphone authenticator that uses a time-based one-time password (TOTP). What type of authentication is she implementing?

    A. Two-factor authentication (2FA)

    B. Something you know

    C. Three-factor authentication (3FA)

    D. MFA

5. Which type of communication connectors provide the *BEST* defense and security to leaky authentication vulnerabilities?

    A. Bayonet-Neill-Concelman (BNC)

    B. Standard connector (SC)

    C. `RJ-45`

    D. `RJ-11`

6. Aika, a security engineer, desires to set up secure authentication systems with the fewest vulnerabilities. Which of the following does she *AVOID*?

    A. Extensible Authentication Protocol (EAP)

    B. Challenge-Handshake Authentication Protocol (CHAP)

    C. Protected Extensible Authentication Protocol (PEAP)

    D. Password Authentication Protocol (PAP)

7. Of the following, which is the strongest password?

    A. `Partner`

    B. `C@t456789`

    C. `@b(D3?`

    D. `antiestablishmentarianism`

8. 4-foot fencing that surrounds an organization's parking lot would be of which control type and in which control category?

    A. Physical type and deterrent category

    B. Physical type and preventative category

    C. Technical type and deterrent category

    D. Administrative type and corrective category

9. Aika, a security analyst with *BARA Corp*, is made aware that electro-magnetic interference (EMI) is extending 100 meters outside of the building. What can she install to minimize EMI leakage?

    A. AirHopper

    B. Tempest filter

    C. Van Eck radiation

    D. Van Eck phreaking

10. An authentication system that connects via a dial-up modem and uses the User Datagram Protocol (UDP) protocol on ports `1812` and `1813` is known as what?

    A. Prodigy

    B. Terminal Access Control Access-Control System (TACACS)

    C. Kerberos

    D. Remote Authentication Dial-In User Service (RADIUS)

11. What are two critical issues with signature-based intrusion detection systems (IDSs)? (Choose 2)

    A. They cannot detect all malware.

    B. Encryption makes it difficult to detect malware.

    C. Zero-days.

    D. Signature-based IDSes are very expensive.

12. Corey is a security manager creating a corporate security document that states laptops must maintain the latest patches and use ClamAV malware detection, the LibreOffice suite, and the Thunderbird email client. This document *BEST* fits which category?

    A. Policy

    B. Standard

    C. Guidelines

    D. Procedures

13. Nneka receives an email that her email box is filling up. In the message is a link for her to click so that the issue can be resolved. The link is *MOST LIKELY* to activate which kind of attack?

    A. Denial of service (DoS)

    B. Pharming

    C. Phishing

    D. Social engineering

14. Kyrie is a security analyst that belongs to the LinkedIn group *Secure your Business*. He gets to know some of the others in the group and shares information about his corporate network. Within 2 weeks, his organization is hit with ransomware. Which attack did the hacker use?

    A. Spoofing

    B. Honeynet

    C. Watering hole

    D. Honeypot

15. Breanna is a systems administrator who ensures all systems are secured by not only making backup tapes but also testing backup tapes. What would make this process more secure?

    A. Implement separation of duties.

    B. Implement collusion.

    C. Implement job rotation.

    D. Restrict users from using computers while backups are being made.

16. Giannis is a network engineer setting up a firewall to separate the business' intranet from the internet. For initial setup just after power-on, which is the *BEST* default rule of the firewall?

    A. Allow all traffic.

    B. Deny all traffic.

    C. Allow all traffic except any related to sports, gambling, or pornography.

    D. Deny all traffic except any related to news and social networking.

17. A Linux feature known as SELinux enables which type of access control?

    A. Discretionary access control (DAC)

    B. Access-control list (ACL)

    C. Role-based access control (RBAC)

    D. MAC

18. Markizai is a barber seeking to visit his daughter at the Central Intelligence Agency (CIA). He's instructed to go through a door that locks behind him, and the door in front is also locked. While locked in the room, he hears over the speaker that metal is detected, and he is being detained. What is the name of this room?

    A. Panic room

    B. Mantrap

    C. Chroot jail

    D. Temporary lockup

19. Colt is an administrative assistant at *90 Days Corp* and needs to print his boss's schedule. Which *BEST* describes the relationship?

    A. Colt is the subject, the printer is the object

    B. Colt and the printer are subjects

    C. Colt and the printer are objects

    D. Colt is the object, the printer is the subject

20. Which system uses a series of distinguished names, common names, and domain components, as shown here?

    ```
    dn: cn=Ted Jordan,dc=jordanteam,dc=com
    ```

    A. Active Directory (AD)

    B. Lightweight Directory Access Protocol (LDAP)

    C. Domain Name System (DNS)

    D. Dynamic Host Configuration Protocol (DHCP)

21. Hillary, a grandmother, receives a phone call from *FlyWithMe Airlines* stating she has been granted 100,000 award miles. So that the miles can be added, she gladly provides her password to the *FlyWithMe* associate. What type of attack is this?

    A. Social engineering

    B. Pharming

    C. Phishing

    D. Vishing

22. Grant is a new employee of *DifQu Corp* and is provided his identity card to access the building, and login credentials to do his programming job. What is this process called?

    A. Enablement

    B. Bringing a new employee online

    C. Identity management

    D. Provisioning

23. Rina is a Navy Lieutenant and has secret access to all objects, including fighter jets. She requires top-secret access to complete a portion of her work but is not allowed. This is enforcing which policy?

    A. Least privilege

    B. Need to know

    C. SSO

    D. Federation

24. Landon is a security engineer analyzing biometric devices to access the security operations center (SOC). Device A has a crossover error rate (CER) of 3.5. Device B has a CER of 3.1. Which of the following is true for *BEST* security?

    A. He should use device A because the CER is higher.

    B. He should use device B because the CER is lower.

    C. Use both devices to simplify access to the SOC.

    D. Since the CERs are similar, he should use the lower-cost device.

25. Biometric systems, such as fingerprint scanners, do which of the following when enrolling a new user if designed in the *MOST* secure manner?

    A. Save an image of the user's fingerprint.

    B. Convert the user's fingerprint into a hash and encrypt the hash.

    C. Save an image of the user's fingerprint and encrypt the fingerprint.

    D. Convert the user's fingerprint into a hash.

26. Palm-vein scanners are highly accurate authentication systems because they capture millions of points from the palm, and they also do which of the following?

    A. Collect deoxyribonucleic acid (DNA).

    B. Collect a sweat sample.

    C. Detect keystroke dynamics.

    D. Perform a liveness test.

27. Which feature reduces the risk of attackers abusing privileged accounts because higher-level privileges are time-limited?

    A. Rule-based access control (RBAC)

    B. JIT access

    C. MFA

    D. Least privilege

28. A synchronous token device is utilized to aid in dual-factor authentication by providing what type of output?

    A. One-time password (OTP)

    B. Time

    C. Date

    D. User password

29. An authentication device that contains private keys, certificates, and even fingerprints would be which of the following?

    A. Token

    B. Smart card

    C. Automated teller machine (ATM) card

    D. Memory dual inline memory module (DIMM)

30. Security devices used to protect packaged goods or clothing from shrinkage or loss prevention are called what?

    A. ATM cards

    B. Smart cards

    C. Memory cards

    D. Radio-frequency identification (RFID) tags

31. Sergei is a hacker who enjoys taking train rides for free. He does this by tricking the ticketing system into thinking he has money on his card. Which attack does he use to recharge the card and simulate it has money?

    A. Differential power analysis

    B. Side-channel attack

    C. Electromagnetic analysis

    D. Timing analysis

32. Won Kim just gave Sameeha access to a file so that they can work together on a project. Sameeha can view the file but cannot make modifications. What is the problem?

    A. Won Kim did not grant Sameeha read authorization.

    B. Won Kim did not grant Sameeha write authorization.

    C. Won Kim did not grant Sameeha delete authorization.

    D. Won Kim did not grant Sameeha copy authorization.

33. Ilhan is a systems administrator finishing setup on a new server. After testing, her users cannot access any files on the system. Why is that?

    A. The users are using incorrect passwords.

    B. The users do not have login credentials for the system.

    C. The system is set up as default-to-no-access until access policies are defined.

    D. She is limiting access to monitor authorization creep and need-to-know.

34. SSO systems have which characteristics?

    A. Provide a single username and password to access each system.

    B. Provide a single username with various passwords to access resources.

    C. Provide multiple usernames and passwords to access resources.

    D. Provide a single username and password to access the entire network.

35. Which two of the following are *NOT* virtual private network (VPN) protocols?

    A. TACACS+

    B. Layer Two Tunneling Protocol (L2TP)

    C. TACACS

    D. Point-to-Point Tunneling Protocol (PPTP)

36. After a user completes authentication with their secret key, the user is allowed access to a service with which of the following?

    A. Service Provisioning Markup Language (SPML)

    B. A session key

    C. Security Assertion Markup Language (SAML)

    D. A secret key

37. A user's digital identity is composed of three parts. These are which of the following?

    A. Passwords, personal identification number (PIN), mother's maiden name

    B. Cards, tokens, office key

    C. Fingerprint, iris, palm vein

    D. Attributes, entitlements, and traits

38. Kenhap is a traveling sales rep who often uses hotel computers to email expense reports. He receives an urgent phone call from tech support that *only* his account has been compromised and he is forced to create a new password. What *MOST LIKELY* occurred?

    A. He fell victim to a phishing attack.

    B. A keylogger compromised his credentials.

    C. He was the victim of a social engineering attack.

    D. His password was compromised in a mantrap.

39. Extensible Markup Language (XML) is often used for the federation of identities. Which two of the following take advantage of XML features?

    A. TACACS

    B. Simple Object Access Protocol (SOAP)

    C. Information Systems Audit and Control Association (ISACA)

    D. eXtensible Access Control Markup Language (XACML)

40. Marta is seeking to access photos that she's uploaded to the cloud. She's given the option to authenticate with her Google, Facebook, or Yahoo account. This is using features of which protocol?

    A. SAML

    B. OpenID

C. Open Authentication (OAuth)

D. Online Certificate Status Protocol (OCSP)

41. A type of RBAC that allows for defining a subset of roles based on a superset role is named which of the following?

    A. Superuser

    B. Subset-based

    C. Superset-based

    D. Hierarchical

42. Anna is a network security engineer, and her manager recognizes an overwhelming amount of phishing attacks coming from a remote country. Which access-control model is *BEST* used to deny these attacks?

    A. MAC

    B. Role-based access control (RBAC)

    C. Attribute-based access control (ABAC)

    D. Rule-based access control

43. Blake is a security engineer taking the Linux+ exam. The screen opens with a Bash shell interface in which he is allowed to *only* use the ls, pwd, cd, touch, rm, chmod, and sudo commands. Which type of user interface (UI) is this?

    A. Viewing

    B. Constrained

    C. Read-only

    D. Menu

44. Lionel is told by his manager to open a specific email only if he doesn't receive a package that afternoon and to otherwise delete the email without reading it. This is an example of which type of access control?

    A. Context-dependent

    B. Rule-based

    C. Package-based

    D. Content-dependent

45. Which of the following would *NOT* be considered an SSO system?

    A. Kerberos

    B. Diameter

    C. RADIUS

    D. Circumference

46. An audit finds that Danielle's access card is used to enter a building at 4:55 P.M. 10 minutes later. she's accessing a building 50 miles (100 kilometers) from the first location. What *MOST LIKELY* occurred?

    A. She successfully accessed both buildings at different times.

    B. Her manager's card is often misread as hers because they are in the same department.

    C. The time is improperly set on one of the buildings.

    D. Her card was cloned.

47. Pascal retired from *SMR Corp* 6 months ago. He realizes there are personal photos on the corporate computer that he would like to download. To his surprise, he is able to log in and download his photos. What could have *BEST* prevented this access?

    A. Disabling remote logon capability

    B. Proper deprovisioning

    C. Automatically disabling the account if the wrong password is used three times

    D. Enforcing password changes every 30 days

48. Which of the following is *NOT* true of TACACS+ over RADIUS?

    A. Communicates using the UDP protocol.

    B. Separates authentication, authorization, and accounting procedures.

    C. Encrypts username, password, and accounting messages.

    D. MFA is available.

49. Which of the following is an example of technical control?

    A. Computer usage policy

    B. Proxy firewall

    C. Bollard

    D. Internet use policy

50. *MLP Corp* is under a widespread phishing attack stating that users' email boxes are full and they must click a link to fix the problem. Which is the *BEST* solution?

    A. Program a packet filtering firewall.

    B. Install software-based firewalls on each personal computer.

    C. Install and program a circuit-level gateway within the corporate local area network (LAN).

    D. Security-awareness training and phish auditing.

51. What does geo-velocity mean when it comes to SSO?

    A. A user's password is so simple, they can authenticate within microseconds.

    B. A user is authenticating from locations far from where they last logged in.

    C. A SSO system allows users to authenticate from more locations than the average system.

    D. A user's current location can be determined from where they authenticate.

52. Luis, a systems engineer, gets called in daily to reboot the accounting server because it crashes every afternoon. Which solution does he put in place to resolve this issue?

    A. Luis replaces the motherboard, network cards, and memory cards.

    B. Luis implements log rotations, automated backups, and the removal of old log files.

    C. Luis doubles the hard-drive size.

    D. Luis makes no change because rebooting the server daily is the normal operating procedure.

53. One way to mitigate hackers attempting to cover their tracks by clearing logs is to do which of the following?

    A. Immediately write logs to Redundant Array of Inexpensive Disks (RAID) 0 or RAID 10 systems.

    B. Immediately write logs to RAID 1 or RAID 5 systems.

    C. Immediately write logs to write once, read many (WORM) media.

    D. Save changes by doing incremental backups.

54. Eden is a security engineer seeking methods to mitigate data loss and prevent password compromise by keyloggers. Which is her *BEST* solution?

    A. Have users sign a data loss-prevention document.

    B. Automatically prevent passwords that are too short and dictionary words.

    C. Disable Universal Serial Bus (USB) ports.

    D. Install trojan horses on user systems known to use poor passwords.

55. Istvan is a new security manager and is pretty certain that a backup tape missing yesterday was there today. What can he *BEST* do to mitigate his discomfort?

    A. Put backup tapes in a locked cabinet that only he has control over.

    B. Check recent surveillance of the area.

    C. Ensure that backups are encrypted.

    D. Hold a meeting with his immediate staff and ask who is removing backup tapes.

56. Sniffers are utilities that can listen to network traffic and can collect data, usernames, and passwords. What are two examples of sniffing tools?

    A. John the Ripper

    B. Wireshark

    C. Tcpdump

    D. Snort

57. Amandine contacts her corporate help desk because an app she installed on her computer is not functioning normally. The manager of tech support steps in and states they cannot help her with the app. What is the *MOST LIKELY* reason?

    A. The application is too difficult a problem for the help desk to resolve.

    B. Amandine has not installed the latest patch for the app.

    C. Amandine is using a Linux computer instead of a Windows one.

    D. She is using some form of shadow Information Technology (IT).

58. Jacqueline, a systems administrator, has just completed installing the Kerberos system into the corporate network. Which is her *BEST* next step?

    A. Create user accounts and create passwords.

    B. Test the system.

C. Notify users the system is ready for use.

D. Employ an MFA system.

59. Mobile device management (MDM) helps system administrators manage the security features of smartphones. Which three of the following are features that are managed using MDM?

A. Remote wipe

B. Encryption

C. Patch updates

D. Contact list updates

60. Neymar is a network engineer and suspects a new switch appearing on the network is fraudulent. What is one step he can take to test whether it is legitimate?

A. Use the `ping` command to validate the switch.

B. Use the inventory management system to validate the certificate.

C. Log in to the switch using the default login name and password.

D. Run a hardware inventory to verify the model number is consistent with company policy.

61. Which of the following would be considered an administrative control?

A. Encryption

B. Perimeter security

C. Data backups

D. Non-disclosure agreement (NDA)

62. Jasmin is an administrative assistant for *LHW Corp* and has access to all client data except for social security numbers and information regarding medical conditions. This is an example of what type of access control?

A. People-based

B. Rule-based

C. Context-dependent

D. Content-dependent

63. Mursel is a network engineer who is programming a wireless access point to allow only `05:06:11:aa:a1:88` and `22:11:de:dd:af:fe:23` Media Access Control (MAC) addresses. Which access control model *BEST* describes this?

    A. DAC

    B. RBAC

    C. ABAC

    D. MAC

64. Emily is scanning and saving her tax records to her thumb drive using the convenient multifunctional device at her hotel. Months later, she discovers her identity has been stolen. What *MOST LIKELY* occurred?

    A. A hacker attacked the multifunction device.

    B. A hacker launched a man-in-the-middle (MITM) attack on the network.

    C. A hacker planted a phishing attack on the multifunction device.

    D. A hacker recovered her documents using a dumpster dive attack.

65. A public key infrastructure (PKI) offers which type of trust to users?

    A. Peer-to-peer

    B. Transitive

    C. Coaching

    D. Trust metrics

66. Sasha is an engineer with *EBL Energy*, a regulated industry. He learns at an industry seminar that outsourcing their identity management (IDM) could save them time and money. What is his next *BEST* step?

    A. Find the identity-as-a-service (IDaaS) vendor that presented at the seminar and schedule installation.

    B. Contact three IDaaS vendors, select the one with the best value, and schedule installation.

    C. Work with his manager to construct a statement of work (SOW) and a request for proposal (RFP) to various IDaaS vendors.

    D. Determine if IDaaS fits with EBL Energy's security policy.

67. Leida is using a customer relationship management (CRM) application that requests access to her Google address book. Which protocol is this *MOST LIKELY* using?

A. Registry Authority (RA)

B. OAuth

C. Key Distribution Center (KDC)

D. Ticket Granting Ticket (TGT)

68. Which are two protocols that use XML for the federation of identities?

A. SPML

B. RADIUS

C. Kerberos

D. SAML

69. Devante is part of an intern rotation program where he works in four departments in 12 months. Which risk should be *MOST* considered by the security team?

A. Non-compete agreement

B. Need to know

C. NDA

D. Authorization creep

70. Jamaun is a network engineer who installs a new firewall for the organization. Unfortunately, it does not work because all traffic is blocked. What should he do?

A. Return the firewall for a full refund and use a different manufacturer and model.

B. Reboot the firewall.

C. Reboot the gateway system.

D. Write ACL rules because firewalls are set up as deny by default.

71. Lisa attempts to withdraw $500 from her bank using her ATM card, but she is denied access to her money, even after verifying that there is enough money in her account. What is the *MOST LIKELY* reason that she cannot withdraw her money?

A. She is using a foreign ATM that does not accept her card.

B. She has a transaction-type restriction that allows her to withdraw no more than $300.

C. She used the wrong PIN to access her account.

D. She needs to clean the magnetic strip on her ATM card and try again.

72. Reesie and Carl have the same role that allows them to add hard drives and printers, but not networks or filesystems. Reesie has full access to files that belong to the security team, but Carl only has read access to those files in the DAC system. Why doesn't Carl have full access to the security team's files?

    A. There is a bug in the access-control system and it requires a patch update.

    B. Even though he and Reesie share a security role, he is not part of the security group.

    C. Carl could access the files if he were in the right location.

    D. Reesie has secret access, but Carl only has confidential rights.

73. Russell frequently logs in as root to access Secure Shell (SSH) servers across the internet. The security team hears about this and asks him to log in remotely as a regular user and then use sudo if he needs elevated privileges. Why does the security team recommend this?

    A. Complexity makes it harder for hackers to break into systems.

    B. To reduce the risk of Russell's privileges being compromised.

    C. To reduce the risk of the root password being compromised.

    D. The security team is usually bullied; making such claims helps them keep their power.

74. An example of a device that blocks cars from entering, but allows people through, is known as which kind of device?

    A. Fence

    B. Mantrap

    C. Bollard

    D. Turnstile

75. Eric is a security specialist who needs some administrative rights to add printers and modify networks. Which the *BEST* security control for him in this case?

    A. Role-based access control (RBAC)

    B. Rule-based access control

    C. MAC

    D. ABAC

76. Which utility assures that an application is interacting with a human?

    A. GOTCHA

    B. CAPTCHA

    C. SaveYa

    D. Blockchain

77. Kalani, a security administrator, suspects that many users are using poor passwords after overhearing a conversation that the best passwords to use are favorite dogs or flowers. What is her next *BEST* step?

    A. Immediately launch a password audit.

    B. Change her password.

    C. Inform each department head to conduct password audits.

    D. Ask management for approval to conduct a password audit.

78. Linux systems have a feature that allows a user to elevate their privilege temporarily, *without* knowing the root password. Which command performs this function?

    A. su

    B. sudo

    C. sudoers

    D. administrator

79. Asuelu is a systems administrator training a summer intern to assist with creating new user accounts. He needs the intern to provision 10 new accounts, so he provides the intern temporary rights with which type of account?

    A. Ephemeral account

    B. Superuser account

    C. Standard account

    D. Root account

80. Which of the following biometric authentication devices is the *MOST* intrusive to users, having the ability to collect protected health information (PHI)?

    A. Palm-vein scan

    B. Retina scan

    C. Iris scan

    D. Facial scan

81. Mimi has just received a call from the help desk that her password needs to be updated. A few days later, she notices her account has been compromised. Which kind of attack *MOST LIKELY* occurred?

    A. A hacker impersonated tech support.

    B. Tech support asked Mimi for her password.

    C. The password request was done by phone instead of using a self-service password reset.

    D. Social engineering attack.

82. Yung enjoys using social media and answering all the fun questions about himself. His credit union account was recently hacked and money was stolen from his account. What *MOST LIKELY* occurred?

    A. His credentials and other private data were stolen during a credit union hack.

    B. Hackers launched a DOS attack on the credit union to obtain his login credentials.

    C. Hackers obtained his credentials by launching a Structured Query Language (SQL) injection attack on his computer.

    D. Hackers used information from social media to discover his credentials and his mother's maiden name.

83. Renee is notified that she has just made a purchase of $120 from Walmart that she does not recognize. Her email reports several messages of bad login attempts to other online stores. What is *MOST LIKELY* occurring?

    A. A hacker broke into her computer and stole all her online store credentials.

    B. Her Walmart credentials were discovered on `pastebin`, and hackers are attempting to use these elsewhere.

    C. Walmart sent her the message in error.

    D. There is no issue because she simply forgot about the purchase.

84. Which two of the following statements are true?

    A. A false negative is the same as a Type I error.

    B. A false positive is the same as a Type II error.

    C. A false negative is the same as a Type II error.

    D. A false positive is the same as a Type I error.

85. Larissa is a security auditor who has borrowed someone's ID card. She uses the card to access the office building because the guard allows her to after viewing the card. This access would be described as what?

    A. True positive

    B. False positive

    C. True negative

    D. False negative

86. Which are two examples of biometric controls for authentication?

    A. Keystroke dynamics

    B. Birthday

    C. Height

    D. Thumbprint

87. Which of the following is the *BEST* process for a user to access a resource?

    A. Identification > Authorization

    B. Identification > Authentication > Authorization > Accounting

    C. Identification > Authorization > Authentication > Accounting

    D. Identification > Authentication > Accounting > Authorization

88. Which two of the following are administrative control types?

    A. Acceptable use policy (AUP)

    B. ACL

    C. Exchange Online Protection (EOP)

    D. SSO

89. TACACS+ uses which communication protocol to support authentication, authorization, and accounting?

    A. UDP

    B. TCP

    C. Internet Control Message Protocol (ICMP)

    D. Assessment & Protection (A&P)

90. Toffin is a virtual reality (VR) artist at *Fakeia Corp*. His manager suspects he is giving away software licenses every Monday to a secret contact that sells them online, and they split the money. On Monday morning, Toffin is told to leave and not return for a week. This is known as _____?

    A. Voluntary vacation

    B. Expulsion

    C. Suspension

    D. Mandatory vacation

91. Maya is a security engineer assigned the task of installing a Debian-based online shopping cart that is improperly set up and unpatched for research purposes. What type of computer is she installing?

    A. Web server

    B. Honeypot

    C. Shopping cart

    D. Linux server

92. Which two of the following transmits username and password information in plain text across the network?

    A. Secure Copy Protocol (SCP)

    B. Telnet

    C. SSH

    D. File Transfer Protocol (FTP)

93. Leosel is an inexperienced hacker who performs this type of attack and gets caught by the authorities. Which attack did she run?

    A. Offline rainbow attack

    B. MITM attack

    C. Online brute-force attack

    D. Passive sniffing attack

94. Which access-control system uses a series of layers to distinguish rights— for example, top-secret versus secret—and only allows users with the proper authorization to access those documents?

    A. RBAC

    B. ACL

    C. MAC

    D. DAC

95. Uhura, a security engineer, has installed a biometric system to authenticate users. The device has a relatively high false accept rate (FAR). Which result can she expect?

    A. Too many unauthorized users will be granted access.

    B. Unauthorized users will be blocked.

    C. The FAR will be equal to the CER.

    D. The false reject rate (FRR) will be relatively high.

96. Scotty has just joined DAP Products as a new employee and his accounts must be set up through identity proofing and enrollment. What is the correct order for providing his credentials?

    A. Resolution, verification, validation, authentication

    B. Resolution, validation, verification, authentication

    C. Validation, verification, authentication, resolution

    D. Verification, validation, authentication, resolution

97. Which of the following lists five of the seven control types?

    A. Deterrent, monitoring, access, recovery, authentication

    B. Authentication, corrective, detective, logging, monitoring

    C. Deterrent, corrective, logging, compensating, authorization

    D. Deterrent, detective, corrective, compensating, recovery

98. Which SSO system uses a concept called *tickets* to manage authentication?

    A. RADIUS

    B. Kerberos

    C. SAML

    D. TACACS

99. Greer is a security engineer seeking authentication solutions. Which of the following would be the *MOST IMPORTANT* for her to consider?

   A. Impact and the likelihood of an attack

   B. Threats and vulnerabilities

   C. Single Loss Expectancy (SLE) and Annual Loss Expectancy (ALE)

   D. Which biometric system to consider

100. Which of the following is the *BEST* example of 2FA?

   A. Fingerprint scanner

   B. Bank ATM card

   C. The Global Positioning System (GPS)

   D. Logging in to your bank with a password, and they also request your birth city

Quick answer key

1. C	16. B	31. B	46. D	61. D	76. B	91. B
2. A D	17. D	32. B	47. B	62. D	77. D	92. B D
3. B	18. B	33. C	48. A	63. B	78. B	93. C
4. A	19. A	34. D	49. B	64. A	79. A	94. C
5. B	20. B	35. A C	50. D	65. B	80. B	95. A
6. D	21. D	36. B	51. B	66. D	81. D	96. B
7. B	22. D	37. D	52. B	67. B	82. D	97. D
8. A	23. A	38. B	53. C	68. A D	83. B	98. B
9. B	24. B	39. B D	54. C	69. D	84. A B	99. A
10. D	25. B	40. B	55. A	70. D	85. B	100. B
11. B C	26. D	41. D	56. B C	71. B	86. A D	
12. B	27. B	42. D	57. D	72. B	87. B	
13. C	28. A	43. B	58. B	73. C	88. A C	
14. C	29. B	44. A	59. A B C	74. C	89. B	
15. A	30. D	45. D	60. B	75. A	90. D	

Answers with explanations

1. **Answer: C** Candace's best next step is to contact Harvard's verification department. Information required is the student's name and—often—their tax ID number. References may be friends from college, but they could also be catfish accounts. Most employers never physically touch a new employee's diploma but get the information from their resume. Most credit checks do not contain college graduation information.

2. **Answer: A and D** Administrative controls (which some call operational) include policies, contracts, agreements, and so on. A firewall is an example of technical control (also known as logical control), and this includes devices such as switches, SSO, and so on. Physical controls limit people or vehicles, such as fences, gates, turnstiles, and so on.

3. **Answer: B** A retinal scanner is a biometric type of control that is very accurate—so accurate that it can detect if people carry some disease or ailment, such as cancer or **Acquired Immunodeficiency Syndrome** (**AIDS**), so because of privacy concerns, it is not often used. Iris scanners just look at iris details, not blood vessels, so they are not as accurate as retinal scanners.

4. **Answer: A** This is an example of something you know (password) and something you have (TOTP). This is tough because MFA is a correct answer, but when given the option, choose the more specific answer.

5. **Answer: B Standard connector** (**SC**) for fiber optic cable, which does not give off EMI, making it much less vulnerable to MITM attacks. BNC connectors are designed for coaxial cables, which emit EMI. RJ-45 is used for Ethernet and twisted-pair cables, and RJ-11 is for telephone modem cables, which also emits EMI.

6. **Answer: D** PAP does not encrypt username and password information. The others do. PEAP and EAP can also accept certificates.

7. **Answer: B** Hackers first test for simple passwords that come from the dictionary, so A and D are out. Then, they start with shorter-length passwords, using brute-force methods by trying all possible characters; in other words, after dictionary words, length is more important than complexity. (See `https://www.grc.com/haystack.htm` for more information.)

8. **Answer: A** Physical types control whether people or vehicles are allowed or denied access. For example, turnstiles and K-rated fencing are physical controls. Categories include deterrents, detective, and so on. Deterrents discourage criminal activity. Detective categories, such as alarm systems, detect activity.

9. **Answer: B** An EMI contains meaningful data that a hacker can decipher. AirHopper is an attack that collects emissions from mobile phones. Van Eck phreaking, also known as Van Eck radiation, is a form of eavesdropping that tempest filters mitigate.

10. **Answer: D** Prodigy is a distractor. Kerberos and TACACS are SSO systems, but neither uses dial-up access; they use the TCP protocol for better reliability and do not use ports `1812` and `1813`.

11. **Answer: B and C** Signature-based IDSes rely on matching malware *signatures* to label it as an attack or not. When signatures are encrypted, no match can be detected. Since zero-days are known exploits without solutions, they are undetectable by IDSes.

12. **Answer: B** Policies are higher-level, visionary documents with few details of how the policy is achieved. Procedures discuss how updates are accomplished and how software is installed. Guidelines are non-mandatory recommendations.

13. **Answer: C** Emails that appear to be from system administrators are cleverly spoofed to hide the identity of the hacker. These are technically social engineering attacks, but in the CISSP exam, if there is a more specific option, select that answer. Pharming is an attack on the DNS—when putting a **Uniform Resource Locator** (**URL**) into a browser, the user is redirected to the hacker's domain.

14. **Answer: C** Honeypots and honeynets are tools to attract hackers to conduct malware studies. Spoofing is pretending to be someone or something else. Watering-hole attacks build trust through public newsgroups.

15. **Answer: A** For best security, another worker should test the backups to mitigate the possibility of internal threats. Job rotations would help because this mitigates collusion, but only after implementing separation of duties. Snapshots allow users to work while backups are being made.

16. **Answer: B** After all traffic is blocked (by default), then program the trusted traffic into the firewall. To allow or deny traffic initiated by your users, use a proxy server to allow or deny specific types of traffic.

17. **Answer: D** MAC enforces access depending on the object level (for example, top-secret, secret, confidential, and so on).

18. **Answer: B** A mantrap locks a person in a room if they appear to be an offender. A panic room is a safe room where people can hide while their primary area is under attack. A chroot jail limits where users can maneuver in a filesystem after logging in to a computer. Temporary lockup is an area in local jails to detain suspects.

19. **Answer: A** Subjects are the users actively accessing some device, file, or another user. The resource is the object.

20. **Answer: B** LDAP is similar to Microsoft's AD but runs on all hardware. In this example, Ted Jordan is one of the namespaces for LDAP.

21. **Answer: D** A couple of close possibilities, but social engineering is too general, so choose the more specific answer for the real exam.

22. **Answer: D** Identity management is a system in place to maintain the identities of staff but bringing the employee online, and modifications as staff change jobs are known as provisioning.

23. **Answer: A** Need to know is similar to least privilege but contains the user's rights based on their role. SSO grants a user access to the network with a single username and password. Federation grants a user additional services; for example, a user logs in to their bank, and then the user's credentials are *federated* to the check-printing company, and not entered again.

24. **Answer: B** CER is where the false-acceptance rate meets the false-rejection rate. Since the question asks for the *best security*, option **B** is your only possibility.

25. **Answer: B** This is the best option because if a hacker is able to attack the saved credentials, they have to first decrypt them, and then determine which pattern made the hash.

26. **Answer: D** Palm-vein scanners mitigate spoofing by examining blood flow.

27. **Answer: B** Privileged accounts are those that have some or all administrator rights. For JIT accounts, users only use the privilege when needed, and usually for some limited period.

28. **Answer: A** A synchronous token generates an OTP that expires and regenerates every 30 seconds (for most devices). The user password is a *something-you-know* type authentication that combines with the *something-you-have* token to complete dual-factor authentication.

29. **Answer: B** A token provides an OTP and does not contain private keys, certificates, or fingerprints. An ATM card contains a PIN. Memory DIMMs are not authentication devices but are the computer's **random-access memory** (**RAM**).

30. **Answer: D** Shrinkage is a term used in the retail industry that defines loss, usually due to shoplifting. RFID tags attached to items assist with inventory management and sound an alarm if someone is taking it without paying.

31. **Answer: B** Differential, side-channel, and timing analysis are all side-channel type attacks that can be used against smart cards.

32. **Answer: B** Write authorizations allow Sameeha to modify the contents of the file. The other options have nothing to do with changing file contents.

33. **Answer: C** On the real exam, look for answers related to policy because it is very important to follow management decisions in the real world.

34. **Answer: D** A SSO system allows a user to access network resources with one login name and password, easing usability.

35. **Answer: A and C** L2TP is a recommended VPN protocol because it uses **IP Security** (**IPsec**) for encryption. TACACS and TACACS+ are SSO systems.

36. **Answer: B** When the user authenticates with the **KDC**, a secret key connects to the **ticket-granting service** (**TGS**). Access to a service, such as printing or email, is secured with a session key. SPML and SGML are markup languages used to federate identities across different vendors.

37. **Answer: D** Attributes include job titles, clearance levels, and so on. Entitlements include rights to files or services, and so on. Traits include biometric information.

38. **Answer: B** A phishing attack is carried out by the user clicking on a malformed link in an email (this was not mentioned in the question). Keyloggers are common in hotel computers because of all of the vast **personally identifiable information** (**PII**) to be collected. Social engineering attacks are non-technical by definition. Mantraps lock a person in a room if they appear to be a threat.

39. **Answer: B and D** TACACS is for corporate environments and is not designed for identity federation. ISACA is an organization that competes with the developer of the CISSP exam called **International Information System Security Certification Consortium** (**ISC2**) and offers cybersecurity certifications.

40. **Answer: B** SAML uses XML to help federate identities between business organizations. OAuth authorizes applications to obtain data from other vendors. OCSP is used as a more efficient **certificate revocation list** (**CRL**).

41. **Answer: D** The superuser has all privileges, similar to an administrator account.

42. **Answer: D** Application firewall rules permit and deny emails based on data within messages and use rule-based access control to watch for specific keywords, patterns, and heuristics.

43. **Answer: B** Constrained interfaces limit which user's command can run and where they can maneuver through the filesystem.

44. **Answer: A** There is no such system as a package-based system. The access control does not depend on the content of a package or email, but on whether a package is received. **Rule-based access control** (**RBAC**) is found in firewalls and switches.

45. **Answer: D** SSO allows a user access and authorizations for all of the resources on the network with a single username and password. SSO systems include RADIUS, Diameter, Kerberos, TACACS, TACACS+, and more.

46. **Answer: D** If there were faulty equipment or a faulty card, the system would be giving off dozens of alerts daily for everyone. Since this is a singular issue, it is most likely her card was cloned.

47. **Answer: B** Proper deprovisioning would back up and remove the account altogether. The other options keep the account opened.

48. **Answer: A** All of the others are true of TACACS+ over RADIUS. TACACS+ communicates via the more stable TCP protocol, and RADIUS uses UDP. Neither of them is compatible with TACACS.

49. **Answer: B** Policies (for example, a computer usage policy and an internet usage policy) are administrative controls, and bollards (which are devices that block vehicles from entering, but not people) are physical controls.

50. **Answer: D** Technical solutions can help to minimize spam and phishing attacks, but staff training to recognize and not click links is the most effective way for the few messages that get through.

51. **Answer: B** Option D is an example of geo-location, and is the ability to determine the location of a device when the user authenticates. Geo-velocity validates authentication also based on *when* the user logged in, and asks, for example, *can the user log in from Canada, and then two minutes later log in from Nigeria?*. A user cannot travel 5000 miles in two minutes, so the second authentication would be denied. The others options are distractors.

52. **Answer: B** This is an example of another issue that occurs in the real world when log files start growing, eventually filling the hard drive and causing the server to crash. Increasing hard-drive size only delays the issue.

53. **Answer: C** Writing logs to WORM systems makes the data undeletable or immutable. RAID systems and backups still allow data to be altered on the hard drive.

54. **Answer: C** USB downloaders and USB keyloggers are common hacker tools, and even installing *audit-based* trojans will not help a password from getting stolen with a USB keylogger.

55. **Answer: A** If there is an insider threat, they will not reveal themselves at a meeting, and they have access to encryption keys. Surveillance can often be unclear.

56. **Answer: B and C** John the Ripper is a password-cracking tool, and Snort is an IDS.

57. **Answer: D** Shadow IT is when staff use unsupported software or conduct unsupported activities. Companies provide a whitelist of allowed applications they support; otherwise, the user is on their own.

58. **Answer: B** Before notifying users and provisioning accounts, make sure the system works.

59. **Answer: A, B, and C** Users maintain their contact lists, but MDM features can handle doing remote backups of a user's contacts.

60. **Answer: B** One way to authenticate devices within the network is with certificates. The other methods verify there is a switch but do not validate that the switch is authorized.

61. **Answer: D** Encryption is a technical control. Perimeter security and backups are physical controls.

62. **Answer: D** People-based does not exist. Context-dependent depends more on the situation, such as the hour or location. Rule-based is used as part of ACLs.

63. **Answer: B Rule-based access control (RBAC)** is used commonly in switches and routers permitting and denying access based on MAC addresses, IP addresses, geographic location, and more.

64. **Answer: A** Emily did not make hard copies, so dumpster diving is out. Phishing cannot be done on a multifunction device. MITM would possibly work if she were emailing the documents. Many multifunction devices save copies of records on an internal hard drive.

65. **Answer: B** A PKI uses a **relying party (RP)** that has collected privacy details from an individual or vendor, and because of this, users trust the website they're visiting. Peer-to-peer is available with **pretty good privacy (PGP)** where each party trusts the others implicitly.

66. **Answer: D** Always follow the policy. There may be security and regulatory issues that make it impossible to outsource **IDM** through an IDaaS organization. If management gives the okay, then an SOW and an RFP can be generated.

67. **Answer: B** A **registry authority (RA)** is part of a PKI for registering owners of internet domains. The **KDC** issues session keys or tickets as part of Kerberos, using a **TGT**.

68. **Answer: A and D** SAML and SPML both use XML for **federated identity management (FIM)**.

69. **Answer: D** Authorization creep could happen as Devante moves from department to department, and administrators neglect to remove rights and privileges from previous departments.

70. **Answer: D** ACL rules will allow Jamaun to select which traffic to allow into the corporate network.

71. **Answer: B** The question states that she is at her bank, so it is not a foreign ATM, and if she had forgotten her PIN, she would not be able to see her balance.

72. **Answer: B** Secret and confidential access only make sense on) MAC systems. The question states that they are using DAC. The location may make sense if the system were an ABAC system.

73. **Answer: C** When Russell follows the security team's standard, the root login and password are never used on the Linux or Unix systems, making it impossible for hackers to decrypt the information through an MITM attack.

74. **Answer: C** Fencing, mantraps, and turnstiles all deny people access, but vehicles can storm through those devices.

75. **Answer: A Role-based access control (RBAC)** allows administrative rights to specific functions and allows junior administrators to perform functions without knowing the administrator or root password.

76. **Answer: B** CAPTCHA is either skewed characters that a user has to type, a puzzle to be solved, or item recognition to assure that a human is interacting with the application or website and that it is not a robot or synthetic transaction.

77. **Answer: D** Before launching a password audit, make sure to obtain management approval; otherwise, it could be that the auditor is a hacker. Training staff would also be an important component.

78. **Answer: B** The su command allows the temporary elevation of privileges but requires knowing the root password. The sudoers file is a database of users allowed to use sudo, and which elevated commands they can run.

79. **Answer: A** An ephemeral account is a JIT access feature that sets up a one-time-use account that performs some administrator function, and then the account is deleted. Superuser and root accounts are the same and would allow the intern to have all privileges with no time limit. A standard account cannot add new users.

80. **Answer: B** Retinal scanners can detect medical conditions such as cancer or AIDS, and therefore can be considered a **Health Insurance Portability and Accountability Act (HIPAA)** violation.

81. **Answer: D** When taking the CISSP exam, this is as close as you will get to a "choose all of the above" question. Here, options A, B, and C represent social engineering. Also, the question asks for the *type of attack*.

82. **Answer: D** Options B and C are out because SQL injection attacks would be done on the credit union server, not the user's system, and DOS attacks make systems unavailable. Option A is a possibility, but for a question such as this, use what is given; so, when taking the CISSP exam, focus on the question, and here they mention social media, which leads to D.

83. **Answer: B** If the hacker had stolen all of her credentials, there would be no bad login attempts at other online stores because they would have the correct passwords. It is more likely that Walmart was hacked, and user credentials were discovered there.

84. **Answer: A and B** A Type I error is also known as a false rejection, and Type II is also known as a false acceptance.

85. **Answer: B** For authentication systems, a true positive means *good (person) allowed*, therefore positive means *allow*, and negative means *disallow*. Since she used a false ID card to gain entry, this triggers a false-positive response. When an employee uses their access card but are denied access, this triggers a false-negative response. A true-negative response is when a threat is denied entry. Learn more on this here: https://youtu.be/1TNWAiFROrA?t=12.

86. **Answer: A and D** Height is too inexact for biometric controls. There would be too many false acceptance errors because many people are the same height. There is no biometric device that knows the exact date someone was born; birthdays are something-you-know authentication, not something-you-are authentication.

87. **Answer: B** The process is also known as **Identification and Authorization, Authorization, and Accountability (IAAA)**. The user identifies themselves with their username. Authentication can be done with a password, which confirms the user. Authorization is the rights or privileges the user has been granted by the administrator. Accounting is a record of their activity.

88. **Answer: A and C** An AUP is a document detailing what users can do on the corporate network; an EOP is a policy stating the organization will be fair to all employees regardless of race, sex, color, religion, and so on; an ACL is a *technical-type* authentication system that contains rules to allow or deny access to devices such as firewalls, switches, and so on; SSO is a *technical-type* authentication system allowing users to access multiple services with the same user ID and password.

89. **Answer: B** TACACS (pronounced *Tak-as*) uses port 49 to handle authentication requests to the TACACS authentication server. A&P was a popular grocery store chain in the 1970s.

90. **Answer: D** Expulsion and suspension occur as punishment for a misdeed. In this case, Toffin is only suspected. Voluntary vacation occurs when Toffin requests time off, not when he is being told to take time off. With mandatory vacations, the organization can investigate activities while the internal threat is gone.

91. **Answer: B** There are distractors in the questions and answers. When taking the real exam, focus on the most *secure* answer or the answer that speaks the most to security, so even though all of the responses are true, she is setting up a honeypot to distract hackers.

92. **Answer: B and D** Telnet and FTP were created before encryption was popular. For remote logons today, use SSH instead of Telnet, and SCP or SFTP instead of FTP.

93. **Answer: C** Online attacks send multiple alerts to IDSs. Brute-force attacks, attempting every possible password, collect all the information needed to locate the offender. All of the other attacks help hackers hide from their targets because they are offline. Rainbow tables contain password hashes with matching plain-text passwords.

94. **Answer: C Role-based access control** (**RBAC**) provides access to objects based on a user's job title or position. If they are a junior administrator, for example, they are allowed to mount hard drives and set up printers but have no rights to reboot computers. ACLs are a feature of **rule-based access control** (**RBAC**), where a defined rule grants whether users are allowed access, for example. MAC separates objects into different layers, and DAC allows users to set whatever rights they want on files they own.

95. **Answer: A** A FAR defines the percentage of unauthorized users granted access. An FRR defines the percentage of authorized users denied access. Where these values cross, this is known as the CER. The lower the CER, the better the biometric device.

96. **Answer: B** Scotty resolves and proves his identity by providing his government credentials, such as a driver's license. The **human resources** (**HR**) department ensures the credentials are valid, and can further validate Scotty by doing background checks. He can now receive his credentials and authenticate into computers or enter the building with his new badge.

97. **Answer: D** The seven control types include compensating, corrective, directive, deterrent, detective, preventative, recovery. Logging would be a detective type of control, and contracts and policies are considered directive controls. Fake cameras are considered deterrents that discourage threats.

98. **Answer: B** Kerberos tickets grant access to services and allow users to authenticate without passwords crossing the network, mitigating MITM attacks.

99. **Answer: A** Risk management starts with *risk assessment*, where event impact and likelihood occur. The next step is *risk response*, to determine whether to mitigate or avoid the risks. *Contingency planning* is next, as a backup plan if something goes wrong. Finally, *tracking and reporting* ensure the risk management plan stays current. Learn more about the risk management process here: `http://www.phe.gov/about/amcg/contracts/documents/risk-management.pdf`.

100. **Answer: B** The ATM card requires the user to have a card (something you have) and a PIN (something-you-know). Fingerprinting and GPS would be considered single-factor authentication. Logging in to your bank is requesting two items from one factor (something you know), so this is also considered single-factor authentication.

6
Security Assessment and Testing Domain 6 Practice Questions

Questions from the following topics are included in this domain:

- Designing and validating assessments and tests
- Conducting security control testing
- Collecting security process data
- Analyzing test output data and generating reports
- Conducting and facilitating security audits

To pass the CISSP exam, you must score high in the Security Assessment and Testing domain. Domain 6 has a 12% weighting on the exam and requires you to understand how to design and validate assessments and audits. Audits need to be done within the organization and, externally, acting as if a black hat hacker were performing them.

Security control testing includes vulnerability scanning and assessment, penetration testing, and observing activity through log files. It also covers understanding where management is involved in the security process, including disaster recovery and business continuity.

Code review and testing, misuse case testing, and running synthetic transactions on web applications will also be covered in this chapter. Understanding these software topics puts you a step ahead in preparing to pass the entire exam, since it is a primer to domain 8, Software Development Security.

Questions

1. The key difference between a vulnerability scan and a penetration test is which of the following?

    A. There is no difference between the two as they both search for vulnerabilities.

    B. Vulnerability testing is done only in physical environments to ensure the exit and safety doors are not vulnerable.

    C. Penetration testing is done only in logical environments to ensure firewalls are not vulnerable to attack.

    D. A vulnerability scan searches for vulnerabilities, but a penetration test exploits vulnerabilities.

2. Vivianne is a security tester working with management to determine which systems and departments to examine for an assessment. They also need to explain which processes need to be monitored. This is an example of which phase of the penetration test?

    A. Executing exploits

    B. Conducting documentation

    C. Defining the scope

    D. Running reconnaissance

3. Antoine is an auditor who needs to conduct an audit remotely from home because of a worldwide pandemic. An issue is discovered during the planning phase. What must be resolved?

    A. There is no such thing as a remote audit. All audits must be conducted onsite.

    B. Antoine currently uses dial-up internet at his home.

    C. Wireless internet at the company site is secure.

    D. The equipment operator does not like appearing on camera.

4. Which two of the following Service Organization Controls (SOC) reports are Type I and Type II reports? (Choose two.)

   A. SOC 1

   B. SOC 2

   C. SOC 3

   D. SOC 4

5. Sadio is the president of *Generic Plastics*. To win a bid with a Fortune 500 company, *Generic Plastics* are requesting their SOC 2 reports, stating they need more detail than the SOC 3 provides. SOC 2 reports are internal-only reports. What should he do?

   A. Inform the Fortune 500 company that SOC 2 reports are Generic Plastics-internal only.

   B. Provide the SOC 2 reports to the Fortune 500 company, but do not inform the board.

   C. Follow the policies of the Fortune 500 company.

   D. Follow the policies of Generic Plastics.

6. Before auditing work begins, each organization must understand the Terms of Engagement (ToE). Which of the following is *NOT* part of the ToE?

   A. Pricing

   B. Scope

   C. Responsibilities

   D. Requirements

7. Pernille just ran a scan on her website and discovered that a hacker dropped files into her web server. The result of this test is considered which of the following?

   A. False positive

   B. False negative

   C. True positive

   D. True negative

8. Diego is an IT manager getting reports that three smaller departments have suffered from ransomware attacks. Because of the company having proper backups, no payments were made. What is his next *BEST* step?

   A. Pay the attackers.

   B. Run phishing exercises.

   C. Respond with ransomware attacks against the hackers.

   D. Have staff sign an agreement on not clicking on ransomware links.

9. As part of a physical audit, Wendie discovers several notes in wastebaskets revealing social security numbers, tax identification numbers, birth dates, and home addresses. Which attack did he execute to discover this issue?

   A. Social engineering

   B. Phishing simulation

   C. Wastebasket check

   D. Dumpster diving

10. Level one merchants are required to conduct network scans how often to comply with PCI-DSS?

   A. Quarterly scans by an Approved Scanning Vendor (ASV)

   B. Bi-annual scans by internal auditors

   C. Annual scans by internal auditors

   D. Annual scans by an ASV

11. DeMarcus is an ethical hacker attacking *HART Hospital*, as authorized by their chief information security officer. Federal investigators notice the attack and raid DeMarcus' facility and arrest him. What is the *MOST LIKELY* reason for him being arrested?

   A. All hacking is against the law, including ethical hacking.

   B. He was attacking HERT Hospital instead of HART Hospital, which was unapproved.

   C. He was attacking the human resources department instead of the financial department, as per the agreement.

   D. He started the attack before getting his Get-Out-of-Jail-Free-Card document.

12. When attackers use Google searches, *WHOIS* results, and Wikipedia articles to learn about their potential victim, they are using what kinds of materials?

    A. Privately accessible

    B. Double-blind

    C. OSINT

    D. Library

13. A hacker dials multiple phone numbers, attempting to find modems and fax machines. What is this attack called?

    A. Sandstorm

    B. War dialing

    C. War driving

    D. WarVOX

14. Good vulnerability reduction practices include all the following, *Except* for what?

    A. Patch updates

    B. New software

    C. Closing unused ports

    D. Firmware updates

15. *RMFco* announced they have resolved a zero day in their code. What should their clients do next?

    A. Wait to hear how early adopters are doing with the new security patch.

    B. Download the security patch, but do not install it until the CEO approves.

    C. Wait for RMFco to make a rollup patch with all their latest patches.

    D. Download the new security patch, test it, and install it on their production systems.

16. An application has been written where two processes are running at the same time. For process A to calculate properly, it needs data from process B. If process A calculates before process B completes, this is an example of which condition?

    A. Race condition

    B. Buffer overflow

    C. Process exhaustion

    D. Application development

17. The main difference between a business continuity plan (BCP) and a disaster recovery plan (DRP) is which of the following?

    A. The BCP requires testing, but the DRP does not because it is not as critical as business continuity.

    B. The DRP ensures the core business functions operate during a disaster; the BCP details steps to restore to normal operations after a disaster.

    C. The BCP ensures the core business functions operate during a disaster; the DRP details steps to restore to normal operations after a disaster.

    D. There really is no difference because they both reduce downtime.

18. Which of the following SOC reports not only affirms that security controls are in place, but also lists the effectiveness of the security controls?

    A. SOC 2 – Type I

    B. SOC 2 – Type II

    C. SOC 3 – Type I

    D. SOC 3 – Type II

19. Virgil is a certified ethical hacker hired to find vulnerabilities in the GRC Bank website as if he were a malicious attacker. What type of testing is he conducting?

    A. Purple box testing

    B. Black box testing

    C. Gray box testing

    D. White box testing

20. The practice of conducting timely network vulnerability scans helps to discover which two exposures? (Choose two.)

    A. Open ports

    B. Poor passwords

    C. Unauthorized services

    D. File modifications

21. Amel is a security professional who believes hackers are within her network. She is concerned they are successfully covering their tracks by modifying log files. What are two steps she can take to mitigate altered log files? (Choose two.)

    A. Run consistent network scans.

    B. Install mantraps in the most vulnerable locations of the building.

    C. Write to WORM media.

    D. Periodically copy log files to remote locations.

22. Paul is a hardware technician who needs to replace the hard drive on the server. To complete this job, all users must be off the server. However, he has noticed that there are three users still on the system, since he has been checking remotely every 10 minutes. What is a better way for him to determine whether users are still logged on?

    A. Physically walk to each user's office and visibly determine whether they are still logged on to the server.

    B. Email all logged-on users, asking them to reply to the message once they are ready to log off the server.

    C. Text the users, asking them to call or text Paul once they have logged off the server.

    D. Create a synthetic transaction that polls for users every 5 minutes and then texts Paul when there are no users on the server.

23. Members of a software development team inspect each other's programming for bugs, bloat, and poor assumptions. This is an example of which activity? (Choose two.)

    A. Vericoding

    B. Code review

    C. Static code analysis

    D. Dynamic code analysis

24. A hacker compromises Kasey's account and uses malware to gain administrator rights. What is the term for when a hacker elevates their privileges?

    A. Verification

    B. Validation

    C. Privilege escalation

    D. Privilege creep

25. Frankie is taking 3 months of leave from *AMCO Inc.* to stay with his family because they just had a child. How should his accounts be managed while he is gone?

    A. Make no changes to his account access.

    B. Suspend his login credentials.

    C. Make no changes to his account access but enforce a password change upon his return.

    D. Delete his account.

26. Tab is a systems administrator putting together a backup strategy to secure his files. Which of the following statements is correct?

    A. In general, differential backups are no different than incremental backups.

    B. In general, making full backups every day is not recommended.

    C. In general, differential backups require more tapes to restore, but daily differential backups are faster.

    D. In general, incremental backups require more tapes to restore, but daily incremental backups are faster.

27. Restoring systems back to standard operations after a disaster is known as disaster recovery. What is the process called where vital functions operate immediately after a disaster?

    A. Business continuity

    B. MTBF

    C. MTTR

    D. Disaster recovery

28. Kosovare runs a security training class for her team, teaching them to ask people "Did you forget your badge?" if they see someone wandering around the building without their badge. What can she do to be certain that staff are following their training?

    A. Run example scenarios in class, pretending someone does not have a badge.

    B. Hire an ethical hacker to wander around the building without a badge.

    C. Leave a badge lying in the parking lot and see if someone tries to use it.

    D. Ask security *not* to check for badges and allow anyone into the building.

29. Several signs and emails warn staff not to pick up and use USB drives found in parking lots, or elsewhere. These types of security notices fall under which category?

    A. Training

    B. Professional development

    C. Awareness

    D. Education

30. Sari just opened her new *SocCo* soccer warehouse business and is ready to take orders on her brand-new multi-function fax machine. A few months later, she receives several complaints that someone representing *SocCo* is demanding payments for fees already paid, and desires repayment by gift cards. What is the *MOST LIKELY* problem here?

    A. Attackers collected customer information by hacking her fax machine.

    B. Her bill collection company mistakenly called clients because they never reconciled payments with SocCo.

    C. The clients never paid their bills, and the bill collection is in order.

    D. One of her staff mistakenly called the clients, thinking their accounts were past due.

31. The practice of capturing and analyzing live user transactions from a website or application to monitor the user experience, or measure the performance of the application, is known as what?

    A. RPM

    B. DNF

    C. YUM

    D. RUM

32. Oguchi is a hacker who has crafted an email to collect bank account numbers from victims when they click the link inside it. He sends this email to the COOs and CFOs of *Standard Federal*. What type of attack is this?

    A. Whaling

    B. Spear phishing

    C. Vishing

    D. Phishing

33. *QWRK Inc.'s* software product has just released an update for their application. Soon, the hotline is overwhelmed with calls about a defect. What is the *MOST LIKELY* thing to have occurred?

    A. Users have not upgraded to the latest release of the application.

    B. A developer did not test the code before pushing it to the Git master branch.

    C. QWRK's hotline is the victim of a Telephony Denial of Service (TDoS) attack.

    D. Several hundred customers had their caps lock key on when they tried to enter their new passwords.

34. When an architect, designer, or developer reuses parts, components, or code instead of validating new replacements, the individual is engaged in which activity?

    A. Band-aiding

    B. Technical debt

    C. Refactoring

    D. Poor testing

35. Hedvig is a developer who just completed unit testing for her product. Once this test has passed, which test should she run to ensure the entire product is valid before releasing it to production? (Choose two.)

    A. End-to-end testing

    B. Performance testing

    C. More unit testing

    D. Integration testing

36. Integrating validating security with applications that are part of the DevOps cycle is also known as what? (Choose two.)

    A. DevOps

    B. Rugged DevOps

    C. DevSecOps

    D. Development

37. Gregg is a security manager crafting a preparedness audit for the company. To run the audit, he gets help from his staff and members of the human resources and legal departments. Which type of audit is this?

    A. Internal

    B. External

    C. Third party

    D. Combination

38. Which of the following is *NOT* a requirement of the payment card industry data security standard (PCI DSS)?

    A. Protect stored cardholder data.

    B. Collect the logins and passwords of each online customer.

    C. Restrict physical access to cardholder data.

    D. Regularly test security systems and processes.

39. When simulating an attack on an organization with penetration testing, which test should be done *FIRST*?

    A. Both tests should be done at the same time.

    B. External penetration test when done with automated tools; otherwise, internal penetration test is done first.

    C. External penetration testing.

    D. Internal penetration testing.

40. What is one of the *BEST* ways of ensuring the business continuity plan stays up to date?

    A. Updating BCPs is not required if desk checks are done properly.

    B. Keep the BCP updated as part of change management.

    C. Conduct quarterly reviews of the BCP.

    D. Conduct annual reviews of the BCP.

41. Which individual is responsible for data classification?

    A. Data processor

    B. Data custodian

    C. Data user

    D. Data owner

42. Paul is a security administrator reviewing audit logs from a security information and event management (SIEM) device. This activity would fall under which category?

    A. Detective

    B. Corrective

    C. Preventative

    D. Recovery

43. A computer job is running multiple threads. The value from thread A is passed to thread B a few seconds after the value is defined. If the value is altered within the few seconds before it reaches thread B, and thread B uses this new value, what kind of error occurs?

    A. Bug

    B. TOCTOU

    C. Docker

    D. Race condition

44. Irene is a network manager whose team has recently installed 50 IP cameras. Practicing good security, all default logins and passwords were changed to strong credentials. It is later discovered that one of the cameras is being used as an attack vector to breach the corporate network. What did the team miss?

    A. They forgot to change the credentials of the breached camera.

    B. A team member installed a 51st camera with the default credentials.

    C. Malware is within the cameras that go back to the manufacturer.

    D. The camera had a hardcoded password.

45. Steph is a security administrator who only wants to be notified of valid staff not gaining entry (false negative) when alerts reach three per minute. This level of notification would be considered a what?

    A. False negative counter

    B. Control zone

    C. Baseline

    D. Clipping level

46. Mix is the chief security officer (CSO) of *MLX Corp*, and he is helping the security managers find the best security controls to protect their assets. Which technique does he advise the security managers to use to select the best controls?

    A. Calculate single loss expectancies.

    B. Rank threats and vulnerabilities.

    C. Conduct risk analysis.

    D. List all assets and recommended safeguards.

47. Carli is a security auditor providing results of her audit to the firm. A good audit report contains what types of data? (Choose two.)

    A. Likely threats and vulnerabilities

    B. A list of known attackers and locations

    C. An estimate of repair fees that an auditor can provide

    D. Probability and impact of the exploitation

48. Gyasi measures single loss expectancies, along with likelihoods, to evaluate whether he should purchase insurance or provide his own mitigations to protect corporate assets. These measurement indicators are known as what?

    A. KCI

    B. KGI

    C. KRI

    D. KPI

49. *XYZ bank* has been shut down due to a tornado that destroyed the building. Staff have attempted to call their managers on their cell phones, but a few numbers have changed, so they have reached the wrong people. Also, no one is familiar with first aid or CPR to assist the injured. How could the bank have been better prepared?

    A. Hire an on-site nurse.

    B. Keep the phone and extension lists updated.

    C. Run a desk check.

    D. Train the staff on the best escape routes.

50. Two programs that contain lists of known cybersecurity vulnerabilities, displaying an identification number of each vulnerability and description, would be which of the following? (Choose two.)

    A. CVD

    B. NVD

    C. MITRE

    D. NIST

51. Which of the following is *NOT* a requirement of the payment card industry data security standard (PCI DSS)?

    A. Maintain a firewall to protect cardholder data.

    B. Securely store credit card numbers and CVC codes.

    C. Do not use default settings or default passwords.

    D. Use and regularly update antivirus software.

52. Alyssa is a security system administrator taking a Linux class and learning how to hack networks with a utility called Kali. This type of learning falls under which category?

    A. Awareness

    B. Professional development

    C. Training

    D. Education

53. Which groups are *MOST* responsible for data leaks of personally identifiable information (PII)?

    A. Hackers and script kiddies

    B. External hacktivists

    C. Nation-sponsored hackers

    D. Employees and contractors

54. Arnie is a software developer and suggests to his supervisor to delay the project 1 week so that he can update the application with security mitigations. Why should his supervisor take this advice?

    A. Because delays are normal in software development projects.

    B. It costs significantly less to resolve security issues earlier in the process than later.

    C. Customers are trained to expect projects to always be delayed.

    D. You should always strive for perfect security.

55. An open sourced utility that runs vulnerability scans and penetration tests on a website is called what?

    A. OWASP APPSEC

    B. OWASP ZAP

    C. OWASP API

    D. OWASP WEBGOAT

56. Which of the following is *NOT* a risk of creating an application with open source components?

    A. When developing under the LGPL license, the application must also be open sourced.

    B. The developer may stop supporting the component.

    C. The license may require fees if the primary application uses a for-profit model.

    D. The open source code may contain some proprietary content.

57. Frances has just completed version 1.0.1 of their website and has switched over to the new version. Customers are complaining their purchases are failing. What is Frances' next *BEST* step?

    A. Revert to version 0.99.1 of the website, even though it performs at 10% of normal operations.

    B. Keep version 1.0.1 of the website running, quickly find a fix, and update the website to 1.0.1 when it's complete since the changes are minimal.

    C. Revert to version 1.0.0 of the website and do further testing of 1.0.1 before uploading it.

    D. Keep version 1.0.1 of the website running, quickly find a fix, and update the website to 1.0.2 when it's complete.

58. Bug number 535 was fixed with patch number 1. Bug number 435 was fixed with patch number 2. After customers installed patch number 2, several calls to support stated bug number 535 was returned. What type of testing was *NOT* done in this scenario?

    A. Acceptance testing

    B. Regression testing

    C. Performance testing

    D. Unit testing

59. What is a key problem with getting too many false positives and false negatives on a system?

    A. Alerts eventually get ignored.

    B. Such systems will not pass NIST standards for compliance.

    C. The system is functional but requires extra attention.

    D. The system is about to fail.

60. Which function assists administrators in determining how many shoppers did *NOT* complete a sale on the website?

    A. User activity telemetry

    B. Transaction telemetry

    C. Application telemetry

    D. Dependency telemetry

61. Maurice operates a website selling car parts. From time to time, customers click on the link for reporting a problem with the website. One customer wrote that she cannot find a part for her 1980 Chevy Chevette. What is the next step Maurice must take?

    A. Ignore the message because it has nothing to do with a website issue.

    B. Contact Chevy to see if he can get the part for her.

    C. Ignore the message because he does not sell parts for Chevy cars.

    D. Contact the customer.

62. You can monitor a website's storage, users, and system loads for effectiveness with which of the following utilities?

    A. Alerts and logs

    B. Events and logs

C. Metrics and logs

D. Thresholds and logs

63. A feature that's available in cloud systems monitors specific metrics to determine if more memory, CPU, or disk space is needed for an application to run efficiently. Once the loads return to normal, the system requirements return to normal. What is this feature called?

A. On-demand self-service

B. Autoscaling

C. Measured service

D. Resource pooling

64. Cloud vendors maintain data and applications using which life cycle steps?

A. Migrate --> secure --> monitor --> protect --> configure --> govern

B. Migrate --> secure --> protect --> monitor --> configure --> govern

C. Migrate --> secure --> protect --> monitor --> govern --> configure

D. Migrate --> protect --> secure --> monitor --> configure --> govern

65. In the arena of software development and using the principles of continuous integration (CI), developers work in which order before releasing finished code to production?

A. Test --> build --> code

B. Build --> code --> test

C. Code --> test --> build

D. Code --> build --> test

66. Sacha is a software developer in the area of research and development and requires beta application updates, and sometimes alpha releases. This would make him what type of user?

A. Early adopter

B. Mature user

C. Canary user

D. End user

67. What is the process called where one set of systems runs in a test environment, but gets switched to a production environment when testing completes? The systems that were running in production are now in the test environment.

    A. Blue-green deployment

    B. Purple deployment

    C. Test-prod deployment

    D. Red-blue deployment

68. Hugo runs the business continuity planning board. After completing other testing, he is ready to run a full test in the production environment. Which test should he choose to run?

    A. Structured walkthrough test

    B. Full interruption test

    C. Desk check test

    D. Checklist test

69. One key advantage of virtual machines related to security is which of the following?

    A. The ability to run applications

    B. The ability to take snapshots

    C. The ability to run the Windows operating system

    D. The ability to run the Linux operating system

70. Earnie is developing a website and has concerns that the website will look different on a smartphone, a computer, and a tablet. What kind of testing can he do to ensure the website will look good on all devices?

    A. Website testing

    B. Interface testing

    C. Code review

    D. Misuse case testing

71. Several engineers at *Desel Corp* are getting phone calls from a salesperson to make a $5,000 investment in gold. What caused this?

    A. Vishing

    B. War dialing

C. PhoneSweep

D. An engineer responded to an advertisement in a magazine.

72. Alejandro has noticed that a standard system file is missing. What utility can he use to help determine who deleted the file?

A. Folder auditing

B. Directory auditing

C. File auditing

D. Server auditing

73. What are two key differences between internal and external auditors? (Choose two.)

A. Internal auditors have a black box view of the organization.

B. External auditors are more effective because they are not affected by internal bias.

C. Internal auditors can measure effectiveness based on a recent baseline.

D. External auditors are more affected than internal auditors by the politics of the organization.

74. Two free, open source utilities that security administrators use to verify whether users are prone to phishing attacks are called what? (Choose two.)

A. Hak5

B. Gophish

C. Kali

D. King Phisher

75. What steps should be followed for an internal audit to ensure that the security study is beneficial?

A. Define audit --> Define threats --> Assess current status --> Resolve --> Prioritize

B. Define audit --> Define threats --> Prioritize --> Assess current status --> Resolve

C. Define threats --> Define audit --> Assess current status --> Prioritize --> Resolve

D. Define audit --> Define threats --> Assess current status --> Prioritize --> Resolve

76. Users have been split into two groups to test whether a single difference in a social media website keeps users more interested in the website and on it for longer. What is this testing called?

    A. Negative testing

    B. A/B testing

    C. Red/blue teams

    D. Penetration testing

77. Which of the following is *NOT* a software tool that analyzes source code for bugs and security vulnerabilities?

    A. Compiler

    B. SonarQube

    C. WhiteSource

    D. Veracode

78. Griedge is a network administrator who keeps router and switch firmware updated. She scans each update for malware and verifies the hash values. Users have noticed anomalies in the network and have discovered that hackers have gained entry. What caused this?

    A. A hacker was able to infect the routers and switches with malware after the firmware updates.

    B. A hacker was able to get malware installed in the firmware source code.

    C. An inside attacker infected the routers and switches with malware after the firmware updates.

    D. Untrained users unintentionally installed malware on their routers and switches after the firmware updates.

79. Yuki uses measurements based on all possible security alerts and monitors them weekly against her baseline and metrics to ensure she can reasonably protect the organization. These measurement indicators are known as what?

    A. KCI

    B. KGI

    C. KRI

    D. KPI

80. Ewa, a chief security officer (CSO), has just discovered that unreleased designs of their next-generation vehicle are in the *Car 'n' Driver* magazine. What can she do to mitigate future design leaks to the public?

    A. Implement DLP.

    B. Implement MAC.

    C. Implement a forward proxy server.

    D. Install and program a firewall.

81. Nilla is the manager of the business continuity plan board and wants to run a very simple, low-effort drill that ensures most of the vital pieces are in place in case of a disaster. Which test does she seek to run?

    A. Full interruption test

    B. Cutover test

    C. Parallel test

    D. Desk check test

82. Data remediation and reconciliation projects help keep records clean and consistent. Systems that monitor records for inconsistencies, and alert administrators of inefficiencies, are known as what?

    A. Remediation systems

    B. Reconciliation systems

    C. Continuous auditing and analytics

    D. Information governance

83. Nikita is a systems administrator who is in charge of recovering data on a server because the hard drive has crashed. She starts the recovery process and learns that the backup tapes are blank. What did the team neglect to do?

    A. Test the RAID 0 (zero) system.

    B. Perform backup verification.

    C. Use the correct backup tape size.

    D. Enable encrypted and compressed backups.

84. Debinha is an application developer who has completed a program that accepts credit cards. She simulates being a hacker, attempting to steal credit card information. This is an example of what kind of testing?

    A. Normal case testing

    B. Misuse case testing

    C. Static code analysis

    D. Code review

85. A centralized system that analyzes, correlates, and retains log files for the entire corporate network is known as which device?

    A. TACACS

    B. LDAP

    C. Kerberos

    D. SIEM

86. Jozy is a security analyst reviewing log files as part of a standard audit. He has noticed that apparent threats have attempted access at 2 A.M. on system A, but at 4 P.M. on system B. He checks the date on both systems and sees that it's incorrect on one of them. Which utility needs to be set up or tuned properly?

    A. NTP

    B. BIND

    C. DNS

    D. NAMED

87. Timely log reviews are conducted because they help security professionals uncover which kinds of issues? (Choose two.)

    A. Detect attackers attempting to break into the network.

    B. Zero days.

    C. Whether users are using strong passwords.

    D. Whether files are being modified via integrity checks.

88. Buffer overflow attacks occur because of poorly written applications. Attackers can exploit this vulnerability and can potentially gain access to the entire computer. They are called buffer overflow attacks because these attacks occur where?

    A. Spaces on hard drives where files have been marked for removal

    B. The main memory of the computer

    C. Unused space in applications

    D. Unused space within files

89. Cobi is a new business owner and has just purchased 100 prospect leads from *Glengary Leads*. The prospects are guaranteed to be interested in real estate opportunities. What is his *Greatest* risk?

    A. That only 90% of prospects will have interest in real estate opportunities.

    B. That only 50% of prospects will have interest in real estate opportunities.

    C. The lead list is stale because Glengary Leads has a poor reputation.

    D. That only 10% of prospects will have interest in real estate opportunities.

90. Tobin is a security manager and has learned that a new software management application has been introduced to the company. Staff are excited to use it because it will double production at half the cost of past methods. What is her *BEST* recommendation?

    A. Test the software for vulnerabilities before rolling into production.

    B. Because of past user testimonials, roll the application into production immediately.

    C. Because of user demand, roll the application into production immediately.

    D. Because of financial pressures, roll the application into production immediately.

91. Any testing that's performed where the evaluator has zero knowledge of the environment is also known as which kind of test?

    A. White box testing

    B. Red box testing

    C. Opaque testing

    D. Blind testing

92. Which *BEST* represents the five-step penetration testing process?

    A. Reconnaissance --> Assess vulnerabilities --> Scan --> Exploit --> Reporting

    B. Reconnaissance --> Scan --> Exploit --> Assess vulnerabilities --> Reporting

    C. Reconnaissance --> Scan --> Assess vulnerabilities --> Exploit --> Reporting

    D. Reconnaissance --> Exploit --> Assess vulnerabilities --> Scan --> Reporting

93. Dzsenifer is an ethical hacker who has been hired by *RCG Credit Union* to find security vulnerabilities as if she were a high-level executive at the bank. What type of testing is this?

    A. Gray box testing

    B. White box testing

    C. Black box testing

    D. Red box testing

94. Which two common vulnerabilities are typically found during internal scans?

    A. Wireshark results

    B. Open network ports

    C. Unpatched systems

    D. Nessus results

95. Which Service Organization Controls (SOC) reports related to security and privacy do *NOT* focus on financial controls? (Choose two.)

    A. SOC 1

    B. SOC 2

    C. SOC 3

    D. SOC 4

96. What are two aspects of compliance audits? (Choose two.)

    A. They prove that the auditee is following regulatory requirements.

    B. They must be exclusively performed by third-party auditors.

    C. They must be exclusively performed by internal auditors.

    D. They prove that the auditee is following their policies.

97. Internal audit teams have what advantage over third-party auditing?

    A. Internal auditors have the best understanding of the technology, people, and processes.

    B. Internal auditors have exposure to other security methods that are used by other organizations.

    C. Internal auditors are not concerned with the impact of submitting a negative audit.

    D. Internal audits are looked at more favorably by regulators over third-party audits.

98. Davici is an auditor. As part of their inspection, they must review a room where no cameras are allowed due to the risk of a fire occurring. What is his next *BEST* step?

    A. Conduct the audit within the room and shoot fewer pictures because the risk of a fire occurring is low.

    B. Conduct the audit within the room and sketch drawings where required.

    C. Skip the room; if the rest of the audit passes, provide a positive complete certification.

    D. Cancel the audit and delay the final certification.

99. Rose has conducted an audit for *MMOH Enterprises*, but because of a missing part, she cannot complete the audit. The part will arrive next week. What is her next *BEST* step?

    A. Pass MMOH as a completed audit and apply for the certificate of success.

    B. Fail MMOH Enterprises and schedule the next 3-year audit.

    C. Schedule a time when the audit can be completed.

    D. Redefine the scope of the audit.

100. What is the next step of the audit process after conducting the audit?

    A. Document the results.

    B. Inform management.

    C. Determine the goals.

    D. Select audit team members.

Quick answer key

1. D	16. A	31. D	46. C	61. D	76. B	91. D
2. C	17. C	32. A	47. A D	62. A	77. A	92. C
3. B	18. B	33. B	48. C	63. B	78. B	93. B
4. A B	19. B	34. B	49. C	64. B	79. A	94. B C
5. D	20. A C	35. A D	50. A B	65. D	80. A	95. B C
6. A	21. C D	36. B C	51. B	66. C	81. D	96. A B
7. C	22. D	37. A B	52. C	67. A	82. C	97. A
8. B	23. B C	38. B	53. D	68. B	83. B	98. B
9. D	24. C	39. C	54. B	69. B	84. B	99. C
10. A	25. B	40. B	55. B	70. B	85. D	100. A
11. D	26. D	41. D	56. A	71. D	86. A	
12. C	27. A	42. A	57. C	72. C	87. A D	
13. B	28. B	43. B	58. B	73. B C	88. B	
14. B	29. C	44. D	59. A	74. B D	89. C	
15. D	30. A	45. D	60. A	75. D	90. A	

Answers with explanations

1.   **Answer: D** Both types of testing are done in physical, logical, and administrative environments, and both search for vulnerabilities, but penetration testing takes the extra step of running exploits, ideally doing no harm.

2.   **Answer: C** After defining the scope of an audit, penetration testing includes reconnaissance, enumeration, vulnerability analysis, launching the exploit, and documenting the final report for management.

3.   **Answer: B** This question is intentionally vague because the real exam contains some questions like this where certain likely assumptions must be made; that is, to conduct a remote audit, there will need to be a live video feed. Dial-up internet is too slow for viewing the video stream from the audit site. Remote audits are allowed, if necessary, for example, during a worldwide pandemic. Corporate policies should cover whether an employee can be on camera. You can learn more about audits at https://iaf.nu/articles/FAQ/288.

4.   **Answer: A and B** The SOC 3 report, which is provided by suppliers, contains general information that's usually posted on a website to prove that an organization practices good security protocols. SOC 4 reports do not exist.

5. **Answer: D** Policies may allow internal data to be released, depending on certain sized deals or relationships. If they have such a policy, they must provide the SOC 2 reports to the Fortune 500 company, so following Generic Plastics' policies is the best answer here.

6. **Answer: A** Pricing is part of the offer letter, after the terms of engagement (often called the rules of engagement) are completed. Scope, objective, definitions, responsibilities, how to handle changes, and requirements are all part of the written terms of engagement.

7. **Answer: C** A true negative rarely gives an alert because no problem has been detected. An example of a false positive is when a user attempts to download a file but is denied because the system incorrectly sees them as a threat. A false negative would not have reported a website breach. To learn more about true and false positives and how they work, visit `https://bit.ly/3cTBFIU`.

8. **Answer: B** Ransomware against hackers is considered a hack-back and is against the law. An employee agreement will not help. Most users are fooled into clicking ransomware links since they appear to be normal.

9. **Answer: D** Dumpster diving is more detailed than social engineering, even though dumpster diving is a type of social engineering. The wastebasket check is a false option. Phishing simulations are done via email.

10. **Answer: A** Approved scanning vendors (ASVs) are required to run penetration and internal scans, and then report the results to their acquiring financial institution. Level 1 merchants process more than 6 million credit card transactions annually, so they are desirable targets for hackers. Learn more here: `https://semafone.com/blog/a-comprehensive-guide-to-pci-dss-merchant-levels/`.

11. **Answer: D** Running approved penetration tests is not against the law. Once chief management has agreed to the test, they need to provide a *Penetration Test Approval* document to the ethical hacker in case they appear malicious to authorities. This includes the contact information of top management so that the authorities can contact them and ensure the hacking was approved.

12. **Answer: C Open source intelligence (OSINT)** uses common free, legal, and publicly available tools to learn about the target.

13. **Answer: B** Sandstorm's *PhoneSweep* and *WarVOX* are applications that are used to conduct war dialing. War driving is where you scan for Wi-Fi hotspots, usually while driving a car.

14. **Answer: B** New software generally contains bugs and needs to be updated and patched immediately. The others are good vulnerability reduction practices.

15. **Answer: D** Zero days are major security issues that hackers exploit, and there is no fix for the vulnerability yet. Once a fix is created, the update needs to occur as soon as possible.

16. **Answer: A** A buffer overflow attacks memory due to poor coding and allows the attacker to control the process. Process exhaustion occurs when a process hangs because it has run out of resources. Application development is basic computer coding and is not a negative condition.

17. **Answer: C** Business continuity plans and disaster recovery plans must be tested to ensure the organization can operate and recover after a major disaster, such as a fire or tornado.

18. **Answer: B** SOC 3 reports do not have differing types, and SOC 2 – Type I shows that security controls are in place.

19. **Answer: B** Malicious hackers have no internal knowledge of the environment. White box testing simulates an internal attacker because they have full knowledge of the environment. Gray box means the hacker has some knowledge of the internal environment. Purple box is a false option.

20. **Answer: A and C** Poor password testing is done with tools such as *Cain & Abel* or *John the Ripper*. File modifications are checked with integrity checkers such as *Nessus*. Open ports are checked with tools such as *Nmap*.

21. **Answer: C and D Write-once read-many (WORM)** media cannot be modified once written. This media prevents attackers from deleting their entries. Also, hackers cannot delete entries from remote systems they cannot access. *Mantraps* lock a threat in a room until security staff arrives. *Network scans* search for open ports and services.

22. **Answer: D** This is a great case for using synthetic transactions. Physically walking to each user could take too much time because they could be 100 miles away from Paul. Email and texting are good, but the user might forget to contact Paul after logging off.

23. **Answer: B and C** Dynamic code analysis is where we validate results when users run the application. *Vericoding* is a false option.

24. **Answer: C** Verification ensures all the components are in place, while validation ensures that all the components are effective. Privilege creep is the accumulation of privileges that you might obtain as you move from department to department within an organization.

25. **Answer: B** Temporarily suspending access protects Frankie's data. At the same time, the account is not vulnerable to hackers since it has been temporarily closed. Timely password changes are important, but if the account is left open while he is gone, it is still vulnerable to attack.

26. **Answer: D** Many companies make daily full backups, which simplifies recoveries because only one tape is needed. Differential backups require fewer tapes to restore than incremental, but daily backups generally take longer.

27. **Answer: A Mean time between failure (MTBF)** is a prediction as to when hardware will fail. **Mean time to repair (MTTR)** is the average time it takes to repair an item after a failure. MTBF and MTTR are related to events or incidents, not business-wide disasters.

28. **Answer: B** Asking security not to check for badges leaves the entire building insecure; this should never be done. Leaving a badge in the parking lot to see if it will be abused is testing a different scenario; we are concerned with people *not* wearing a badge. Example scenarios in the class are good, but an ethical hacker runs a live case scenario and can provide a report on the experience.

29. **Answer: C** Professional development and education are formalized programs where students can obtain credit hours toward a certificate or degree. Training includes classes that are designed to teach an individual a new skill. Awareness is exposure to different subjects so that people can recognize security issues and respond to them better.

30. **Answer: A** Multi-function printers attached to company networks are vulnerable to attacks and can grant a hacker access to the entire network, where they can exploit customer records. Bill collection companies and staff would not request payment via gift cards.

31. **Answer: D Real-user monitoring (RUM)** measures user and application performance. **Yellowdog Updater, Modified (YUM)**, **Red Hat Package Manager (RPM)**, and **Dandified YUM (DNF)** are Linux package management tools.

32. **Answer: A** Spear phishing is close, but since he is targeting **Chief Operating Officers (COOs)** and **Chief Financial Officers (CFOs)**, this is whaling because they are high-level executives that have more knowledge about the organization. Phishing is similar, but phishing attacks are sent to a broad community, and vishing is done by phone, not email.

33. **Answer: B** The hotline was not overwhelmed until the new software was released, so customers performed the update. The attacker behind a TDoS attack would not hang on the phone line long enough to open a service call about a defect. Most systems warn users that their *Caps Lock* key is on when entering their passwords.

34. **Answer: B** Poor testing, band-aiding, and code refactoring, such as reusing code and making small changes so that it works in the new software, are all components of technical debt. These quick fixes are left unvalidated and can end up costing much more to fix as the project moves closer to production.

35. **Answer: A and D** End-to-end testing checks the entire system, while integration testing validates that the different units work together. More unit testing is not necessary, and performance testing tests the product under varied loads, but not in terms of functionality.

36. **Answer: B and C** DevOps is the combination of development and operations, which includes testing and release to production. You can learn more about *rugged DevOps* here: https://insights.sei.cmu.edu/blog/build-devops-tough/.

37. **Answer: A** Internal audits are conducted by the organization's staff. External audits occur via a business supplier to ensure their security meets the policy. Since all the testers work for the organization, this is not a third-party audit because this requires hiring an outside organization to conduct the audit. A combination audit would be run by company resources and third-party resources. You can learn more here: https://quality-one.com/auditing/.

38. **Answer: B** Maintaining account information for online customers is not a requirement of PCI-DSS.

39. **Answer: C** External penetration testing simulates a threat from outside the company and helps expose vulnerabilities that can be exploited. Then, an internal penetration test is performed to simulate what an attacker can do after exploiting external vulnerabilities. The internal test also simulates an insider attack. These tests can be performed by corporate teams or professional third-party organizations.

40. **Answer: B** As new systems and software are added to the environment, always ask what effect this change will have on business continuity. This is normally done within the change management process. Most teams run change management weekly, so updates are frequent.

41. **Answer: D** Data users can access the data if they meet the correct classification level. The data custodian is in charge of making good backups. The data processor uses this information to send postal mail and emails. The data owner is legally accountable if the data is breached.

42. **Answer: A** SIEM devices are **Intrusion Detection Devices (IDS)**, not **intrusion prevention devices (IPS)** such as firewalls. A corrective device corrects the asset state after an exploit; for example, a water sprinkler is a corrective device in case of a fire. Backup tapes are examples of recovery devices that return the asset to its normal state.

43. **Answer: B** This is a bug, but there is a more specific answer. **Time-of-check to time-of-use (TOCTOU)** is the result of a race condition where the value is *not* verified immediately before it's used by the next computational thread. Docker is a utility that's used to clone a virtual machine image.

44. **Answer: D** Hardcoded passwords are written into the firmware. The best way to remove these is with a security firmware update from the manufacturer. They changed all the credentials, so they did not miss one. Also, they only installed 50 cameras according to the question. If malware was followed back to the manufacturer, several cameras would have been breached.

45. **Answer: D** A baseline is considered an expected normal level for alerts; this value could be higher or lower than the clipping level. False negative counters and control zones are both false options.

46. **Answer: C** Listing assets and safeguards, ranking threats and vulnerabilities, and calculating **single loss expectancies (SLEs)** are all phases of the risk analysis process.

47. **Answer: A and D** A good technical audit also lists the recommended actions to take to reduce the impact of exploitation. A list of attackers and locations is too numerous, and changes by the minute. The auditor must not be the repair person because this is poor separation of duties, and therefore insecure.

48. **Answer: C** **Key control indicators (KCIs)** are used to evaluate a security control and if it stays within a certain tolerance level. **Key risk indicators (KRIs)** measure whether risks fall within tolerances that have been measured against **SLEs**. **Key performance indicators (KPIs)** are a leading indicator for evaluating whether the organization is on target to achieving a goal. **Key goal indicators (KGIs)** are lagging indicators that are evaluated once a goal has been reached.

49. **Answer: C** Part of the desk checking process is to make sure phone numbers are updated, training programs are implemented on escape routes and first aid, and to determine whether everyone knows their role as part of a disaster.

50. **Answer: A and B** MITRE is a community-driven effort that tracks and provides the **common vulnerabilities and exposures (CVE)** list. The **national vulnerability database (NVD)**, provided by NIST, syncs the CVE list of vulnerabilities to their list.

51. **Answer: B** The **card verification code (CVC)** that is on the back of most credit cards should *not* be saved by the merchant.

52. **Answer: C** Professional development and education are formalized programs where students can obtain credit hours toward a certificate or degree. Training includes classes that are designed to teach an individual a new skill. Awareness is exposure to different subjects so that people can recognize security issues and respond to them better.

53. **Answer: D** Nation-sponsored hackers and other hackers often persuade employees to leak data by offering them money or making threats. Script kiddies are people who are new to hacking and generally harm themselves more than others. Hacktivist are driven by a cause; for example, they may really want people to use stronger passwords. Learn more about data breaches here: `https://www.pandasecurity.com/en/mediacenter/security/who-is-to-blame-data-breaches/`.

54. **Answer: B** According to NIST and the Poleman Institute, repairs that might cost $80 to fix during development end up costing $240 to fix at build time. If you were to repair during the **quality assurance (QA)** process, it would cost $960, and after production, it would cost $7,600. You can learn more about defect costs here: `https://owasp.org/www-pdf-archive/APAC13_Keynote_HyojinChoi.pdf`.

55. **Answer: B** Features include an intercepting proxy server, automation tools, fuzz testing, and script support. OWASP *Webgoat* is an intentionally vulnerable website you can practice on with OWASP ZAP. OWASP AppSec Pipeline applies DevOps and Lean principles for designing secure applications. OWASP API Security Project focuses on mitigating vulnerabilities in **application programming interfaces (APIs)**.

56. **Answer: A** Free software, although usually *free* of charge, allows users specific *freedoms* in terms of liberties; for example, the right to view the source code. The **Lesser General Public License (LGPL)** allows the developer to keep their source code closed, if desired, whereas the **General Public License (GPL)** requires that applications using GPL code must also open source their applications. The other risks can harm the developer financially. You can learn more here: `https://www.gnu.org/licenses/lgpl-3.0.html`.

57. **Answer: C** Revert to a known-good version so that the organization does not lose sales. The other options risk losing business and customer goodwill.

58. **Answer: B** Regression testing ensures no functionality is lost or that past fixed problems are not reintroduced into the system. Acceptance testing focuses on meeting requirements. Performance testing checks how the system responds to different loads. Unit testing checks an individual module; this usually results in regression problems because examiners do not continue with a full functional or integration test.

59. **Answer: A** All alerts, including true alerts, can eventually be ignored. The other options are not true because getting false alerts is common across common systems.

60. **Answer: A** User activity telemetry informs administrators of click streams that have been started and abandoned. Transaction telemetry is a false option; there is a feature called **transaction traceability** that monitors workloads. Application telemetry monitors error messages and the response times of web apps. Dependency telemetry monitors varied response times, such as networks or databases.

61. **Answer: D** The next step is to contact the customer to learn more about the issue and determine which part she needs. This is because if Maurice contacts Chevy first, he will not know which part to order. If Maurice ignores customers' issues, they will eventually feel like he does not care about them, and they will shop elsewhere.

62. **Answer: A** Alerts use thresholds and metrics to immediately inform administrators that a system requires attention. Events are entries that go into log files.

63. **Answer: B** On-demand self-service does not operate automatically but requires manual intervention when it comes to adding resources. Measured services can provide more services manually, but not automatically. Resource pooling allows multiple tenants to share resources; if one user overloads the system, it will affect all the users.

64. **Answer: B** Migration refers to moving data to the cloud vendor. Securing data is ensuring that the software can defend known threats. Protection ensures the data is always available; part of this is making backups. Monitoring tracks the health and availability of data. Configuring ensures that the application is set up to run efficiently. Governance ensures that applications correspond to the policy that has been set up.

65. **Answer: D** Coding, building, and testing are the correct steps to take when developing code before releasing it to production. Most releases start smaller with some form of beta testing before being released to a wider audience.

66. **Answer: C** Canary users desire bleeding-edge features as soon as possible. Early adopters use applications after some testing and may use higher generation beta software, but not early releases. End users only use applications after thorough testing, often using older software versions because they do not trust newly released gamma software.

67. **Answer: A** The production systems may be on the green servers and being tested on the blue servers. Once testing is complete, blue gets switched to production, and green becomes the test environment. The other options are false options. Red-blue teams are used in ethical hacking exercises, where red is the threat and blue is the defender. Purple members maximize the effectiveness of the hacking exercise. You can learn more here: `https://blog.christianposta.com/deploy/blue-green-deployments-a-b-testing-and-canary-releases/`.

68. **Answer: B** Walkthroughs are what they sound like, where the team *walks through* a scenario without touching the production systems. Desk checks and checklist tests allow the team to discuss scenarios and make educated guesses as to how to best recover from disaster. Full interruption tests use live systems to evaluate responses to a disaster.

69. **Answer: B** Snapshots are instant backups. Virtual machines can make snapshots daily, or even more frequently. When data needs to be recovered, it is as simple as reverting to a snapshot, which is much faster than recovering from a backup tape.

70. **Answer: B** Website testing is too general an answer. Interface testing is specifically what needs to be done: testing the website with each device. A code review is where the source code is inspected by a team, while misuse testing is intentionally trying to break the software's security.

71. **Answer: D** The question asked what *caused* the attack, not the *type* of attack being performed. The technique the boiler room operators are using is known as war dialing. They dial through all the extensions the original investor *gave them* by responding to the advertisement. This is a type of vishing attack because the attackers are selling investments they do not own. *PhoneSweep* is a tool that's used for war dialing.

72. **Answer: C** Server, directory, and folder auditing are too broad for validating the entire server, directories, and folders, respectively. File auditing just validates files and informs Alejandro who modified, created, or deleted a file.

73. **Answer: B and C** Internal auditors have a white box view of the organization because they know all the details of the company. Internal auditors are more affected by organizational politics, and these relationships could cause them to alter the results so that they're more favorable to companies or business units.

74. **Answer: B and D** Hak5 and Kali provide security toolkits that contain phishing simulators, but these are general-purpose ethical hacking utilities. *Gophish* and *King Phisher* provide phishing simulators with GUI environments showing users that fell victim to the email.

75. **Answer: D** Internal security audits help mitigate data breaches. Conducting an audit at the best value involves the five steps provided in answer D. For more details, visit `https://blog.dashlane.com/conduct-internal-security-audit/`.

76. **Answer: B** A/B testing is a basic controlled experiment where a single difference is tested. Red and blue teams are used as part of penetration testing. The red team acts as the hacker, while the blue team acts as the defender. Negative testing hardens applications, checking to see how they will respond to unwanted input.

77. **Answer: A** A compiler converts source code into machine language and can find coding syntax errors. *SonarQube*, *WhiteSource*, and *Veracode* search for security vulnerabilities, poorly written libraries, and licensing-related issues to keep the source code accurate and consistent.

78. **Answer: B** The update developer created a hash value in the code they believed was credible; therefore, the resulting hash gets marked as trusted, even though the code should be marked as untrusted. Malware protection scanners would have picked up issues in options A, C, and D.

79. **Answer: A** KCIs are used to evaluate security controls and whether they stay within a given threshold. **KRIs** measure whether risks fall within tolerances. **KPIs** are a leading indicator to evaluate whether the organization is on target to achieve the desired goals or objectives. **KGIs** are lagging indicators that are evaluated once a goal has been reached, and they measure how well the goal was achieved. You can learn more here: `https://stratexsystemsadmin.squarespace.com/blog/2013/1/30/kpis-kris-kcis-are-they-different-if-so-does-it-really-matte.html`.

80. **Answer: A Data loss prevention (DLP)** is the best solution for stopping insider attacks like this. **Mandatory access control (MAC)** can help, but the insider leaking the designs may have top-secret clearance. A proxy server enforces security policies, such as which websites can be viewed. A firewall blocks unwanted traffic from entering the corporate network.

81. **Answer: D** Full interruption and cutover tests simulate a disaster using production systems. Parallel tests build up systems that are identical to production systems and simulate a disaster on the secondary systems. A desk check involves the team reviewing and updating a checklist of items that are important in case a disaster occurs.

82. **Answer: C** Continuous auditing and analytics enforces good information governance, which includes remediation and reconciliation to keep records such as social security numbers, phone numbers, pricing, costing, and more clean and consistent.

83. **Answer: B** After encrypted and compressed backups are made, they must be tested. RAID 0 systems don't data mirroring like RAID 1 systems do. If the backup tapes did not physically fit, they would have discovered that much earlier.

84. **Answer: B** Normal case testing assumes that you are attempting to use the software in a normal manner, not as an attacker. Code review and static analysis involves other members of the team reviewing each other's source code for the application.

85. **Answer: D** A **security information and event management system (SIEM)** logs and tracks events over the entire network. **Kerberos**, **LDAP**, and **TACACS** are network-based authentication systems, and they only log authentication events.

86. **Answer: A** The **network time protocol (NTP)** ensures that all the systems are time-synchronized from a standard server. **Domain name service (DNS)**, **NAMED**, and **BIND** are all domain name search utilities.

87. **Answer: A and D** Zero days are undiscovered vulnerabilities, so log reviews cannot detect these. Authentication tools force users to use strong passwords.

88. **Answer: B** Data that's written within unused space is called a SNOW attack, a type of steganography attack that hides attacks in plain sight.

89. **Answer: C** Cobi should validate and verify his suppliers before using them. Cobi starts calling the prospect leads that he bought, and several prospects complain to him that they wish the phone calls would stop because the same leads were sold to several others, and they are calling the same prospects. He will eventually find that Glengary Leads will not honor their guarantee because they will not respond to his requests for a refund.

90. **Answer: A** Applications must be tested and baselined before they are rolled into production; otherwise, the results may be a lot worse than a few unhappy users; for example, a financial shortfall.

91. **Answer: D** White box testing would mean the evaluator has full knowledge of the environment. Red box and opaque are false options.

92. **Answer: C** Reconnaissance allows the attacker to collect information about a target, such as their IP address and location. The scanning phase is where the attacker enumerates the devices that have been found. Next, they need to see which devices are vulnerable. Finally, an ethical hacker will launch exploits without causing harm and report the findings to management.

93. **Answer: B** A high-level executive has complete knowledge of the environment and demonstrates the biggest risk as an internal threat to an organization. A black box test simulates an external attacker having no knowledge of the environment. A gray box test simulates some knowledge of the organization, such as an administrator or engineer. Red box is a false option.

94. **Answer: B and C** *Wireshark* and *Nessus* are tools that are used to discover vulnerabilities.

95. **Answer: B and C** SOC 1 reports focus on financial services and policies, such as proper accounting and bookkeeping standards. SOC 4 reports do not exist.

96. **Answer: A and B** Compliance audits are performed because an organization such as a power plant or brokerage firm needs to show they are following the regulations for their industry.

97. **Answer: A** In general, options B, C, and D are advantages of third-party audits.

98. **Answer: B** Safety first, even when conducting an audit.

99. **Answer: C** Regulations may not allow the audit to be redefined, and audits must be completed before they are certified.

100. **Answer: A** The eight-step process is 1) Determine goals, 2) Choose business unit(s), 3) Determine scope, 4) Select the audit team, 5) Audit planning, 6) Conduct the audit, 7) Document results, and 8) Communicate the results.

7

Security Operations Domain 7 Practice Questions

Questions relating to the following topics are included in this domain:

- Understanding and complying with investigations
- Proper logging and monitoring activities
- Performing configuration management
- Applying fundamental security concepts
- Conducting resource protection and incident management

To pass the **Certified Information Systems Security Professional** (**CISSP**) exam, you must score highly in the *Security Operations* domain. Domain 7 has a 13% weighting on the exam and requires you to understand the differences between events, incidents, and disasters, and how to properly run an investigation. Also, it is important to understand logging and monitoring devices and activities.

A thorough understanding of mitigations to social engineering is also required; so, understanding where and when to use **separation of duties** (**SoD**), mandatory vacations, and job rotations is critical to passing the CISSP exam.

Finally, understanding the importance of protecting data locally and remotely is tested, as well as understanding the 7-step incident management process, including recovery, remediation, and lessons learned.

Questions

1. Paola, a systems administrator, notices that files are rapidly encrypting on several systems she monitors. Which stage of the incident management process is she in?

    A. Detection

    B. Response

    C. Mitigation

    D. Remediation

2. Which of the following profiles *BEST* represents the *prudent person* concept?

    A. A software developer performing code review and dynamic analysis

    B. A systems administrator backing up data to the cloud

    C. A network administrator ensuring Local Area Network (LAN) systems can reach the internet

    D. A technician ensuring the backup generator is filled with fuel

3. Sherida, a systems administrator, was just shocked a third time by one of the systems in the security operations center (SOC). What is her *BEST* next step?

    A. Raise the temperature of the SOC.

    B. Lower the temperature of the SOC.

    C. Adjust the humidity lower in the SOC.

    D. Adjust the humidity higher in the SOC.

4. Which two of the following are mitigations to collusion?

    A. SoD

    B. Job rotations

    C. Mandatory vacations

    D. Employee policies

5. Sofia is a database administrator with the right to create, update, delete, and manage database tables and databases, but she has no right to update network settings or add hard drives. This is an example of which control type?

   A. Job rotation

   B. SoD

   C. Least privilege

   D. Need-to-know

6. Bobdilo, a junior buyer, is paying invoices to a shell company he created. Which are two of the *BEST* ways to detect this fraud?

   A. Mandatory vacation

   B. Need-to-know

   C. Job rotation

   D. Least privilege

7. An attacker from a North Korean network breached a firewall and stole corporate documents. The firewall failed because the attack was detected as a _____.

   A. True positive

   B. True negative

   C. False positive

   D. False negative

8. Intrusion detection systems (IDSes) watch and report anomalies in an organization's network. Only when the errors exceed a minimum clipping level are they reported. This *clipping level* is also known as a _____.

   A. Bridging

   B. Tailoring

   C. Scope

   D. Baseline

9. Kellen is a network engineer tuning the network to meet corporate standards. His supervisor informs him that his security measures are making the network run too slowly and he must remove them. What must be done for the security of the organization?

    A. Kellen must remove the security measures.

    B. Kellen should remove the security measures and re-enable them after his manager goes home.

    C. Kellen should suggest his manager speak with the security manager.

    D. Make Kellen's supervisor the security manager.

10. This process establishes periodic meetings to manage and schedule major software, hardware, and security updates to the organization. This process is known as _____.

    A. Change and configuration management

    B. Upgrade and update management

    C. Patch management

    D. Systems and operational management

11. When a systems administrator attempts to install a new driver and receives a warning that the driver is unsigned, what should be their next step?

    A. Install the driver because serious work needs to be accomplished.

    B. Install the driver because downtime is costly.

    C. Install the driver if policy allows.

    D. Do not install the driver.

12. Which of the following is the *Least* important when securing backup tapes?

    A. Test backup data to confirm the integrity of records saved to tape.

    B. Easy access to tapes outside the SOC for quick availability.

    C. Encrypt backup data on tapes to maintain the confidentiality of data.

    D. Keep versions of backup tapes miles from the originating environment in case of serious incident or disaster.

13. Software, hardware, and Information Technology (IT) services deployed within an organization to make the workplace more efficient, but unapproved by the organization, are considered _____.

    A. Shadow IT

    B. Business-managed IT

    C. Efficient IT

    D. Unapproved IT

14. Critical systems that contain restricted data and/or important financial records should be administered in which manner for *BEST* security?

    A. On-site in a restricted-area environment

    B. On-site where employees only are allowed

    C. Remotely by critical personnel only

    D. Remotely by employees only

15. Which two of the following are examples of physical access controls?

    A. Fence

    B. Acceptable use policy (AUP)

    C. Firewall

    D. Padlock

16. For the *BEST* performance, reliability, availability, and security in a data center, servers and racks should be configured using which kind of system?

    A. Intake and outtake air flows

    B. Warm aisles

    C. Hot and cold aisles

    D. Heating, ventilation, and air conditioning (HVAC)

17. A device that is used to defeat a pin tumbler lock is called what?

    A. Bump key

    B. Keyway

    C. Cylinder

    D. Driver

18. Which two of the following devices are good mitigations for tailgating or piggybacking?

    A. Bollard

    B. Mantrap

    C. Turnstile

    D. Door

19. When considering physical types to help secure an office building or parking lot, which physical type deters the casual intruder?

    A. 4 feet (ft) (120 centimeters (cm)) of ground cover between the sidewalk and parking lot

    B. 4-ft (120-cm) fencing

    C. 6-ft (180-cm) fencing

    D. 8-ft (240-cm) fencing

20. When lighting a parking lot, light posts that house lights with a 40-ft (12-meter (m)) radius spread should be how far apart from each other for *BEST* security?

    A. 80 ft/24 m

    B. 100 ft/30.5 m

    C. 120 ft/36.5 m

    D. 160 ft/49 m

21. Fake video cameras are a type of which security control?

    A. Deterrent

    B. Preventative

    C. Compensating

    D. Detective

22. Which of the following is an electromechanical type of alarm system?

    A. Pressure mat

    B. Microwave

    C. Acoustical

    D. Infrared

23. Ji is a chief information security officer (CISO) with *MARco* and has determined that her organization must only use a list of nine specific applications, and no others. What is this list of allowed-only software called?

    A. Application list

    B. Application whitelisting

    C. Application blacklisting

    D. Allowed-only software

24. Users were having too much trouble completing their assignments, so they decided to install their own software and hardware into the organization without approval from the configuration and change management board. What is the primary reason for the CISO deploying an AUP to stop these practices?

    A. To reduce the risk of rogue access points and evil twins

    B. To ensure unlicensed software does not get installed

    C. To have a policy in place that creates a more secure environment

    D. To ensure backdoors are not inadvertently installed

25. Which step occurs after *Documentation* as part of the change control or change management process?

    A. Change request

    B. Change approval

    C. Change testing

    D. Change implementation

26. Which cloud service is generally provisioned for system administrators?

    A. Platform as a Service (PaaS)

    B. Ransomware as a Service (RaaS)

    C. Software as a Service (SaaS)

    D. Infrastructure as a Service (IaaS)

27. Which of the following predicts how long an electromechanical system will run until it fails?

A. Mean time between failures (MTBF)

B. Mean time to recovery (MTTR)

C. Mean time to failure (MTTF)

D. Mean down time (MDT)

28. Cristian is a systems administrator seeking to create a storage system that continucs to run even though two hard drives fail. Which system is *BEST* suited for him?

A. Redundant Array of Inexpensive Disks (RAID) 0

B. RAID 1

C. RAID 5

D. RAID 6

29. Some security features of a Storage Area Network (SAN) environment include all of the following *Except* which one?

A. Encryption capabilities

B. Support for disk mirroring

C. Capability of mitigating denial-of-service (DoS) attacks

D. Capability of providing backup and restore over a network

30. Which is one of the major differences between grid computing and clusters?

A. Computers within a grid must be the same model and configuration.

B. Some of the computers within a cluster can sit idle while others are processing.

C. Clustering is for high availability (HA), whereas grid computing is not.

D. Some of the computers within a grid can sit idle while others are processing.

31. How do backups and snapshots work together?

A. Snapshots can be made from tape backups.

B. Snapshots can be used to recover a backup.

C. Backups can be made from large snapshots.

D. Snapshots generally take hours to create.

32. Formiga is a networking engineer securing her Wi-Fi network. Which is the *BEST* device she can use to mitigate networking threats?

    A. Host-based IDS (HIDS)

    B. Wireless intrusion prevention system (WIPS)

    C. Network intrusion prevention system (NIPS)

    D. Network-based IDS (NIDS)

33. Bibi is a systems engineer who just received an emergency patch update required for the corporate servers. A day after patching the servers, IT support reported hundreds of trouble tickets created because of poor performance issues. What *MOST LIKELY* occurred?

    A. An application installed a week earlier has a memory leak.

    B. The IPS is detecting too many false negatives.

    C. The IDS is detecting too many false negatives.

    D. Bibi neglected to test the patch in a sandbox before installing it on production systems.

34. Which of the following is true when observing malicious network traffic?

    A. Honeypots are a network of dozens of tiny honeynets.

    B. Honeynets are designed to distract hackers while researchers learn of their activities.

    C. Black holes are designed to distract hackers while researchers learn of their activities.

    D. Honeynets drop packets without notifying the sender.

35. Zack is a security engineering intern who just learned about the incident management process. Which of the following causes him to implement this process?

    A. A user is caught watching child pornography.

    B. A desktop computer has crashed due to malware.

    C. An independent contractor has not signed the working agreement.

    D. An employee's badge is found to be defective when entering the building.

36. *Surge Corp* has detected an attack on their network whereby personally identifiable information (PII) was leaked to an overseas organization. What is the next step in the incident management process?

    A. Preparation

    B. Detection

    C. Response

    D. Mitigation

37. Giulia is a security administrator who notices a workstation is performing abnormally. Using a security toolkit, she determines that a rootkit is on the system. What is the *BEST* way for her to remove this?

    A. Use a virus removal tool to delete the rootkit.

    B. Use a malware removal tool to delete the rootkit.

    C. Use a rootkit removal tool to delete the rootkit.

    D. Wipe the hard drive clean and reinstall the operating system.

38. Which of the following *BEST* describes the recovery point objective (RPO)?

    A. Acceptable data loss in units of gigabytes (GB)

    B. Acceptable data loss in units of time

    C. The amount of time to recover from a disaster

    D. The amount of time to recover before reputational loss for the business

39. The main difference between the recovery time objective (RTO) and work recovery time (WRT) is which of the following?

    A. WRT occurs before a disaster, while RTO occurs after a disaster.

    B. RTO occurs before a disaster, while WRT occurs after a disaster.

    C. RTO results in data recovery after a disaster, while WRT tests recovered data before returning to normal operations.

    D. WRT results in data recovery after a disaster, while RTO tests recovered data before returning to normal operations.

40. Sebastian is a security administrator who convinced the CISO that they should make an investment in an empty building as a recovery site because space would be hard to find in the case of a disaster. Which kind of facility is this?

    A. Hot site

    B. Warm site

    C. Cold site

    D. Cloud site

41. Which technology monitors user and system behaviors, and recognizes changes in behavior that could signal an internal threat?

    A. Security Information and Event Management (SIEM)

    B. IPS

    C. Unity and Entity Behavior Analytics (UEBA)

    D. IDS

42. Which two of the accounts listed here are privileged accounts and deserve a greater degree of security?

    A. Root

    B. Administrator

    C. Security Account Manager (SAM)

    D. Shadow

43. Mana is the CISO of *Jones Dishwashers*, and fears data of their new designs could be leaked to their overseas competitors. Which two of the following solutions does she select to monitor and mitigate data exfiltration?

    A. Data leak prevention (DLP)

    B. Update malware protection

    C. Host-based IPS (HIPS)

    D. Disable Universal Serial Bus (USB) adapters

44. Security professionals seeking threat-intelligence information can search and obtain lists of common vulnerabilities and exposures (CVEs), severity scoring, and patch availability from which website?

    A. `https://www.cve.com`

    B. `https://nvd.nist.gov`

    C. `https://www.cve.org`

    D. `https://www.cve.mil`

45. Walker is the chief security officer (CSO) and is implementing information security continuous monitoring (ISCM) to better monitor security for the company. He has considered which assets to protect, has determined vulnerabilities, and has determined which tools to use for continuous monitoring. What is the next step of the ISCM?

    A. Update

    B. Define

    C. Establish

    D. Implement

46. *BRM Corp* manufactures buttons for major clothing companies and uses the HAL 3000 computer to manage their designs and other data files. Even though the system is 10 years old, they are purchasing 30 more of the same system. What is the reason for this?

    A. The HAL 3000 model is on the end-of-life (EOL) list, and BRM's software only runs on the HAL 3000.

    B. The HAL 3000 supports a tape drive that is no longer available on future HAL models.

    C. Management is investing in the fact that the value of the HAL 3000 will double in 5 years.

    D. Their HAL 3000 users do not want to learn how to use a new model.

47. Cyber-extortion insurance coverage covers all of the following losses because of ransomware *Except* for which one?

    A. Cost of forensic experts who recommend preventative measures after an attack

    B. Business loss due to blockage of data because of a crypto-malware attack

C. Business loss due to blockage of the website because of a DoS attack

D. Business loss due to blockage of the building entrance because of a protest

48. Which of the following steps are *NOT* part of forensically protecting evidence from a hard drive?

A. Duplicate the hard drive.

B. Save critical files for the manufacturing department to a remote system.

C. Hash the hard drive.

D. Write-protect the hard drive.

49. When interrogating a suspect or interviewing a witness, how many investigators should ideally be in the room during the questioning?

A. One

B. Two

C. Three

D. Four

50. Which of the following is *NOT* a digital forensic tool used to examine a system after an incident?

A. dd

B. Wireshark

C. Autopsy

D. Minesweeper

51. Garmas is a security manager who damaged a hard drive intended to be used as evidence due to an incident. How should he proceed with this evidence?

A. Explain to the judge what happened, and the judge determines whether it can be allowed.

B. Enter the hard drive as evidence because no one will notice the damage to the hard drive since it is all internal.

C. Enter the duplicated (backup) hard drive as evidence since the data is the same.

D. Destroy the hard drive because it can no longer be used as evidence.

52. When a system requires forensic investigative techniques to be used, which data is the most volatile and the most difficult to preserve?

    A. Hard drive

    B. Network

    C. Memory

    D. Swap space

53. Disk-mirrored systems allow for continuous availability in case of a disk failure. This is an example of which type of replication?

    A. Asynchronous

    B. Synchronous

    C. Tape

    D. Remote tape

54. Cyber insurance covers all of the following business liabilities *Except* for which one?

    A. Illegal download of driver license numbers

    B. Theft of health records

    C. Damage to a mantrap from a break-in

    D. Credit card number exfiltration

55. Which of the following backup types make for the fewest number of tapes to restore after making several months of backups?

    A. Full

    B. Differential

    C. Incremental

    D. Partial

56. When following an ICSM process, what is the next step after analyzing and reporting the results?

    A. Implement

    B. Respond

    C. Review

    D. Update

57. Which of the following would *not* be considered an indicator of compromise (IOC)?

    A. Common login activity

    B. Changing hash values

    C. Unusual network activity

    D. Changes in the hosts file

58. Zak is a security engineer tasked with protecting log files and assuring log files are not modified by hackers. Which is the *BEST* solution to mitigate data loss from log files?

    A. Save log data to hard drives.

    B. Save log data to write-once, read-many (WORM) media.

    C. Save log data in the cloud.

    D. Save log data to backup tapes.

59. Guro is a CISO considering security devices that automatically monitor activities using behavior analytics. Which is the *BEST* device for her to consider?

    A. UEBA

    B. Closed-circuit television (CCTV)

    C. User activity monitoring software (UAMS)

    D. Keylogger

60. An important difference between a hot site and a mirrored site is which of the following?

    A. A hot site can recover a downed data center within minutes, and a mirrored site can recover a downed data center within seconds.

    B. A hot site is corporate-owned, but a mirrored site is offered through third-party providers.

    C. A hot site can recover a downed data center within hours, and a mirrored site can recover a downed data center within minutes.

    D. A mirrored site is corporate-owned, but a hot site is offered through third-party providers.

61. As part of disaster recovery planning (DRP), a dentist on the third floor of his building creates a reciprocal agreement with a dermatologist in her second-floor office. What is the major security flaw in their planning?

    A. They need a wired network connection between the two offices.

    B. They need a wireless network connection between the two offices.

    C. They are in the same building.

    D. They have minimal IT skills.

62. A facility from where to run operations that runs days after a disaster is called which of the following?

    A. Mirrored site

    B. Hot site

    C. Warm site

    D. Cold site

63. Jeannie is a systems administrator required to recover data after a disaster. Every time staff calls her, they get notified that her phone number has changed. What went wrong with the business continuity planning (BCP) process?

    A. Her phone number was changed.

    B. Phone numbers were not confirmed as part of DRP testing.

    C. She provided her personal instead of business phone number.

    D. The company provided corporate-owned personally enabled (COPE) phones.

64. When looking at the DR process, the maximum tolerable downtime (MTD) is the sum of the RTO and which function?

    A. WRT

    B. RPO

    C. MTTR

    D. MTBF

65. Which situation requires the deployment of a DR process?

    A. Ransomware worms through the entire organization.

    B. Personal health information (PHI) is extracted from a medical billing company by a hacker.

C. An intern lost a data file they created yesterday.

D. An engineer's workstation keeps intermittently shutting down.

66. *Purge Corp* has finally returned to normal operations after repairing systems involved in an attack where PII was stolen. What is the next step of the incident management process for the organization?

A. Mitigation

B. Reporting

C. Recovery

D. Remediation

67. *Generic Medical College* suffers an incident where a male teacher follows ladies into bathrooms, takes a photo, and runs out. He is finally caught, and newspapers are asking employees for information. All staff, except for public relations, should be trained to say which of the following?

A. The attacker was apprehended, and the police will get back with answers to your questions.

B. The attacker was apprehended, and public relations will get back with answers to your questions.

C. The attacker was apprehended, and the chief executive officer (CEO) will get back with answers to your questions.

D. No comment.

68. Which of the following is the *BEST* mitigation to zero-day attacks?

A. Antivirus software

B. NIPS

C. Vulnerability scanning

D. Application control software

69. Anderson, a network engineer, installs a firewall and opens ports 80 and 443. He can reach the website, but testing the File Transfer Protocol (FTP) service from the Wide Area Network (WAN) results in access being denied. What *MOST LIKELY* caused this issue?

A. The first rule of the firewall is allow-all.

B. The first rule of the firewall is deny-all.

C. The last rule of the firewall is deny-all.

D. The last rule of the firewall is allow-all.

70. A SIEM system, which monitors security alerts for applications and the network, falls under which class of devices?

A. HIPS

B. HIDS

C. NIPS

D. NIDS

71. What are two key differences between a BCP and a DRP?

A. A BCP restores the business to normal operations after executing a DRP.

B. A DRP restores the business to normal operations after executing a BCP.

C. A BCP keeps critical corporate functions operating immediately after a disaster.

D. A DRP keeps critical corporate functions operating immediately after a disaster.

72. When comparing scale-out technologies with scale-up technologies, what is the main difference?

A. Scale-out technologies increase processing power by adding more central processing units (CPUs) instead of additional servers, as is done with scale-up technologies.

B. Scale-up technologies increase processing power by adding more CPUs instead of additional servers, as is done with scale-out technologies.

C. Scale-up technologies are associated with distributed architectures.

D. Scale-out technologies grow by adding more memory and disk to a system.

73. Clusters provide all of these security features *Except* for which one?

A. Guaranteed uptime

B. Load balancing

C. Scalability

D. Server failover

74. When data is striped across hard drives, that means the data is saved in which manner?

A. Portions of data are written across one drive.

B. Portions of data are written across several drive partitions.

C. Portions of data are written across multiple drives.

D. Portions of data are written to the drive and memory.

75. Which version of RAID is *NOT* designed for failover but is great for performance?

A. RAID 0

B. RAID 1

C. RAID 4

D. RAID 5

76. Which of the following should *NOT* be part of a service-level agreement (SLA)?

A. The types of media backup data is saved on

B. Remedies for breach of the agreement

C. Metrics on how services will be measured

D. Protocols to change metrics

77. The process of scheduling the install of a change occurs at which step of the change management process?

A. Change approval

B. Change documentation

C. Change testing

D. Change implementation

78. Casey, an information technology intern, opens a case with the corporate support department, but they refuse to assist her. This is *MOST LIKELY* for which reason?

A. Interns are required to get technological assistance from their supervisor.

B. She is seeking assistance for software not on the whitelist.

C. Interns are required to get technological assistance from their assigned peer.

D. Part of being an intern is figuring out technology issues on your own.

79. Aron is a CISO and proposes to his security team the idea of using a virtual machine (VM) snapshot to deploy a virtual desktop infrastructure (VDI). The snapshot image is also known as a(n) what?

A. Gold master

B. Least privilege

C. VM cache

D. Application whitelist

80. One major difference between using security guards instead of guard dogs is which of the following?

    A. Guard dogs can only focus on specific areas.

    B. Guard dogs only protect specific doors and window spaces.

    C. Security guards are trained for specific tasks.

    D. Security guards can exercise judgment.

81. The primary difference between electromechanical alarm systems and volumetric systems is which of the following?

    A. Volumetric systems are triggered when there is a break in the circuit.

    B. Electromechanical systems are better for the home than the office.

    C. Volumetric systems can better detect an individual.

    D. Electromechanical systems can better detect an individual.

82. Video cameras that scan large parking lots generally use which of the following for better detection?

    A. A high focal length

    B. A low focal length

    C. A low shutter speed

    D. A high shutter speed

83. One method for an attacker to defeat a barbed-wire fence without major injury includes all of the following *Except* for which one?

    A. Covering the barbs with a thick coat or mat

    B. Slowly climbing the fence

    C. Cutting through fencing with wire cutters

    D. Jumping or vaulting over the fence

84. Improving building security by growing thorny plants, ensuring grounds are well kept, and growing spiky bushes as natural barriers are considered which type of design?

    A. Crime prevention through environmental design (CPTED)

    B. CCTV

    C. Common criteria

    D. Perimeter intrusion detection and assessment system (PIDAS)

85. What is the *primary* difference between piggybacking and tailgating?

    A. Tailgating is with the consent of the authorized individual.

    B. Piggybacking is with the consent of the authorized individual.

    C. Piggybacking occurs with only one unauthorized individual.

    D. Tailgating occurs with more than one individual.

86. What is the *primary* purpose of configuring a data center using a hot and cold aisles configuration?

    A. Increase server capacity.

    B. Reduce exhaust recirculation.

    C. Improve the availability of computing services.

    D. Reduce cooling costs.

87. Locks share three components. Which of the following is *NOT* one of these components?

    A. Locking device

    B. Switching device

    C. Operating mechanism

    D. Latching device

88. Weston is a security administrator required to wear an identification badge while working at the corporate office. What is the security purpose of wearing a company badge?

    A. If he does not wear a badge, he is not employed with the organization.

    B. It shows other staff and officials he is likely an employee, and his role.

    C. He has the right to access restricted areas of the organization.

    D. Guarantees that he is an employee, and displays his role.

89. A system that attempts to stop threats from entering the parking lot, although the attacker gets past that and then gets stopped by the security guard, but the attacker gets past the guard and then gets stopped at the elevator because they do not know the entry code, but they succeed in circumventing that, yet are ultimately denied because they do not know the elevator exit code, is known as which concept?

    A. Failed security

    B. Elevator security

C. Layered security

D. Obfuscated security

90. The *BEST* utility to use for remote access to an office from home is called _____.

    A. Telnet

    B. FTP

    C. Remote login (`rlogin`)

    D. Virtual private network (VPN)

91. Asisat is an engineering intern with *Mekdune Co.* and suggests at the team meeting that the company could save money installing free, pirated versions of software. Why does the company reject her suggestion?

    A. Free, pirated software is illegal and may contain malware.

    B. The company prefers using supported software; free, pirated software comes without tech support.

    C. It is difficult to get patches and updates for free, pirated software.

    D. The company likes her suggestion, but the president's relatives run the software company they buy applications from.

92. Which of the following is *NOT* a security control type?

    A. Physical

    B. Authoritative

    C. Administrative

    D. Technical

93. Riley is a systems administrator tasked with installing a new application approved by configuration and change management. When he attempts to install it, he is warned that the application is unsigned. How should he proceed?

    A. Install the software if the release notes from the change management department approve it for this specific application.

    B. Install the software because it is critical for the function of a project.

    C. Contact the vendor for the signed version of the application and install the signed version.

    D. Do not install the software.

94. For best security, after an important server crashes, which of the following should occur *FIRST*?

    A. Reboot to normal operations.

    B. Contact the systems administrator.

    C. Reboot to safe mode or single-user mode.

    D. Reboot and test before allowing full access.

95. The user who handles security assessments, manages password policies, and reviews audit logs, should be handled by whom?

    A. Security administrator

    B. Network administrator

    C. Systems administrator

    D. Operations administrator

96. Kadidiatou is a chief security officer reviewing details of the International Organization for Standardization (ISO) *27002* security framework and determines she can ignore the security controls related to parking because the organization has no parking lot. This process is known as _____.

    A. Tailoring

    B. Scoping

    C. Supplementing

    D. Baselining

97. Carl, a systems administrator, installs a new service that requires port 49050 to be used. The service continually fails until he realizes the firewall must be programmed to allow port 49050. From Carl's perspective, when the firewall blocks this new service, it is considered a _____.

    A. True negative

    B. True positive

    C. False positive

    D. False negative

98. Phillip is a writer and belongs to an industry that requires him to take 5 days off as paid vacation every year. What is this called, and why are staff required to do this?

    A. Mandatory vacation—this is done as a health measure to improve attitude.

    B. Mandatory vacation—this is done as a security measure to mitigate fraud.

    C. Required vacation—this is done to keep staff fresh and positive.

    D. Required vacation—this is done to help build up business with their travel agent clients.

99. Ante is the finance director of *Chi Co.* and is requesting bike part designs for financial planning purposes. The engineering director gives him the costs he wants, but not the designs. The engineering director is enforcing which control type?

    A. Least privilege

    B. Prudent person

    C. Need-to-know

    D. SoD

100. Preki is a systems administrator in charge of making backups for the lab. After making backups, he also tests them to verify backups were made. What could be done to improve this process?

    A. Move the backups to the cloud.

    B. Encrypt the backups.

    C. Assign a different administrator to verify backups.

    D. Create snapshots and then back up the snapshots.

Quick answer key

1. A	16. C	31. C	46. A	61. C	76. A	91. A
2. A	17. A	32. B	47. D	62. C	77. D	92. B
3. D	18. B, C	33. D	48. B	63. B	78. B	93. A
4. B, C	19. B	34. B	49. B	64. A	79. A	94. B
5. C	20. A	35. A	50. D	65. A	80. D	95. A
6. A, C	21. A	36. D	51. A	66. D	81. C	96. B
7. D	22. A	37. D	52. B	67. D	82. B	97. C
8. D	23. B	38. B	53. B	68. D	83. B	98. B
9. D	24. C	39. C	54. C	69. C	84. A	99. C
10. A	25. C	40. C	55. A	70. D	85. B	100. C
11. C	26. D	41. C	56. B	71. B, C	86. C	
12. B	27. A	42. A, B	57. A	72. B	87. D	
13. A	28. D	43. A, D	58. B	73. A	88. B	
14. A	29. C	44. B	59. A	74. C	89. C	
15. A, D	30. D	45. D	60. D	75. A	90. D	

Answers with explanations

1. **Answer**: **A** Paola is at the phase of discovering the event. Responding is her next step, where the incident is triaged. Mitigation involves containing the event. Remediation involves **root-cause analysis (RCA)**.

2. **Answer**: **A** Software developers performing code review (due care) and dynamic analysis (due diligence) represent responsible and cautious practices on the part of the coders. The others represent due care or due diligence, but not both; backups must be tested, networks must be protected, and generators must be tested.

3. **Answer**: **D** Electrostatic discharge is due to the humidity being too low in the room. It would be best for her to adjust it to about 50%; much higher would cause corrosion and rust. Adjusting temperatures too high or too low could harm the computers and void their warranties.

4. **Answer**: **B, C** Mandatory vacations require one of the staff to take leave for 5 to 10 working days while someone else does their job. Job rotations do the same, but permanently. Either could expose malicious activities. If two individuals are colluding, policies are being ignored. Collusion mitigates SoD; for example, if the tech that makes backups colludes with the tech that verifies backups, they can both agree to make *fake* backups, leaving the company exposed to data loss attacks.

5. **Answer: C** Least privilege is having the right to do your job. SoD would mean that Sofia can create databases, but a different database administrator would delete databases. She is not working in multiple departments, so job rotation is out, and the question states nothing about hidden knowledge.

6. **Answer: A, C** Employees committing fraud are very concerned about being caught, so being able to monitor their activities is of the utmost importance. Mandatory vacation and job rotation take them away from their day-to-day job, risking they will get caught. Least privilege and need-to-know allow Bobdilo to do his job.

7. **Answer: D** When bad traffic is allowed, the condition is a *false negative*. When good traffic is blocked, the condition is a *false positive*. A *true positive* occurs when malicious traffic is denied. A *true negative* occurs when benign traffic is allowed.

8. **Answer: D** Bridging is used to extend a network; for example, a Wi-Fi network that doesn't have enough range. Tailoring involves tuning parameters to fit the organization's needs. Scoping narrows a set of standards to fit the organization's needs.

9. **Answer: D** Kellen is working as part of the network department, which has conflicting responsibilities with security. Because of this, security must always be a different chain of command from networking, systems administration, and so on; so, moving Kellen to the security department will best allow him to implement corporate policies.

10. **Answer: A** Change and configuration management meetings generally occur once or twice a month, depending on the organization, to plan and test patches, software updates, hardware updates, and applications before release to the entire organization.

11. **Answer: C** Oftentimes, organizations verify and validate specific drivers that are unsigned and are approved for installation. As a best practice, unsigned drivers and applications should not be installed until they are approved through the change management process.

12. **Answer: B** Making tapes easy to access also makes them available to attackers, such as internal threats. For better security, keep the backup tapes within an SOC in a locked cabinet.

13. **Answer: A** To learn more, see this article by the *Journal of Information Technology Management*: http://jitm.ubalt.edu/XXX-4/article1.pdf.

    Reference: *Shadow IT and Business-Managed IT: Practitioner Perceptions and Their Comparison to Literature, Andreas Kopper et al., Journal of Information Technology Management, Volume XIX, Number 4, 2019.*

14. **Answer: A** Organizations such as the University of Cincinnati utilize a **Critical Server Security Standard** (**CSSS**) to manage equipment deemed to have high security. Learn more here:

    `https://www.uc.edu/content/dam/uc/infosec/docs/Standards/Critical_Server_Security_Standard.pdf.`

    Reference: *Critical Server Security Standard, University of Cincinnati, Office of Information Security, revised March 2017.*

15. **Answer: A, D** Even though a firewall can be physically touched, it is a programmable device and therefore a technical control, not a physical one. An AUP is an administrative control.

16. **Answer: C** Hot and cold aisles have servers in rows so that air exhaust faces each other for the best cooling efficiency of the facility. HVAC is part of every data center. The others are distractors.

17. **Answer: A** A bump key enters the keyway and forces the driver pins into the cylinder for just a moment so that the cylinder turns, enabling an intruder to defeat the lock without damaging it. Learn more at `http://www.cs.ucf.edu/courses/cis3360/spr2014/ppt/Ch02-Locks.pptx.`

18. **Answer: B, C** Bollards are posts that keep cars from crashing into buildings. Doors are not good mitigations because this is usually how piggybacking and tailgating occur; the authenticated individual holds the door open for the unauthenticated individual. Some mantraps hold multiple people, but they must be authenticated before being allowed into the building; otherwise, they are locked in the room until the authorities arrive.

19. **Answer: B** When using ground cover, the more distance between the parking lot and the sidewalk, the better for security. 8-ft fencing deters all but the most determined threat.

20. **Answer: A** Options of 100 ft/30.5 m or greater would leave dark zones in the parking lot; it would be too dark for a camera to film.

21. **Answer: A** A real video camera acts as a detective device because it can record and act as a deterrent; therefore, some devices can encompass multiple control types. Compensating provides a countermeasure, like a sprinkler system when there is a fire. A preventative control such as a firewall blocks an activity from occurring.

22. **Answer: A** The others are volumetric alarm type systems. Electromagnetic-type systems work by causing a break in the circuit, such as using magnetic contacts. Microwave, acoustical, and infrared systems detect that a pattern has been disturbed.

23. **Answer: B** Application blacklisting is a list of software *not* allowed to be installed on computers. Application lists and allowed-only software are both distractors.

24. **Answer: C** An AUP details what a user is and is not allowed to do with the IT infrastructure.

25. **Answer: C** The change control or change management process follows this format: 1) Change request 2) Change approval 3) Change documentation 4) Change testing 5) Change implementation 6) Change reporting.

26. **Answer: D** IaaS is generally for systems administrators since they will manage the operating system and application installation after obtaining their desired hardware implementation from the cloud vendor. SaaS is generally for users of email, customer relationship software, and so on, and PaaS is generally for software developers. RaaS allows an attacker to purchase malware from a ransomware developer.

27. **Answer: A** MTBF is unlike MTTF because MTTF is the predicted time of failure for a non-repairable system. MTTR is the anticipated amount of downtime to get a device running after it fails. MDT defines how long a system is down after failure, including logistical factors.

28. **Answer: D** RAID 0 is designed for performance and not failover. RAID 1 uses multiple drives for failover, but if the same primary and secondary drive fail simultaneously, the system fails. RAID 5 also fails if two drives fail at the same time.

29. **Answer: C** If a SAN is targeted with a network DoS attack at its network connection, access to the drives is unavailable.

30. **Answer: D** Grid computing is designed for disparate systems to work together solving multiple problems, whereas clusters are multiple systems that work together providing a single service.

31. **Answer: C** Snapshots are the fastest way to capture the current state of data. After a snapshot is created, it can be backed up to a tape or disk with a backup utility while users are on a live system. There are no concerns about data changing when saving a snapshot, even though users are on the system.

32. **Answer: B** A WIPS is the best device to use in this case. A NIPS and a NIDS are not the best options when a WIPS is available. A HIDS only monitors threats on a server or workstation.

33. **Answer: D** It is very important to test patches before they are installed on production systems. If the issue were an application, trouble tickets would be generated earlier. False negatives are undetected, so they are not reported.

34. **Answer**: **B** Black holes drop packets without notifying the sender, and honeynets are several honeypots designed to learn how hackers move through networks during an attack.

35. **Answer**: **A** Viewing child pornography is against the law and requires legal authorities to be contacted. In such cases, it is important to follow the incident management process, including having a strong chain-of-custody process to keep a guilty person from going free in court proceedings. The others do not affect the at-large security of the organization.

36. **Answer**: **D** Preparation is not part of the incident management process, but security is an important day-to-day activity an organization must accomplish. The description shows detection and response, so the next step is mitigation of the exploit by containing the damage.

37. **Answer**: **D** Rootkits are nefarious in that they infect even malware detection, compromising it and making it appear there is no malware on the system, even after thorough scans.

38. **Answer**: **B** The amount of time to recover from a disaster is the RTO. If the MTD is exceeded, the organization risks reputation loss. The RPO describes the earliest point where data can be recovered in units of time.

39. **Answer**: **C** RTO and WRT both occur after a disaster, with RTO focusing on data recovery and WRT focusing on returning to normal operations.

40. **Answer**: **C** A hot site has equipment and recent backups, so within minutes to hours, IT is functioning after a disaster. A warm site has enough equipment and data to recover within days of a disaster. A cold site is an empty room and could take weeks to recover from a disaster. Cloud sites can be set up as mirrored, hot, or warm.

41. **Answer**: **C** A SIEM system, an IDS, and an IPS monitor threats across a network and within systems, but a UEBA device specifically monitors changes from normal operations to detect all threats.

42. **Answer**: **A**, **B** Privileged accounts are those that have some or all of the administrator rights, which can stop any process, remove any file, or install any application; these accounts deserve the utmost level of care. The root user is the administrator on Linux, Mac, and Unix systems. The administrator is the root user for the Microsoft operating system. The SAM and shadow files contain the encrypted passwords for users on Microsoft and Linux/Unix systems, respectively.

43. **Answer**: **A, D** DLP can monitor hashes of internal data and compare it to data leaving the company. Disabling USB adapters makes thumb drives unusable within their corporate environment, disallowing data to leak this way. Malware protection and HIPS systems are designed to block external threats—that is, malware.

44. **Answer**: **B** CVEs are sponsored by the **Department of Homeland Security** (**DHS**) and the **Cybersecurity and Infrastructure Security Agency** (**CISA**). The database is compiled into the **National Vulnerability Database** (**NVD**), managed by the **National Institute of Standards and Technology** (**NIST**).

45. **Answer**: **D** Walker has defined and established which tools to use. The next phase is implementation. The objective of ISCM is to continuously monitor the effectiveness of security controls. ISCM is a management process that defines the threat and risk tolerance of an organization and continuously measures effectiveness.

46. **Answer**: **A** Remember when taking a security exam to focus on the answer that provides the most security. In this case, since they have a critical application that depends on the EOL hardware, new unsupported models will make their buttons unavailable to their customers.

47. **Answer**: **D** Ransomware requires the victim to pay a ransom as the business's operations are held hostage. Cyber extortion coverage also includes monies to pay ransom demands (less deductible) and costs to hire data hostage negotiators. To learn more, visit `https://www.irmi.com/term/insurance-definitions/ransomware`.

48. **Answer**: **B** After an incident, write-protect the hard drive, hash the hard drive, duplicate the hard drive, and ensure that the hashes of both hard drives match. Analysis can now be done on the duplicate hard drive by authorities (although they will likely take both hard drives as evidence). Saving critical files is not part of the forensic process.

49. **Answer**: **B** Especially for cases where there is no camera recording the interview, the investigators act as witnesses for each other during the process. The two should plan the interviewing process together, and ideally one should be female, the other male. Learn more here: `https://rm.coe.int/guide-to-investigative-interviewing/16808ea8f9`.

    Reference: *A Brief Introduction to Investigative Interviewing – A Practitioner's Guide*, M. Boyle, J. C. Vullierme, 2015.

50. **Answer: D** Autopsy analyzes hard drives and smartphones to investigate what happened in the device. Wireshark performs network packet captures to analyze the network. DD is used to duplicate and image hard drives. To learn more, visit `https://h11dfs.com/the-best-open-source-digital-forensic-tools/`.

51. **Answer: A** Do not destroy the hard drive, but explain what happened. Often, the judge will accept the evidence with an explanation. The judge may ask if there's a duplicate that can be used as evidence. The other responses are inappropriate.

52. **Answer: B** Data traveling a network can be saved within log files if running a NIDS. Data from cache and memory is the next most volatile and can be recovered with forensic memory analyzers.

53. **Answer: B** Synchronous replication provides real-time duplication and is the fastest way to recover from hard-drive failure versus asynchronous and tape replication. Asynchronous recovery would be the next fastest because the data can only be seconds or minutes out of sync.

54. **Answer: C** General liability insurance covers bodily injury and property damage. Cyber insurance is generally a separate purchase from general liability. Cyber insurance helps with notifying customers about a breach and recovering compromised data. To learn more, visit `https://www.nationwide.com/lc/resources/small-business/articles/what-is-cyber-insurance`.

55. **Answer: A** If doing a full backup every day that only requires one tape, the restore will simply be one tape, no matter when the corruption of the hard drive occurs; so, doing a full backup daily results in just using that tape for the recovery, even if months go by. Differential is the next fewest because it backs up changes made since the last full backup, and incremental would involve the most tapes, backing up the changes that only occur daily.

56. **Answer: B** After analyzing and reporting results, management responds with how to manage the risk—that is, mitigate, transfer, accept, or avoid—before reviewing and updating the process. The ISCM steps are define, establish, implement, analyze, respond, review, and update.

57. **Answer: A** An IOC is a type of threat intelligence that monitors for extreme changes in network activity, changes to **Domain Name System** (**DNS**) data, uncommon login patterns, and so on. These—and others—could mean malware is in the network or hackers on a system.

58. **Answer: B** WORM media mitigates loss or alteration of data saved to it. Other forms, such as the cloud, hard drives, and tapes, can be modified.

59. **Answer: A** UAMS, CCTV, and keyloggers all require manual intervention to monitor user activities. UEBA combines behavior analysis with **machine learning (ML)** and reports anomalies. To learn more, visit `https://www.csoonline. com/article/2998174/user-entity-behavior-analytics-next- step-in-security-visibilty.html`.

60. **Answer: D** The downtime between the two facility models is the same. The primary difference is that one is corporate-owned, versus purchasing services through an IT provider.

61. **Answer: C** If the building is struck by some disaster such as a tornado or an earthquake, their data will be lost because they are not using a separate site for their backups.

62. **Answer: C** Mirrored sites can be up and running within seconds to minutes after a disaster. Hot sites take minutes to hours to run after a disaster. Warm sites are up and running within days of a disaster, and cold sites are up and running within weeks of a disaster.

63. **Answer: B** This question asks about *the process*, not the activity, so phone number changes and personal versus business numbers are out. BCP processes can be tested, from checklists all the way to live simulations. Going through this process can uncover vulnerabilities, including the verification of phone numbers.

64. **Answer: A** RTO is the time it takes to restore lost data after a disaster occurs. WRT is the time to verify system integrity before resuming production. MTD is the total amount of downtime that can occur without harming the reputation of the organization, and is the sum of RTO and WRT. RPO is an allowable amount of data loss in units of time. MTTR and MTBF are not functions used within the DR process.

65. **Answer: A** An intern losing a data file and a workstation that shuts down are events that can be resolved by opening a service call. Extracted PHI would start the incident management process due to breaking **Health Insurance Portability and Accountability Act (HIPAA)** regulations. Ransomware worms cause a disaster because no one can work until the issue is resolved.

66. **Answer**: **D** The question describes the recovery phase of the incident management process since the organization has returned to normal operations, so the next step is remediation, which helps ensure an attack will never occur again in the exact same way by making mitigations permanent. This is also where new lessons learned are discussed. Learn more here: `https://www.adobe.com/content/dam/cc/en/security/pdfs/adb-incident-response-overview.pdf`.

    Reference: *The Official (ISC)² Guide to the CISSP CBK Reference, 5th edition, Warsinske et al. An Official (ISC)² Publication, p. 554, Apr 2018.*

67. **Answer**: **D** Although having the press contact public relations is a good answer, the organization does not want to risk staff getting into a conversation with the press. *No comment* is simple to remember, easy to say, and helps to slow rumors. The CEO should avoid being the spokesperson; their job is to work with the public relations spokesperson.

68. **Answer**: **D** Vulnerability scanning, NIPS, and antivirus software all use signatures to detect malware, and zero-days is malware with no signature created yet. Application control software in this case is the least bad answer because it can create allow and deny lists based on applications.

69. **Answer**: **C** When an allow-all rule is set, all traffic is allowed, but FTP traffic is being blocked. If the first rule were deny-all, then website traffic wouldn't work, so the last rule of the firewall is apparently set to deny-all.

70. **Answer**: **D** HIPS and HIDS reside as technical controls on servers, laptops, smartphones, and so on. NIPS and NIDS reside on firewalls, switches, routers, and so on. NIDS systems report incidents, and NIPS devices block threats. SIEM devices just report.

71. **Answer**: **B, C** A BCP is followed immediately after a disaster. An executed DRP returns the business to normal operations and follows the BCP.

72. **Answer**: **B** Scale-up systems are designed to add more processing, disk, or memory to a single system, whereas scale-out systems add additional servers. In the cloud, either is straightforward to accomplish.

73. **Answer**: **A** Clusters are groups of servers that appear as one. If all of the servers fail at the same time, the entire system is down.

74. **Answer**: **C** Concatenation occurs when data is written on one drive. RAID 0 systems can be designed as concatenated or striped for better read performance.

75. **Answer**: **A** RAID comes in multiple forms, with RAID 5 being the most popular today because of its failover capability of being able to continue to run even if one drive fails. RAID 4 also uses a parity drive and is designed for failover, as is RAID 1.

76. **Answer**: **A** An SLA contains a description of services provided, expected service levels, measurable metrics, responsibilities of each party, and penalties for breach of the agreement.

    Reference:

    `https://www.cio.com/article/2438284/outsourcing-sla-definitions-and-solutions.html`.

77. **Answer**: **D** After change testing, change implementation involves scheduling the installation and then executing the install. Change reporting occurs after this step to ensure satisfactory performance.

78. **Answer**: **B** Corporate technology support departments work only with software and hardware approved by configuration and change management. If it's unsupported, they are not allowed to spend time on it because of the hundreds of other supported events needing help.

79. **Answer**: **A** Least privilege provides users the minimum rights to do their job. A VM cache saves data within the VM instead of using memory or a disk. Application whitelisting is the software allowed to be installed onto systems. Learn more about gold masters for VDIs here: `http://citeseerx.ist.psu.edu/viewdoc/download?doi=10.1.1.229.2731&rep=rep1&type=pdf`.

80. **Answer**: **D** Security guards are more expensive because of their salary and benefits, while dogs have a better sense of smell and hearing, but dogs can cause too many false positives, being unable to recognize authorized individuals.

81. **Answer**: **C** Volumetric systems include photoelectric, infrared, and acoustical systems that scan a room for an intruder. Electromechanical systems watch for a circuit to break when opening a window or door.

82. **Answer**: **B** Shutter speeds are only important for still cameras, not video cameras. Video cameras record at various frame rates, where 24 **frames per second** (**FPS**) is sufficient. The lower the focal length, the higher the field of view, which is important for scanning large lots.

83. **Answer**: **B** Slowly climbing the fence will not work because the sharp blades of the barbed wire will cut through the intruder's skin. The others are successful ways to defeat a barbed-wire fence with little or no injury.

84. **Answer: A** CPTED uses features of nature, such as hills and lakes, to mitigate human threats. CCTV is used to monitor and record parking-lot activity, lobby activity, and so on. The common criteria verifies and validates security devices to one of seven levels. A PIDAS is fencing that has sensors on it.

85. **Answer: B** Tailgating and piggybacking can occur with one or more individuals, and the main difference is that piggybacking allows an unauthenticated individual into a building with the consent of the authenticated individual.

86. **Answer: C** Increasing server capacity, reducing exhaust recirculation, and reducing cooling costs are all true, and the primary purpose of these is to improve computing availability to users. To learn more, visit `https://citeseerx.ist.psu.edu/viewdoc/download?doi=10.1.1.415.7935&rep=rep1&type=pdf`.

    Reference: *Cold Air Containment, M. Pervilä and Jussi Kangasharju, GreenNet'11, August 19, 2011, Toronto, Ontario, Canada.*

87. **Answer: D** Locking devices include latches and bolts; they physically keep the area secured. Switching devices include keys, cards, or biometrics; they authorize the device to open. The operating mechanism interacts with the switching device to grant access—for example, a cylinder. See more at `https://www.cdse.edu/documents/student-guides/PY104-guide.pdf`.

    Reference: *Student Guide Course: Lock and Key Systems, Center for Development of Security Excellence, page 3, 2012.*

88. **Answer: B** A badge does not guarantee an individual works there because an outside attacker could have found or stolen the badge, or poor deprovisioning could leave an old employee with a badge. Not everyone wearing a badge is granted restricted access.

89. **Answer: C** The others are distractors. Layered security does not depend on a single layer of defense to stop intruders but on multiple layers, in case one or more layers fail.

90. **Answer: D** A VPN encrypts the conversation and **Internet Protocol** (**IP**) headers to hide the user's location. The other utilities listed allow remote access, but are unencrypted protocols. **FTP** is the **File Transfer Protocol**.

91. **Answer: A** Unlicensed software risks the organization using an application that is a trojan, and the company risks legal action, putting them at risk concerning staying in business.

92. **Answer**: **B** Physical controls refer to building security such as bollards, man traps, and security guards. Administrative controls refer to policies such as an AUP and a **non-disclosure agreement (NDA)**. Technical controls refer to devices such as firewalls and DLP systems.

93. **Answer**: **A** Often, there are vendors with cutting-edge software, and they provide no code signing. After thorough testing by change and configuration management, they will document to ignore the warning that the code is unsigned and request the unsigned version be installed.

94. **Answer**: **B** The systems administrator can ensure that recovery occurs in a secure manner. The others could become insecure due to an insider attack or through corruption within the hardware or software.

95. **Answer**: **A** There are too many conflicts of interest for systems administrators, network administrators, and operation administrators to handle issues around security. Implementing security harms system performance and there needs to be a separate chain of management for the organization's long-term future.

96. **Answer**: **B** Scoping involves removing controls that are not applicable. Tailoring involves tuning parameters to meet your needs. Supplementation adds controls to meet the organization's needs if not included in the framework. Baselining defines the minimum acceptable level.

97. **Answer**: **C** When bad traffic is allowed, the condition is a *false negative*. When good traffic is blocked, the condition is a *false positive*. A *true positive* occurs when malicious traffic is denied. A *true negative* occurs when benign traffic is allowed.

98. **Answer**: **B** Required vacation is a distractor. Someone has to do the job of the employee while they are on vacation, and fraud could be uncovered in such cases.

99. **Answer**: **C** Prudent person is not a control type, but does demonstrate when a person or organization practices due care and due diligence. Least privilege would mean that Ante could not even receive the financial data he needs from engineering. SoD states what Ante can and cannot do in the financial department.

100. **Answer**: **C** For best SoD, have a different individual test the backups to mitigate an internal attack; for example, pretending to do backups and leaving tapes blank. The others improve the process, but SoD provides the best security in this case.

8
Software Development Security Domain 8 Practice Questions

Questions from the following topics are included in this domain:

- Understanding and integrating security into the software development life cycle
- Identifying and applying security controls to software development
- Assessing the effectiveness of software security
- Assessing the security of acquired software
- Defining and applying secure coding guidelines and standards

To pass the CISSP exam, you must score high in the Software Development Security domain. Domain 8 has an 11% weighting on the exam and requires you to understand details regarding the **software development life cycle (SDLC)**, development methodologies such as Agile and Waterfall, and change management.

A thorough understanding of security controls, as well as when and where to apply them, is critical to passing the CISSP exam. Such controls include software configuration management, security orchestration, and repositories. You must also understand the difference between dynamic and static testing.

Finally, understanding the importance of securing software from outside vendors is critical. Acquired software includes **application programming interfaces (APIs)**, commercial-off-the-shelf, and even open source. By default, these must go through normal security evaluations.

Questions

1. Several software developers are invited to review each other's source code. This is an example of which type of activity?

   A. Passive testing

   B. Fuzzing

   C. Static analysis

   D. Dynamic analysis

2. Mal, a system administrator, insists that she did not send an email threatening a co-worker. Further analysis shows that the public key of the letter directly relates to Mal's private key. What is this an example of?

   A. Certificates

   B. Non-repudiation

   C. Defense in depth

   D. Repudiation

3. The security approach of complete mediation has which of the following features?

   A. A security design that preserves data integrity

   B. A security design where all access is verified

   C. A security design where a kernel protects the hardware

   D. A security design that uses defense in depth

4. Which organization is responsible for maintaining the top 10 list of web application vulnerabilities?

    A. OSSTMM

    B. OWASP

    C. OEC

    D. OCTAVE

5. The software development team at *Flat Ground Mountain Bank* is planning to test their production application using real customer data. Which process should they use to ensure the privacy of their customers?

    A. Data anonymization

    B. Data protection

    C. Depersonalization

    D. Safe harbor

6. Reference monitors must have all the following features *Except* for which one?

    A. Speed

    B. Verifiable

    C. Tamperproof

    D. Complete mediation

7. Which of the following are foundations of privacy?

    A. Choice, data integrity, security

    B. Verifiable, diverse, transferable

    C. Openness, complexity, nonrepudiation

    D. Encryption, availability, storage

8. All the following are phases of the software development life cycle (SDLC) *except* for which of the following?

    A. Planning

    B. Fuzzing

    C. Design

    D. Maintenance

9. Which software development model is based on manufacturing design, where work proceeds through steps in a linear, sequential process?

    A. Spiral

    B. Scrum

    C. Waterfall

    D. Agile

10. From the following options, which cannot be used as a shared secret?

    A. Something you have

    B. Something you are

    C. Something you know

    D. Something you need

11. Delphine is a security analyst classifying human resources and payroll data for the organization's employees and contractors. Which of the following is her *BEST* classification methodology?

    A. Impact

    B. Privacy

    C. Sensitivity

    D. Likelihood

12. Which of the following is *NOT* considered structured data?

    A. MySQL database of cybersecurity books

    B. LibreOffice spreadsheet of course authors

    C. Log file of SCSI drive errors

    D. XML file of customer names and phone numbers

13. When creating functional requirements for a software application, modeling how software should be used properly by customers helps build software that meets expectations. What are these models called?

    A. Behavioral diagrams

    B. Use cases

    C. Application modeling

    D. Misuse cases

14. Darlene is the CISO of *YRF Charities*, and her team of software developers creates applications for churches. She follows organizational secure coding standards. What does this guarantee?

    A. Error-free code

    B. Complete security functionality

    C. Code is economical

    D. Code sans change orders

15. When not properly handled, overly complex conditional logic can result in which condition?

    A. Infinite loops

    B. Input attacks

    C. Race conditions

    D. Memory leaks

16. Nathan, a software engineer, has developed an application in the C language that allows users to enter their tax identification number. Which of the following is his primary concern?

    A. Users entering an incorrect tax identification number

    B. Lack of library support

    C. Buffer overflows

    D. Malware

17. Owen is a software manager who's leading a team of developers that are making sales marketing software. He tracks and manages the project requirements with a grid. This grid is known as what?

    A. A requirements traceability matrix

    B. A Gantt chart

    C. A Pareto chart

    D. A PERT chart

18. When prioritizing use cases, at a minimum, the use cases must be designed for which of the following?

    A. All requirements

    B. Poorly defined business requirements

    C. Input validation

    D. Security-related requirements

19. Which tool should you use to decompose systems so that you can understand threats better?

    A. UML

    B. NVD

    C. DFD

    D. CVE

20. What is the primary purpose of security reviews within the software development life cycle (SDLC)?

    A. Ensure that threat models are updated at each phase

    B. Ensure the quality of security actions

    C. Ensure the attack models are updated

    D. Ensure all steps of the SDLC are followed

21. Matthew manages the software development of a website with a paywall, and they are running behind schedule. The threat model documentation is mostly complete. What should be their next step?

    A. Complete the threat model documentation in the next phase.

    B. The documentation can be skipped because development has tested positive.

    C. Delay the process until the documentation is complete.

    D. Apply for a waiver from the security team.

22. The characteristics of a trust boundary are found in which of the following?

    A. Cannot be observed

    B. Items share the same rights, access, and identifiers

    C. Items have the same access control list access

    D. Items share identical user accounts

23. The critical security details for the design phase of a new software product are contained in which document?

    A. Security control model

    B. Threat model

    C. Bug database

    D. Configuration file

24. Reducing risk by reusing source code, libraries, and application programming interfaces is an example of which model?

    A. Separation of duties

    B. Leveraging existing components

    C. Least common mechanism

    D. Weakest link

25. Hernan is designing an application that would work great within a single sign-on (SSO) system. What is the *BEST* way for him to manage authentication in the system?

    A. Utilize the existing SSO management system.

    B. Log exception data.

    C. Implement exception management systems.

    D. Create a management interface within the application.

26. Complete mediation can be *BEST* described by which of the following approaches to security?

    A. An approach that minimizes the opportunity to be circumvented.

    B. Layered security.

    C. Integrates authentication and authorization.

    D. An approach that uses defense in depth and least privilege.

27. Which of the following is the *BEST* example of exception management?

    A. Logging and audit data

    B. Psychological acceptability

    C. Separation of duties

    D. Integrity and availability

28. Hash functions are commonly deployed for what purpose?

    A. Confidentiality

    B. Integrity checking

    C. Authentication

    D. Authorization

29. Which of the following technologies is a set of standards that uses radio frequencies over very short distances?

    A. Yagi

    B. Zigbee

    C. NFC

    D. Omni-directional

30. Which architecture mimics desktop applications in terms of functionality and usability?

    A. REST

    B. SOAP

    C. RPC

    D. RIA

31. Which architectural component acts as a communication translator between protocols such as XML, REST, DCOM, and others?

    A. JSON

    B. CORBA

    C. ESB

    D. EDI

32. Which of the following is *NOT* a feature of digital rights management (DRM) that controls the use, modification, and distribution of copyrighted works?

    A. Persistence

    B. Integrity checking

    C. Encryption

    D. Copy restriction

33. The approach of linking to shared libraries when a program executes and loading them into memory is known as what?

    A. Interpreting

    B. Dynamic linking

    C. Early linking

    D. Static linking

34. Which of the following both has compile features and acts as an interpreted language?

    A. Lenovo

    B. Java virtual machine (JVM)

    C. Pascal

    D. Android

35. Isolating test code from direct contact with in-production data and systems goes by the name of which process?

    A. Automation

    B. Revision control

    C. Isolation

    D. Sandboxing

36. What are two of the *MOST* important advantages managed code has over unmanaged code? (Choose 2)

    A. Garbage collection

    B. Runs faster

    C. Security

    D. Error-free

37. Hashing values return the same result for identical inputs. How can you resolve this vulnerability?

    A. Salt the hash.

    B. Revert to MD5 hashing.

    C. Use longer hash functions.

    D. Triple hashing.

38. What are the *BEST* methods for examining and selecting code when you're using disallowed functions (for example, routines prone to buffer overflows)? (Choose 2)

    A. Static code analysis

    B. Misuse case testing

    C. Dynamic code analysis

    D. Code review

39. Attacking memory locations where applications had once run goes by which name?

    A. Buffer overflow

    B. Memory relocation

    C. Data remanence

    D. ASLR

40. One of the important differences between a SIEM platform and a SOAR platform is what?

    A. SIEMs rank threats and generate alerts.

    B. SOARs identify deviations from the baseline.

    C. SIEMs aggregate data from multiple sources.

    D. SOARs use automation to respond to threats.

41. The process that considers decision making from a variety of skill sets, for a specific product, within a specific timeframe, and uses consensus building techniques is considered which of the following?

    A. TCB

    B. SDLC

    C. IPT

    D. CMMI

42. A popular source code repository tool that archives, tracks the history, and maintains revisions of an application is called what?

    A. Pascal

    B. Git

    C. Fortran

    D. Java

43. The goals of software configuration management (SCM) include all the following *Except* which one?

    A. Managing processes and tools for software builds

    B. Conducting source code reviews

    C. Defect-tracking back to the source

    D. Ensuring that the configurations meet all your requirements

44. Edson is a software developer creating applications for the automotive industry. He uses a system called DevOps that allows continuous development, testing, and delivery of new code. This activity is also known as what? (Choose 2)

    A. Continuous development

    B. Continuous delivery

    C. Continuous integration

    D. Continuous installation

45. What is an organization's largest security risk when it comes to using third-party or commercial-off-the-shelf applications?

    A. The application is written in a language prone to buffer overflows.

    B. The developers are slow at releasing security patches.

    C. The application has not been tested for input attacks.

    D. The creator(s) has/ve poor security software design policies.

46. Security tools built into continuous delivery process are known as what?

    A. Security as code

    B. Software-defined security

    C. Commercial-off-the-shelf (COTS)

    D. Open source

47. Marie-Antoinette is a security manager concerned with the amount of entry point sources into the application being developed. What is her number one priority?

    A. APIs

    B. Software versioning

    C. Type-safe code

    D. Cryptographic abilities

48. Khadija is a software developer that just downloaded a signed API from *LYI Corp*. Code signing provides all the following information about the API *Except* for what?

    A. API is authentic

    B. API is free of errors

    C. API is published by *LYI Corp*

    D. API integrity

49. Jacques has just finished writing an application for computer-aided engineering. After running the application, he notices that the output results are incorrect, and now he needs to debug the application even further. What kind of test did he run?

    A. Static analysis

    B. Code review

    C. Dynamic analysis

    D. Code walkthrough

50. When running a functional test, the examiner will conduct all the following tests *Except* for which one?

    A. Unit testing

    B. Performance testing

    C. Dynamic testing

    D. Attack surface area testing

51. Maren is a software development manager, and her team is at the final testing for the software before releasing it to production. The final test will simulate the production environment. What is this test called?

    A. Penetration testing

    B. Sandbox testing

    C. Simulation testing

    D. Production testing

52. An important part of customer service for those that use an organization's software product includes which of the following?

    A. Creating new features

    B. Responding to requests

C. Training

D. Getting the latest software development and testing tools

53. Jackson tests security for applications, including those that encrypt data. To validate the encryption functions, he runs all of the following *Except* for what?

A. RNG

B. Secret encryption techniques

C. Encryption algorithms

D. Key distribution

54. Veronica leads the software development team at *TTC Corp* and uses a tool to prioritize which errors must be resolved before releasing the application. What is this tool called?

A. SDLC process requirements

B. Bug bar

C. Trust boundaries

D. Security gates

55. Applications that are written to restore themselves after a security breach are known to have which functionality?

A. Recoverability

B. Reliability

C. Restorability

D. Resilience

56. When coding in .NET on a Microsoft system, compiling with the /GS flag enables which feature?

A. Buffer security check

B. Graphics speedup

C. Enable input validation

D. Graphics security

57. Robbie is the manager of software development and is at a crossroad regarding whether the new application should use managed or unmanaged code. Which of the following are advantages of managed code? (Choose 2)

    A. Type-safe code

    B. Runs on one operating system

    C. Faster execution

    D. Improved memory management

58. Which of the following is *NOT* true regarding declarative security programming and imperative (programmatic) security programming?

    A. Declarative programming describes which security principles to apply, but not how to do it.

    B. Imperative programming techniques create applications with high portability.

    C. Declarative programming uses a container-based approach to aid in security.

    D. Imperative programming *programs* specific security features into an application.

59. What is the technology called that virtualizes security functions into software that enables simpler remote management and simpler deployments?

    A. Continuous integration and continuous delivery

    B. Honeypot

    C. Software-defined security

    D. DevSecOps

60. *TVM Corp's* team of software developers inspects each programmer's source code for proper data sanitation regarding inputs, backdoors, and buffer overflow mitigations. This is an example of which activity? (Choose 2)

    A. Code review

    B. Dynamic code analysis

    C. Code identification

    D. Static code analysis

61. What is an organization's largest security risk when it comes to using open source applications?

    A. The source code is visible by anyone in the world.

    B. The operations department does not install version updates and patches in a timely manner.

    C. The creator(s) of the application may not have used secure software development procedures.

    D. The creator(s) decide to discontinue further development of the application.

62. Which of the following is the biggest risk for an organization converting from a Waterfall development to continuous integration and continuous delivery?

    A. The risk that management cannot track project activity

    B. The risk that developers will reuse metrics before they are reassessed by management

    C. The risk that developers do not understand the sprint process

    D. The risk that high-priority bugs will go unresolved

63. What technique is used to detect buffer overflows?

    A. Fairy

    B. Canary

    C. Sparrow

    D. Gnome

64. What is the primary difference between software configuration management (SCM) and a revision control system (RCS)?

    A. RCS manages the software and the hardware hosting system.

    B. SCM primarily focuses on application configurations, not source code.

    C. RCS primarily focuses on application configurations, not source code.

    D. SCM performs defect tracking, whereas RCS does not.

65. Source code repositories that archive, track history, and maintain revisions of applications have all the following features *Except* for what?

    A. Compilers

    B. Bug tracking

    C. Code review

    D. Personal repository

66. Which system uses customized playbooks to automate the mitigation of cybersecurity incidents, thus resulting in faster incident response and system operations being streamlined?

    A. SOAR

    B. IDS

    C. IPS

    D. Firewall

67. Which of the following is *NOT* a key difference between standard work groups and integrated product teams (IPTs)?

    A. Work products are created collectively in standard work groups.

    B. Consensus is essential in IPTs.

    C. Work products are individually focused on standard work groups.

    D. Teams delegate work in IPTs.

68. Ingrid is an ethical hacker attempting to exploit a victim by running a string that includes %252E%252E%255C within her browser. What type of attack is she attempting to run?

    A. SQL injection

    B. Directory traversal

    C. Percentage injection

    D. Buffer overflow

69. The trusted platform module (TPM) resides on the computer's motherboard and manages at least which two features for system users?

    A. Availability

    B. Encryption

    C. Hashing

    D. Software platforms

70. Which of the following describes the infrastructure of using certificates and asymmetric keys for mutual verification?

    A. OSCP

    B. GPG

    C. PGP

    D. X.509

71. Which of the following provides a system for websites to grant access by using a relying party, allowing users to log into unrelated websites without having to create separate identities?

    A. MySQL

    B. SAML

    C. OpenID

    D. OSCP

72. Which process creates machine language-based object files from source code?

    A. Linking

    B. Compiling

    C. GUI

    D. Interpreting

73. The service-oriented architecture (SOA), which allows disparate applications to communicate across a network, has all the following features *Except* for which one?

    A. Interoperability

    B. Uniform testing framework

    C. Modularity

    D. Platform neutrality

74. Which of the following is *NOT* a characteristic of cloud computing?

    A. Resource pooling

    B. Provisionable

    C. Broad network access

    D. Measured service

75. Which of the following is *NOT* one of the cloud deployment models?

    A. Personal

    B. Private

    C. Hybrid

    D. Community

76. Designing a simpler system that makes it easier for the team and others to understand design objectives is an example of which principle?

    A. Open design

    B. Single point of failure

    C. Least common mechanism

    D. Fail safe

77. The Open Web Application Security Project Software Assurance Maturity Model (OWASP SAMM), which provides a vendor-neutral, measurable, and effective secure development life cycle, contains which five business functions?

    A. Governance, design, implementation, verification, operations

    B. Governance, threat assessment, implementation, verification, operations

    C. Strategy, threat assessment, secure build, architecture, incident management

    D. Policy, secure requirements, deployment, testing, operations

78. Creating standardized designs, and running standardized code for similar or repeatable functionalities, goes by which design philosophy?

    A. Open design

    B. Economy of mechanism

    C. Complete mediation

    D. Psychological acceptability

79. Mapi is part of a development team creating a smartphone gaming application. She can reuse source code from previous video games to simplify her task. How should the development manager respond?

    A. Never reuse code because it is poor practice.

    B. Never reuse code because it brings bugs into the application.

    C. Test and validate the reused code as if it were new code.

    D. Never reuse code because it is inherently insecure.

80. Pamela is leading a software development team in a modeling exercise that lists the appropriate security mitigations for various threats. Which mitigations are preferred?

    A. Acceptance of the vulnerability

    B. Encryption

    C. Novel, state-of-the-art security controls

    D. Commonly used standard corporate security controls

81. Which of the following is *NOT* an appropriate mitigation method for threat management?

    A. Accept the vulnerability.

    B. Redesign to avoid vulnerabilities.

    C. Modify the security requirement to disregard the threat.

    D. Apply normal mitigation.

82. Malesa is a software developer that commonly works with multithreaded applications. As a result, she must create controls to mitigate race conditions. What are these controls called?

    A. Single threading

    B. Race windows

    C. Atomic actions

    D. Mutual exclusion

83. Kenneth is a software manager that is implementing mitigations for common attacks for his new application. This will be represented with which types of diagrams? (Choose 2)

    A. Security

    B. Misuse case

    C. Abuse case

    D. Use case

84. Cle leads the software development team at *TRY Corp* and uses the software development life cycle for his projects. He always starts with the planning and business requirements. These requirements get converted into what for the software developers?

    A. JavaScript

    B. Functional requirements

    C. Security concerns

    D. White box testing

85. Which of the following is *NOT* a type of data on a web server?

    A. Preserved

    B. Personally identifiable information

    C. Personal health information

    D. Classified

86. Data in any organization has a life cycle so that it can be managed and disposed of properly. Which of the following is *NOT* a stage of the data life cycle?

    A. Degaussing

    B. Generation

    C. Retention

    D. Disposal

87. What is a specific risk called that is *NOT* found during an audit?

    A. Audit risk

    B. Control risk

    C. Inherent risk

    D. Detection risk

88. Reggie is a security director and analyzes whether software meets legal and regulatory policies. These policies are examples of which type of requirements?

    A. Internal requirements

    B. External requirements

    C. Customer requirements

    D. Job requirements

89. Policy elements related to integrity include which of the following?

    A. Systems that control risk

    B. Determine who is authorized to see specific data segments

    C. Obtain error detection and correction

    D. Ensure systems are available for authorized users

90. Which tool can be *BEST* used to examine the vulnerabilities of input interfaces?

    A. Bug bar

    B. Attack surface analysis

    C. Threat model

    D. Fuzz testing framework

91. Microsoft has put which system together that helps users analyze common software threats?

    A. SMART

    B. DREAD

    C. STRIDE

    D. Waterfall

92. Which of the following are *NOT* phases of the Microsoft SDL process? (Choose 2)

    A. Requirements

    B. Security

    C. Validation

    D. Training

93. HITECH and HIPAA are frameworks that have been designed to protect which of the following?

    A. PII

    B. PHI

    C. PCI

    D. PFI

94. What is the fifth level of the CMMI maturity model?

    A. Incomplete

    B. Initial

    C. Defined

    D. Optimizing

95. *Glue Corp* is based in the US, while *Horse Ltd.* is based in the UK. Which of the following principles needs be invoked to facilitate data sharing?

    A. GDPR

    B. Safe harbor

    C. FISMA

    D. UNTC

96. Of the following, which is *NOT* a technological risk?

    A. Regulatory

    B. Privacy

    C. Encryption

    D. Change management

97. The software design principle of keeping things simple is related to which other security principle?

    A. Economy of mechanism

    B. Simple security rule

    C. Layered security

    D. Least privilege

98. Users that create passwords with multiple characters using uppercase characters, lowercase characters, special characters, and a minimum of 12 characters are using which type of security model?

    A. Defense in depth

    B. Security through obscurity

    C. Mutual authentication

    D. Implicit deny

99. A system approach where the separation of elements mitigates accidental sharing of information is called what?

    A. Weakest link

    B. Leverage existing components

    C. Separation of duties

    D. Least common mechanism

100. Static code analysis would fit *BEST* in which testing model?

    A. Black box testing

    B. Gray box testing

    C. White box testing

    D. Opaque box testing

Quick answer key

1. C	16. C	31. C	46. A	61. C	76. A	91. C
2. B	17. A	32. B	47. A	62. B	77. A	92. B, C
3. B	18. B	33. B	48. B	63. B	78. B	93. B
4. B	19. C	34. B	49. C	64. B	79. C	94. D
5. A	20. D	35. D	50. D	65. A	80. D	95. A
6. A	21. C	36. A, C	51. C	66. A	81. C	96. A
7. A	22. B	37. A	52. B	67. A	82. B	97. A
8. B	23. B	38. A, D	53. B	68. B	83. B, C	98. B
9. C	24. B	39. C	54. B	69. B, C	84. B	99. D
10. D	25. A	40. D	55. A	70. D	85. A	100. C
11. C	26. A	41. C	56. A	71. C	86. A	
12. B	27. A	42. B	57. A, D	72. B	87. D	
13. B	28. B	43. B	58. B	73. B	88. B	
14. B	29. C	44. B, C	59. C	74. B	89. C	
15. A	30. D	45. D	60. A, D	75. A	90. D	

Answers with explanations

1. **Answer: C** Code reviews, or static analysis, are used to help others write more efficient code and watch for security vulnerabilities such as buffer overflows or backdoors. Dynamic analysis tests how the code operates when it runs. Fuzzing tests user input into applications, while passive testing monitors software as it runs.

2. **Answer: B** Since her private key matches the public key of the letter, she cannot repudiate that she sent the email. It is still possible that someone sent the email from her account when she stepped away from her computer, and that could be determined through video analysis or other investigations.

3. **Answer: B** Complete mediation designs ensure that access to an object is checked for authority. Whenever a subject accesses an object, the action must be mediated to ensure the subject has the required privilege.

4. **Answer: B** The **Open Web Application Security Project (OWASP)** provides tools to mitigate web application vulnerabilities. The **Open Source Security Testing Methodology Manual (OSSTMM)** provides a penetration testing security model. The **Open Education Consortium (OEC)** advocates for free and open university-level educational materials. **Operationally Critical Threat, Asset, and Vulnerability Evaluation (OCTAVE)** is an approach to managing general information security risks.

5. **Answer: A** Test data management utilizes data anonymization to strip the data of any **personally identifiable information (PII)**. Skipping the anonymization step could leak customer PII unintentionally. Safe harbor, data protection, and depersonalization all protect the data, but the PII could still potentially be leaked because customer information has not been removed.

6. **Answer: A** Reference monitors keep systems secure by constructing and assessing the effectiveness and assurance of security policy enforcement in automated systems.

    Learn more here: https://web.ecs.syr.edu/~wedu/seed/Labs/ Reference-Monitor/.

7. **Answer: A** The fundamental privacy elements are access, choice, enforcement, data integrity, notice, onward transfer, and security. Learn more here: https://www.ncbi.nlm.nih.gov/pmc/articles/PMC5124066/.

8. **Answer: B** The phases of the SDLC are Planning and Requirements, Design, Build, Test, Deploy, and Maintenance. Fuzzing is a component of the test phase to ensure that input validation is taking place and done properly. Learn more here: http://www.austincc.edu/skumpati/BCIS1305/CC06.ppt.

9. **Answer: C** Waterfall is the model that's used in the automotive, road construction, and bridge building industries. It makes it very difficult to return to a previous step in the process because the expense would be huge. Because of the flexibility of software, processes such as spiral, Agile, and Scrum create opportunities to improve software by revisiting earlier steps in the process.

10. **Answer: D** Possible methods of authenticating identities for application use include something you have, something you are, and something you know. Identities can be further proven using the something you do and somewhere you are factors. Learn more here: https://dojowithrenan.medium.com/the-5-factors-of- authentication-bcb79d354c13.

11. **Answer: C** Privacy is not a methodology, but a goal. The **privacy risk assessment methodology (PRAM)** helps organizations respond to privacy risks; one way is to label data according to its sensitivity. Impact and likelihood are part of the PRAM approach. Learn more here: `https://www.nist.gov/system/files/documents/2020/01/16/NIST%20Privacy%20Framework_V1.0.pdf`.

12. **Answer: B** When LibreOffice, Google Chrome Office, Microsoft Office, IBM Lotus, and other files are saved, they are preserved in the binary format of that vendor, which disrupts the format of the spreadsheet. The others are structured, and their formats are understood by a multitude of applications.

13. **Answer: B** Use case diagrams display what an authenticated user can and cannot do depending on their role as a user. Misuse case diagrams display what unauthenticated users cannot do. The others are distractors.

14. **Answer: B** Examples of secure coding standards are published by the Software Engineering Institute/CERT at Carnegie Mellon University. This includes recommendations for secure programming that resolve vulnerabilities that are found within typical source code. *Sans* means *without*.

15. **Answer: A** When complex conditionals aren't checked properly, infinite loops can occur because a statement seen as true when it was last checked may now be false. It now remains in the loop, even though it shouldn't.

16. **Answer: C** C language development is prone to buffer overflow attacks, especially when users can enter input. When successfully exploited, a buffer overflow can allow attackers to exfiltrate data or power off the system. Malware and library support are concerns, but more so to system administrators.

17. **Answer: A** The **requirements traceability matrix (RTM)** is designed specifically for the software industry to track and verify requirements. **Gantt, Pareto**, and **Program Evaluation and Review Technique (PERT)** are generic project management tools that are used to coordinate specific events and tasks for a project.

18. **Answer: B** Use cases are helpful in describing unusually complex and confusing circumstances between the user and the system, which results in better software design. The other options are generally issues that are normally handled in software development; therefore, developing use cases for such events would be redundant.

19. **Answer: C Data flow diagrams (DFDs)** provide the system with the processes, data stores, and data flows between elements so that developers can examine trust between the boundaries that are most vulnerable to attacks. The **Unified Modeling Language (UML)** does not go into this level of detail. The **National Vulnerability Database (NVD)** and **Common Vulnerabilities and Exposures (CVE)** are both tools that can be used during the DFD process as these provide lists of known vulnerabilities.

20. **Answer: D** The primary goal of security reviews is to assure the development team that the SDLC process and the desired security mitigations are effective so that the process can be trusted and tuned for future projects.

21. **Answer: C** Each phase of the **software development life cycle (SDLC)** must be approved by security before advancing to the next phase, which means completing that phase before continuing.

22. **Answer: B** Trust boundaries are areas where systems have equal trust, such as identical rights, privileges, identifiers, and access. Trust boundary violations refers to vulnerabilities where code trusts unvalidated data. Learn more here: `https://owasp.org/www-project-web-security-testing-guide/ assets/archive/OWASP_Testing_Guide_v3.pdf`.

    Reference:"*OWASP Testing Guide*", *OWASP Foundation, p. 155, 2008 v3.0.*

23. **Answer: B** Threat modeling is a process by which potential threats, such as structural vulnerabilities or the absence of appropriate safeguards, can be identified and enumerated, and mitigations can be prioritized. The purpose of threat modeling is to provide defenders with systematic analysis of what controls or defenses need to be included, given the nature of the system, the probable attacker's profile, the most likely attack vectors, and the assets most desired by an attacker. Learn more here: `https://owasp.org/www-community/Threat_Modeling`.

24. **Answer: B** Risk is reduced by using proven components. When each component performs one task, and performs it well, it is considered separation of duties. The least common mechanism states that code that's used to access resources should not be shared; sharing mechanisms creates vulnerabilities. Where the vulnerabilities are highly exploitable is considered the weakest link.

25. **Answer: A** Utilizing the existing SSO system provides many operational advantages as systems administrators can maintain a system they understand. The other options are reinventing the wheel, so thorough security testing would be required to ensure their long-term success.

26. **Answer: A** Authority is verified before use in complete mediation system; for example, verifying that the user has the rights to modify a file before making changes.

27. **Answer: A** When systems crash or fail, detailing when and why these errors occur is important and saved in log files. This is also known as auditing. This aids in proper diagnoses and correction. The others have little to do with exception management.

28. **Answer: B** Hashing functions are also used as part of authentication, but hashing is more commonly used for integrity checking to determine whether files have been altered accidentally or intentionally. File alterations could be as simple as an entry made by a user, or due to malware added by an attacker.

29. **Answer: C Near-field communication** (**NFC**) communicates over very short distances, making it less vulnerable to man-in-the-middle attacks versus Yagi systems, which are very long range, and Wi-Fi, which uses omni-directional antennas. Many home security systems use Zigbee wireless networks.

30. **Answer: D** Rich internet applications (**RIAs**) use the internet to transfer data and use the client to process the data, typically to display graphics, with, for example, JavaScript or Flash. **Remote procedure calls** (**RPCs**) create remote instructions, put them into a message, send them to the server to execute, and return the results to the client. The **Simple Object Access Protocol** (**SOAP**) allows enterprises to integrate messaging with their partners using different programming languages. **Representational State Transfer** (**REST**) makes server-side data available to website administrators.

    Learn more here: `https://www.altexsoft.com/blog/soap-vs-rest-vs-graphql-vs-rpc/`.

31. **Answer: C** An **enterprise service bus** (**ESB**) provides seamless communication between XML, DCOM, REST, CORBA, WSDL, EDI, and others.

32. **Answer: B** The **Digital Millennium Copyright Act** (**DMCA**) defines the copyright laws that DRM enforces. Persistence ensures that rights persist, regardless of where the document is moved. Copy restriction doesn't allow you to make duplicates of the medium. Other features include installation limits, anti-tampering, regional lockouts, and watermarking. Learn more here: `https://www.locklizard.com/rights-management/`.

33. **Answer: B** Dynamic links, also known as late links, are resolved at runtime, where static or early links are built into the compiled application. Interpreted languages may read dynamically linked libraries when they're executed.

34. **Answer: B** Compiled JVM byte code runs universally on any JVM offering the capability to write once and run anywhere, as long as the system runs a JVM. JVMs run on smartphones, computers, tablets, and web browsers.

35. **Answer: D** Sandboxing protects live, in-production systems from changes that could damage critical systems. Revision control systems provide branches to isolate experimental changes from trusted branches. Many automation systems have sandboxing utilities built in as part of their service, allowing developers to segment an experimental area from the trusted environment.

36. **Answer: A, C** Managed code works within a virtual machine; for example, the **Common Language Runtime (CLR)** on Windows. The CLR provides secure features, such as sandboxing, garbage collection, type safety, and memory management. Unmanaged code provides better performance because it runs on the target system it was designed for, but the developer must add their own security features.

37. **Answer: A** Salting creates stronger hashes by making them more random so that a hash is different for identical inputs. The salt is added to the input so that the hash varies. Linux systems salt hashes by default as part of authentication. (Windows systems do not salt their hashes.)

38. **Answer: A, D** Code review and static analysis is where other members of the team review each other's source code within the application. Misuse case testing evaluates software by abusing its intended purpose. Dynamic testing analyzes an application at runtime.

39. **Answer: C** Attackers attempt to get copies of data where applications had once run on memory. This can happen if garbage collection is not done, which overwrites unused memory locations with zeroes. Another mitigation is **address space layout randomization (ASLR)**, which places applications in different areas of memory each time they are executed, making it harder for hackers to find where the data is located.

40. **Answer: D** Security orchestration, automation, and response (SOAR) systems use automation, machine learning, and artificial intelligence to respond to threats. **Security information and event management (SIEM)** systems are similar to SOAR systems, but without the automation.

41. **Answer: C Integrated product teams** (IPTs) bring people together from diverse backgrounds, such as engineering, marketing, manufacturing, software developers, and so on, using consensus to develop an application that best meets the needs of the user. Neither the **trusted computing base** (TCB), the **software development life cycle** (SDLC), or the **Capability Maturity Model Integration** (CMMI) fit the model for IPT. Learn more here: `https://www.mitre.org/publications/technical-papers/integrated-project-team-ipt-startup-guide`.

42. **Answer: B** Git is a revision control system that was developed by Linus Torvalds, the founder of the Linux operating system. Source code hosting facilities that use Git include GitHub, GitLab, Launchpad, and others. The other options are computer languages whose source code can be utilized in a repository.

43. **Answer: B** SCM provides a bigger picture than code management. Code reviews are completed by separate teams outside of SCM. The SCM ensures that the software meets the needs of the environment, including interactions with other applications and disparate hardware.

    Reference: *Software Configuration Management, Coordination for Team Productivity, W. A. Babich, Addison-Wesley, 1986.*

44. **Answer: B, C Continuous integration and continuous delivery** (CI/CD) are important for successful software **development and operations** (DevOps). CI involves developers and testers working together to validate new code. CD is the straightforward release of this new code to users without servers needing to be shut down. Learn more here: `https://www.infoworld.com/article/3113680/5-common-pitfalls-of-cicd-and-how-to-avoid-them.html`.

45. **Answer: D** Any software development not using secure software development practices leaves organizations open to vulnerabilities. The other options are the result of poor software development policies.

46. **Answer: A** Continuous delivery provides an automated framework for software changes, releasing software upgrades, patches, and configuration changes in a predictable format. Security-as-code controls automatically where testing is done, who has access to repositories, manages changes, and more. Learn more here: `https://www.oreilly.com/library/view/devopssec/9781491971413/`. Reference: *DevOpsSec, Jim Bird, O'Reilly Media, Inc, June 2016.*

47. **Answer: A Application programming interfaces** (APIs) are generally black boxes that provide additional features for applications. Since static code analysis cannot be performed, other security measures must be performed to ensure the APIs do not bring insecurities into the application.

48. **Answer: B** Code signing provides authenticity and integrity checking, but not defects within the code.

49. **Answer: C** Jacques is performing dynamic analysis. The others are all types of static analysis where reviewers examine the source code. Debugging his application takes him back to the code review stage since he will be examining the source code again.

50. **Answer: D** Attack surface area testing is part of the **software development life cycle (SDLC)** process. Functional tests are concerned with how the application functions.

51. **Answer: C** A simulation test *simulates* the production environment the software will be released to. Production testing occurs once the software has been released to a live production environment. Sandboxing and penetration testing occur before simulation testing.

52. **Answer: B** Organizations that respond to customer requests are successful because the voice of the customer leads to features they are seeking, and they feel as if they are part of the process. The others are important, but if the customer feels ignored, the firm will eventually lack business.

53. **Answer: B** **Random number generators (RNGs)** are tested for robustness. Side-channel attacks are tested against key distribution systems. Encryption algorithms are analyzed, ensuring the correct versions are used for the needs of the data. Custom-made, secret encryption techniques are not tested because they are inherently insecure. Learn more here: `https://resources.infosecinstitute.com/topic/the-dangers-of-rolling-your-own-encryption/`.

54. **Answer: B** Bug bars are a measure of the minimal level of quality, or bar, before software is released to production. If errors exceed the bar, they must be fixed before the software is released into production.

55. **Answer: A** Recovery testing is part of a non-functional process, and developers study how quickly it recovers, as well as with what functionalities. The other options are improper terminology. Learn more here: `https://www.guru99.com/recovery-testing.html`.

56. **Answer: A** The `/GS` compiler switch enables stack overflow protection using a cookie. This cookie is treated as a canary to determine whether its value changes when the program reaches the end of a function. Learn more here: `https://docs.microsoft.com/en-us/cpp/build/reference/gs-buffer-security-check`.

57. **Answer: A, D** Managed code such as applications that use Java or .NET provide more security by default because the applications run in a **Common Language Runtime** (**CLR**) environment. This provides sandboxing, index checking, and multi-platform capabilities.

58. **Answer: B** Declarative programs use a container-based approach to manage their applications so that security is managed by operational personnel, not development. An imperative programming approach reduces the portability of the applications because of their built-in customization. Learn more here: `https://www.csm.ornl.gov/SOS20/documents/McCormick-SOS20.pdf`.

    Reference: *Imperative, Declarative, Functional and Domain-Specific Programming... Oh My!, Patrick McCormick, SOS 20 Workshop, Los Alamos National Laboratory, March 2016.*

59. **Answer: C** Virtualizing security functions provides many of the same benefits as virtualization in general, including reducing **capital and operational expenses** (**CapEx/OpEx**), smaller device footprints, and easier updating. Learn more here: `https://www.sdxcentral.com/security/definitions/what-is-software-defined-security/`.

60. **Answer: A, D** Dynamic code analysis is the process of validating results when users run the application. Code identification is a distractor.

61. **Answer: C** Any software development not using secure software development practices leaves organizations open to a plethora of vulnerabilities, including malware, backdoors, and hijacking. Many view the visibility of open source software as an advantage because many more developers can spot vulnerabilities via static analysis, and if the creator(s) decide not to develop any further, it is straightforward for someone to take over and continue the effort. The operations department needs to keep all the software updated. Learn more here: `https://devops.com/the-risks-and-potential-impacts-associated-with-open-source/`.

62. **Answer: B** Software managers and developers must understand that although many segments of **continuous integration and continuous delivery** (**CI/CD**) follow the **software development life cycle** (**SDLC**), it does not drive the SDLC. Software and security managers must ensure that the SDLC drives the CI/CD process and define the requirements before design, as in this example. The CI/CD process makes it easier to track project activity, manage bugs, and explain the sprint process.

63. **Answer: B** The canary technique sets a parameter to a known value between the buffer and control data on the stack. If the value changes, it's likely the buffer overflowed and overwrote the canary value, and the application should terminate. The other options are distractors.

64. **Answer: B Software configuration management** (**SCM**) is primarily concerned with how software operates in the environment, not standalone like **revision control systems** (**RCSes**). SCM's goals include configuration management, environment management, and facilitating team interactions.

65. **Answer: A** Source code repositories offer many services, including web hosting, wikis, translation systems, shell server support, mailing lists, forums, and more. Software developers need to provide their own compilers. Learn more here: `https://github.com/features/`.

66. **Answer: A Security orchestration, automation, and response** (**SOAR**) systems aid in cybersecurity by using machine learning to help resolve security events or incidents. **Intrusion detection systems** (**IDSes**), **intrusion prevention systems** (**IPSes**), and firewalls do not use playbooks. Learn more here: `https://searchsecurity.techtarget.com/definition/SOAR`.

67. **Answer: A** Work products are more individually focused on standard work groups. Learn more here: `https://www.mitre.org/publications/technical-papers/integrated-project-team-ipt-startup-guide`.

    Reference: *"Integrated Project Team (IPT) Start-up Guide"*, *Creekmore, Muscella, and Petrun, The MITRE Corporation, October 2008*.

68. **Answer: B** Ingrid is using URL encoding to defeat intrusion detection or prevention systems so that her attack goes unnoticed. `%252` represents "`.`," while `%255C` represents "`\`," which, when decoded, becomes "`..\`." This means "`change directory`." The goal is for the attacker to reach the folder where her exploit resides so that she can execute it and compromise the server.

69. **Answer: B, C Trusted platform modules** (**TPMs**) contain processors to generate and store asymmetric and symmetric keys. They also have hash generators to assist with integrity checking. Other features include a hardware-based random number generator and platform integrity, so that they can detect whether any network cards or hard drives have been replaced.

70. **Answer: D X.509 certificates** contain details about the vendor, such as their name, address, expiration date for the certificate, and more. The **Online Certificate Status Protocol (OCSP)** is used to obtain the status of X.509 digital certificates. **GNU Privacy Guard (GPG)** is the free, open source version of **Pretty Good Privacy (PGP)**, which provides tools for building X.509 certificates.

71. **Answer: C** OpenID is used by Google, Facebook, Microsoft, and others so that users can use those credentials to access other services. **Security Assertion Markup Language (SAML)** is similar to OpenID in functionality but does not use a relying party. The **Online Certificate Status Protocol (OCSP)** is used to obtain the status of X.509 digital certificates. MySQL is an open source relational database management system.

72. **Answer: B** Compiling creates object files that usually end in `<filename>.o` or `<filename>.obj`, but can't be executed by the operating system yet. The next stage is linking, which combines the functions, libraries, and dependencies into a single file that can be executed by the operating system. Interpreted languages don't need to be compiled; for example, **Python** and **Bash**. **Graphical user interfaces (GUIs)** allow users to run programs using a mouse.

73. **Answer: B** Features of the **service-oriented architecture (SOA)** include platform neutrality, modularity, reusability, a contract-based interface, discoverability, and interoperability. Because of the heterogeneity and complexity of SOA and its large number of testing possibilities, multiple tools are required to validate SOA services.

74. **Answer: B** The characteristics of cloud computing include on-demand self-service, broad network access, resource pooling, rapid elasticity, and measured service. Learn more here: `http://blog.mesa.org/2017/08/manufacturing-in-cloud-part-ii-5.html`.

75. **Answer: A** The four cloud deployment models are public, private, community, and hybrid, which is a combination of the first three.

76. **Answer: A** Open design is all about clear communications. The simpler the communications to the design team, the better the design and the better the security of the application. Single point of failure is similar to weakest link in that if there is no backup, the system fails. A fail safe is designed so that if the system fails, it fails in a secure manner.

77. **Answer: A** The OWASP **Software Assurance Maturity Model (SAMM)** provides an effective and measurable way to analyze and improve the secure development life cycle. SAMM was built to be evolutive and risk-driven. The five *business functions* – governance, design, implementation, verification, and operations – are built on top of more than a dozen *practices*, including strategy and metrics, threat assessment, secure build, architecture assessment, and incident management. Learn more here: `https://owasp.org/www-project-samm`.

78. **Answer: B** Reusing components is a representation of economy of mechanism. When applications are written with mild learning curves, they are more likely to be used. This is known as psychological acceptability. Where there is open and constructive communication, you have a system of open design. Conducting authorization checks before an operation proceeds is known as complete mediation.

79. **Answer: C** When reusing code, make sure it goes through the normal SDLC security process. Reusing code can help save time and can often be more secure than writing new code because it is heavily tested.

80. **Answer: D** Organizations that utilize known, tested, and commonly used security controls use systems that they are familiar with and allow staff to compare the results against their past benchmarks. The other options are useful, but the best practice is to use security controls validated by the organization, as well as going through configuration management.

81. **Answer: C** Ignoring the threat does not mitigate the threat and still leaves the application vulnerable. The others are appropriate risk mitigations.

82. **Answer: B** Race windows interpret the environment, which can cause a race condition. This is where an object can be altered by concurrent threads. These are commonly resolved using mutual exclusion and atomic actions. Single threading is a distractor.

83. **Answer: B, C** Misuse and abuse case diagrams display what attackers should *not* be able to do, so that proper mitigations can be put in place during the design and development phases of software development. Misuse case diagrams are slightly more detailed than abuse case diagrams, but both are great at making software more secure. Learn more here: `https://www.cs.auckland.ac.nz/courses/compsci725s2c/archive/termpapers/csia.pdf`.

    Reference: *"Misuse Cases and Abuse Cases in Eliciting Security Requirements"*, *Chin Wei, Department of Computer Science, University of Auckland, October 25, 2005.*

84. **Answer: B** The business requirements are converted into functional requirements, which are like blueprints for which software will be securely designed and tested. At this stage, it is too early to conduct any JavaScript coding because the requirements may call for a different computer language entirely. Security is part of every stage of the SDLC, and white box testing occurs much later in the testing phase.

85. **Answer: A** All data is saved or preserved on a hard drive. The others can all be labeled as PII, PHI, classified, or unclassified.

86. **Answer: A** Degaussing uses a magnet to securely dispose of data. The proper stages of the data life cycle are generation, retention, and disposal.

87. **Answer: D** Detection risk occurs when an auditor fails to find a vulnerability. Inherent risks are risks that are present in source code by default. Control risks are those that the software developer cannot prevent or detect. An audit risk is a distractor. Learn more here: `https://www.investopedia.com/terms/d/detection-risk.asp`.

88. **Answer: B** Laws and regulations are detailed and enforced by outside organizations, making them external requirements. Internal requirements include those that are created and enforced by the organization Reggie belongs to. Customer requirements are product functions that appeal to the client. Job requirements come with a task list for completing an assignment.

89. **Answer: C** Integrity controls log errors and detect items outside a baseline. Availability controls determine who is allowed to access specific data segments, or whether systems are available for authorized users. Risk is analyzed as part of business impact analysis.

90. **Answer: D** Fuzz testing is a process where random inputs are sent to an interface seeking exploitable failures. Bug bars prioritize bugs as to whether they need to be fixed in current or future releases. One way to accomplish this is with the **DREAD** model (**damage, reproducibility, exploitability, affected users, and discoverability**). Threat models define and describe threats to the entire software system; one such model is Microsoft's STRIDE model. Attack surface analysis measures software vulnerabilities.

91. **Answer: C** The Microsoft **STRIDE** model reminds developers to out watch for **Spoofing, Tampering, Repudiation, Information disclosure, Denial of service, and Elevation of privilege**, all of which are common threats. This helps users build better quality and lower cost software.

    Learn more here: `https://www.microsoft.com/security/blog/2007/09/11/stride-chart/`.

92. **Answer: B, C** The Microsoft **security development life cycle** (**SDLC**) consists of the following phases: 1) Training, 2) Requirements, 3) Design, 4) Implementation, 5) Verification, 6) Release, 7) Response. Security is reviewed in each phase of the SDL. Validation is part of the Release phase.

93. **Answer: B** If **personal health information** (**PHI**) is compromised, patients could end up with the wrong prescriptions or procedures. Also, leaked information could affect the patient's employment or employment opportunities.

94. **Answer: D** The maturity levels represent an organization's path toward performance and process improvement. The **Capability Maturity Model Integration** (**CMMI**) maturity levels are Level 0: Incomplete, Level 1: Initial, Level 2: Managed, Level 3: Defined, Level 4: Quantitatively Managed, and Level 5: Optimizing. Optimizing organizations focuses on continuous improvement.

    Learn more here: `https://cmmiinstitute.com/learning/appraisals/levels`.

95. **Answer: A** When working with firms in the European Union, **General Data Protection Regulation** (**GDPR**) principles must apply to all data, no longer Safe Harbor, which allowed for looser relationships regarding data exchange, especially with regards to **personally identifiable information** (**PII**). The **Federal Information Security Management Act** (**FISMA**) is a federal law that requires federal agencies to implement security programs. The United Nations Treaty Collection is a depository of over 500 multilateral treaties.

96. **Answer: A** Regulatory would be an example of a business risk because there is no technical utility to manage such risk, where privacy, change management, and encryption all contain a technical control to manage their risk.

97. **Answer: A** The simple security rule is defined for use within the **Bell-LaPadula** confidentiality model and states that the user must have the correct rights to view an item. Economy of mechanism states that code complexity leads to security vulnerabilities because of the larger attack surface.

    Learn more here:

    `https://us-cert.cisa.gov/bsi/articles/knowledge/principles/economy-of-mechanism`.

98. **Answer: B** One way security through obscurity protects passwords is that they are different from any dictionary word, making them very difficult to crack.

    Learn more here: `https://us-cert.cisa.gov/ncas/tips/ST04-002`.

99. **Answer: D** Prevention of accidental sharing is the point here. The least common mechanism states that any mechanisms that are used to access resources should not be shared. Separation of duties reduces fraud by ensuring that each individual does one small piece of the entire work. Leveraging existing components allows you to reuse low-risk coding elements. Weakest link states that the least secure component harms security for the entire system.

100. **Answer: C** With static code analysis, each participant has a full view of the source code. Since everyone has knowledge of the internals, this best fits with white box testing. Black box testing would best fit dynamic code analysis for code that's been purchased from a vendor that does not provide source code. Gray box testing means that the reviewers have some knowledge of the internals. Opaque box testing is a distractor.

9
Full Practice Exam
Exam 1

This chapter contains practice exam questions from all eight domains, and they are weighted as if you were taking the real CISSP exam, as follows:

- 15% from Security and Risk Management
- 10% from Asset Security
- 13% from Security Architecture and Engineering
- 13% from Communication and Network Security
- 13% from Identity and Access Management
- 12% from Security Assessment and Testing
- 13% from Security Operations
- 11% from Software Development Security

Please give yourself 2 hours (120 minutes) maximum to complete the exam. Based on my experience of training hundreds of professionals to study and pass the CISSP exam, after thorough studying, if you score 85% or more on these practice exams, you are ready for the real exam.

At the end of this exam, you'll find the necessary answer sheet, as well as a list of which questions belong to which domains. For any questions you get wrong, do more research and determine why you chose the wrong answer. Once your research is complete, and if you still have questions, feel free to contact me on Twitter at @jordanteamlearn or at youtube.com/jordanteamlearn by commenting on one of my study videos.

Questions

1. Frederick automatically backs up his smartphone on the cloud. Which of the following does this represent?

    A. Safety

    B. Integrity

    C. Availability

    D. Confidentiality

2. Beth is an auditor determining which department and systems to examine for an audit. She also needs details about which processes to monitor. This is an example of which phase of the audit?

    A. Executing exploits

    B. Running reconnaissance

    C. Defining the scope

    D. Conducting documentation

3. The security approach of complete mediation provides which feature?

    A. A security design where a kernel protects the hardware

    B. A security design where all access is verified

    C. A security design that preserves data integrity

    D. A security design using defense in depth

4. The device that resides on system motherboards to manage encryption and passwords is called what?

    A. HSM

    B. TCG

    C. MBR

    D. TPM

5. What communication connectors provide the *BEST* defense and security for leaked authentication vulnerabilities?

    A. RJ-45

    B. SC

    C. BNC

    D. RJ-11

6. Jorda, a computer engineer, wishes to add routers that make routing decisions based on hop count only. Which protocol should she select?

    A. OSPF

    B. RIP

    C. EIGRP

    D. IGRP

7. Randy has installed firewalls to protect his team from outside attacks. This is a good example of what?

    A. Due process

    B. Due diligence

    C. Due care

    D. Regulatory requirements

8. Passive entities that subjects access are called what? (Choose the *BEST* answer)

    A. Objects

    B. Files

    C. Processes

    D. Computers

9. When a system fails to display leaky banners, information that's useful to a hacker is visible in error messages. This is an example of which type of attack?

    A. Leaky attack

    B. Banner attack

    C. Social engineering

    D. Reading attack

10. Periodic meetings to manage and schedule major software, hardware, and security updates are known as what?

    A. Change and configuration management

    B. Systems and operational management

    C. Patch management

    D. Upgrade and update management

11. Abbe is running the marketing department and finds that her team has sold $300,000 of their yearly goal of $1,000,000. What are the KPI and KGI?

    A. The KPI is 30%, while the KGI is $300,000.

    B. The KPI is $300,000, while the KGI is 30%.

    C. The KPI is $300,000, while the KGI is $300,000.

    D. The KPI is -$700,000, while the KGI is $1,000,000.

12. When attackers use Google searches, *WHOIS* results, and Wikipedia articles to learn about their potential victim, they are using what kinds of materials?

    A. Library

    B. Double-blind

    C. OSINT

    D. Privately accessible

13. Lisa receives an email stating that her email box is filling up. The message contains a link for her to click on so that the issue can be resolved. The link is *MOST LIKELY* being used for which type of attack?

    A. Pharming

    B. Denial of service

    C. Phishing

    D. Social engineering

14. Ashley, a security engineer, encrypts all credit card information on the hard drive because of PCI-DSS. A breach is discovered, where over 5,000 customer credit card details were stolen. What is the *MOST LIKELY* cause of this?

    A. The hacker downloaded the credit card information from the hard drive.

    B. The hacker downloaded the credit card details while processing in RAM.

C. The hacker tricked the customers into providing their credit card numbers.

D. The hacker downloaded the credit card details while traveling across the internet.

15. A single sign-on system is characterized by what?

   A. It provides a single username and password to access each system.

   B. A single username with various passwords to access resources.

   C. Multiple usernames and passwords to access resources.

   D. It provides a single username and password to access the entire network.

16. Which VPN protocol operates at layer 2 of the OSI model using 256-bit encryption?

   A. PPP

   B. L2TP

   C. PPTP

   D. IPsec

17. Landon is a software manager leading a team of developers who are creating wind tunnel simulation software. He tracks and manages the project requirements with a grid. This grid is known as what?

   A. Requirements traceability matrix

   B. PERT chart

   C. Pareto chart

   D. Gantt chart

18. A full-mesh network containing five nodes requires how many connections?

   A. 12

   B. 10

   C. 8

   D. 7

19. Barry is an intern at *Our Days Corp* and needs to print his boss' schedule. Which *BEST* describes Barry and the printer's relationship?

   A. Barry is the subject, while the printer is the object.

   B. Barry and the printer are objects.

C. Barry is the object, while the printer is the subject.

D. Barry and the printer are subjects.

20. Sherrel is a security administrator and believes hackers are within her network but that they are covering their tracks well by modifying log files. What two steps can she take to mitigate altered log files? (Choose 2)

A. Install mantraps in the most vulnerable locations of the building.

B. Run consistent network scans.

C. Periodically copy log files to remote locations.

D. Write to WORM media.

21. Danni, a network administrator, wishes to configure a network using a star type topology. Which of the following should she select?

A. Partial mesh

B. Wi-Fi

C. Bus

D. Token ring

22. Which of the following is an electro-mechanical type of alarm system?

A. Pressure mat

B. Infrared

C. Acoustical

D. Microwave

23. Sam plans to outsource their IT services so that the team can focus on designing smartphones. What is the *BEST* way they can monitor the effectiveness of the service provider?

A. KPI

B. KGI

C. KRI

D. SLA

24. The control that enforces a policy over a subject's (process' or user's) ability to interact with objects (systems or files) is known as the what?

A. Referee

B. Reference monitor

C. Access control system

D. BIBA

25. Retinal and fingerprint scanners do which of the following when enrolling a new user, if designed securely?

A. Save an image of the user's retina or fingerprint, and then encrypt the image.

B. Convert the user's retina or fingerprint image into a hash, and then encrypt the hash.

C. Save an image of the user's retina or fingerprint.

D. Convert the user's retina or fingerprint image into a hash.

26. Chang is a computer engineer who has been enlisted to implement security containers on her systems. These will be divided into top secret, secret, confidential, and unclassified containers. Which system should she implement?

A. Rule-BAC

B. MAC

C. DAC

D. NDAC

27. Which of the following is the *BEST* example of exception management?

A. Logging and audit data

B. Separation of duties

C. Psychological acceptability

D. Integrity and availability

28. Carl is a computer intern creating a storage system that continues to run even though two hard drives have failed. Which system is *BEST* suited for him?

A. RAID 0

B. RAID 1

C. RAID 5

D. RAID 6

29. Which *BEST* describes a UTP cable?

A. UTP cables transfer data using laser signals.

B. UTP cables have two insulated twisted wires.

C. UTP cables have two conductors in concentric circles.

D. UTP cables have a range of 1 km before data signal loss.

30. Marylin has just opened her new *GolfCo* golf supply business and is ready to take orders on her brand-new multi-function fax machine. A few months later, she receives several complaints, stating that someone representing *GolfCo* is demanding payments for fees already paid, and desires repayment by gift cards. What is the *MOST LIKELY* problem here?

A. Attackers collected customer information by hacking her fax machine.

B. The clients never paid their bills, and the collection is in order.

C. Her bill collection company mistakenly called clients because they never reconciled payments with GolfCo.

D. One of her staff mistakenly called clients, thinking their accounts were past due.

31. Ayesha has discovered her staff are spending over 65% of their time on issues related to information technology (IT), instead of designing and engineering smartphones. She wants to outsource IT-related issues to *FiXit Corp*. What type of risk management is this?

A. Risk avoidance

B. Risk transference

C. Risk mitigation

D. Risk acceptance

32. Databases use four transaction properties to guarantee data validity. Which of the following is *NOT* one of these data validity properties?

A. Aggregation

B. Isolation

C. Consistency

D. Durability

33. Abiline has spent days finding tuning, pricing, and performance data to conduct a risk assessment meeting. Now that she has all the necessary data, her team needs to perform what type of risk analysis?

    A. Quantitative

    B. Impact

    C. Likelihood

    D. Qualitative

34. Which of the following is *NOT* a physical access control type?

    A. Data backups

    B. Bollards

    C. Security awareness training

    D. Network segregation

35. Which of the following are VPN protocols? (Choose 2)

    A. Kerberos

    B. PPTP

    C. RADIUS

    D. L2TP

36. Two important advantages managed code has over unmanaged code include which of the following features? (Choose 2)

    A. Security

    B. Error-free

    C. Garbage collection

    D. Runs faster

37. Xenxiu is a security professional who has noticed that a desktop computer is performing abnormally. She determines a rootkit is on the system. What is the *BEST* way for her to remove the rootkit?

    A. Use a virus removal tool to delete the rootkit.

    B. Use a rootkit removal tool to delete the rootkit.

    C. Use a malware removal tool to delete the rootkit.

    D. Wipe the hard drive clean and reinstall the operating system.

38. Which protocol uses sequence and acknowledgment numbers to keep track of communications?

    A. IP

    B. UDP

    C. TCP

    D. ICMP

39. When simulating an attack with penetration testing, which test should be done *FIRST*?

    A. An external penetration test when done with automated tools; otherwise, an internal penetration test should be done first.

    B. Both tests should be done at the same time.

    C. External penetration test.

    D. Internal penetration test.

40. Individuals from all the departments of the organization have met to prioritize risks based on impact, exposure, and likelihood. Which process is this?

    A. BCP

    B. IRP

    C. DRP

    D. BIA

41. Which technology monitors user and system behaviors, and then notices changes in behavior that could signal an internal threat?

    A. IPS

    B. SIEM

    C. UEBA

    D. IDS

42. Shivani is a network engineer, and her manager recognizes hundreds of phishing attacks coming from the country of Hackistan. Which access control model is *BEST* used to deny these attacks?

    A. Mandatory access control

    B. Attribute-based access control

C. Role-based access control

D. Rule-based access control

43. The goals of software configuration management (SCM) include all the following *Except* for which one?

A. Managing processes and tools for software builds

B. Conducting source code reviews

C. Ensuring that the configurations meet all the requirements

D. Defecting tracking back to the source

44. An unlabeled tape drive is found lying on a table in a cafeteria. By default, we should assume that this tape has which type of clearance?

A. Top secret

B. Secret

C. Classified

D. Unclassified

45. Carol is a security administrator who wants to be notified of valid staff not gaining entry to the server room (false negative) when it reaches 5 per minute. This form of notification would be considered which of the following?

A. Control zone

B. False negative counter

C. Baseline

D. Clipping level

46. Out of the following encryption methods, which system is considered impossible to crack?

A. Caesar

B. One-time pad

C. Null cipher

D. Vigenère

47. Paul is part of the network security team, and they are setting up Wi-Fi that allows any employee to connect to the network when at the office. Which feature should he recommend for network security?

    A. DHCP snooping

    B. Encryption

    C. Flood guards

    D. Integrity checking

48. The National Institute of Standards and Technology (NIST) outlines security controls to put in place at federal agencies in which Special Publication report?

    A. 800-50

    B. 800-51

    C. 800-52

    D. 800-53

49. When interrogating a suspect or interviewing a witness, ideally, how many investigators should be in the room during the questioning?

    A. One

    B. Two

    C. Three

    D. Four

50. When it comes to dual-use goods (items that can be used by the military and ordinary citizens), there are special agreements for import/export. One that limits military buildup that mitigates issues related to international security is called *Conventional Arms and Dual-Use Goods and Technologies*. What name is this also known by?

    A. Dual-Use Agreement

    B. Wassenaar Arrangement

    C. Arms Agreement

    D. Import/Export Law

51. For single sign-on systems, what does geo-velocity mean?

    A. A user's current location can be determined from where they authenticate.

    B. A user is authenticating from locations far from where they last logged in.

C. The single sign-on system allows users to authenticate from more locations than the average system.

D. A user's password is so simple that they can authenticate within microseconds.

52. An important part of a service for users of an organization's software product includes which of the following?

A. Training

B. Responding to requests

C. Creating new features

D. The latest software development and testing tools

53. Leroy is a security controls buyer seeking products that perform method testing and design. Which assurance level should he select?

A. EAL6

B. EAL4

C. EAL2

D. EAL1

54. Tiger is a software engineer who has convinced his supervisor to delay the project for 1 month to code security mitigations. Why did his supervisor take his advice?

A. You should always strive for perfect security.

B. It costs significantly less to resolve security issues earlier in the process than later.

C. The customers are trained to expect projects to never be released on time.

D. Because delays are normal in software development projects.

55. Jerry is the CEO of *Tulsa Auto* and has held an emergency meeting with the CISO because their new automotive designs were just published in *Car World Magazine*. He asks the CISO what more can be done since they already have an EDLP solution. Which of the following should be chosen here?

A. Encrypt all hard drives.

B. Upgrade and enhance the EDLP solution.

C. Encrypt all network traffic.

D. Deploy an NDLP solution.

56. When using the information security continuous monitoring (ISCM) process, what is the next step after analyzing and reporting the results?

    A. Implement

    B. Respond

    C. Update

    D. Review

57. Wilma is an email administrator, and her mail server is being used to send forged emails. What technology mitigates this issue?

    A. SMTP

    B. SPF

    C. SASL

    D. SSL

58. Madea is a security manager and is updating policies for staff and vendors. Controls in this area are considered which of the following?

    A. Management

    B. Logical

    C. Technical

    D. Operational

59. Which of these is *NOT* true?

    A. Procedures are the same as written directions.

    B. Standards can define key performance indicators.

    C. Guidelines contain step-by-step instructions that must be followed.

    D. Strategic documents would be considered policies.

60. Joseph is a network engineer and suspects that a new switch on the network is fraudulent. What step can he take to test whether it belongs on the network?

    A. Log in to the switch using the default login name and password.

    B. Use the inventory management system to validate the certificate.

    C. Use the `ping` command to validate the switch.

    D. Run a hardware inventory to verify the model number is consistent with the policy.

61. Kelly is the CSO of *MYA Corp* and has decided to secure his physical perimeter further. What is his *BEST* option for making sure cars cannot crash into the building?

    A. Having 4-foot fencing around the parking lot.

    B. Installing bollards 4 feet apart from each other.

    C. Having an intrusion detection system at the doors.

    D. Implementing a flood parking lot with magnesium lighting.

62. Which of the following is the biggest risk of a company converting from Waterfall development to CI/CD?

    A. The risk that management cannot track project activity

    B. The risk that developers reuse metrics before they are reassessed by management

    C. The risk that high-priority bugs will go unresolved

    D. The risk that developers do not understand the sprint process

63. There is a cloud feature that monitors specific metrics to determine whether more memory, CPU, or disk is needed for an application to run well. Once loads return to normal, system requirements return to normal. What is this feature called?

    A. On-demand self-service

    B. Autoscaling

    C. Resource pooling

    D. Measured service

64. Carl fears he will lose his job if his employer learns he has AIDS. He does not want which of the following to leak?

    A. HHS

    B. HIPAA

    C. HITECH

    D. PHI

65. Which ports are considered the well-known ports?

    A. 1-1023

    B. 0-1023

    C. 0-1024

    D. 1-1024

66. Carlson is an administrator with *CHV Fuel*, a regulated industry. At a fuel conference, he learns that outsourcing their IdM could save them time and money. What is his next *BEST* step?

    A. Work with his manager to construct a SOW and RFP for various IDaaS vendors.

    B. Contact three IDaaS vendors, select the one with the best value, and schedule the installation.

    C. Find the IDaaS vendor that presented at the seminar and schedule installation.

    D. Determine whether IDaaS fits with CHV Fuel's security policy.

67. Cara is securing the internet and allowing staff to work from home via VPNs. This will protect and secure what?

    A. Data in motion

    B. Data in use

    C. Data at rest

    D. Data in network

68. Which is the *BEST* mitigation for zero-day attacks?

    A. Vulnerability scanning

    B. Network intrusion prevention systems

    C. Antivirus

    D. Application control software

69. Which of the following attacks is *BEST* used against an asymmetric system?

    A. Ciphertext only

    B. Known plaintext

    C. Chosen ciphertext

    D. Chosen plaintext

70. A security information and event management system (SIEM), which monitors security alerts across the network, falls under which class of devices?

    A. NIPS

    B. HIDS

    C. HIPS

    D. NIDS

71. What allows a system for websites to grant access by using a relying party (RP), allowing users to log in to unrelated websites without having to create separate identities?

    A. SAML

    B. MySQL

    C. OpenID

    D. OSCP

72. Pradip notices a standard system file is missing. What utility can he use to help determine who deleted the file?

    A. Folder auditing

    B. Server auditing

    C. File auditing

    D. Directory auditing

73. Dave is a hacker who is exfiltrating corporate files to his partner, Mike. What is the *BEST* way for Dave to launch the upload without getting caught?

    A. Mike builds an SSH server so that Dave can launch a covert channel and tunnel HTTP over SSH.

    B. Mike builds an FTP server so that Dave can launch a covert channel using FTP.

    C. Mike builds an SSH server so that Dave can launch a covert channel using SSH.

    D. Mike builds a TELNET server so that Dave can launch a covert channel using TELNET.

74. Naomi needs an administrative control to enhance the confidentiality of data. Which should she choose?

    A. Security guards

    B. Fencing

    C. Data leak prevention system

    D. Non-disclosure agreement

75. Nox is a security engineer who needs some administrative privileges to add printers and modify networks. Which is the *BEST* security control for him in this case?

    A. Role-based access control

    B. Mandatory access control

C. Rule-based access control

D. Attribute-based access control

76. Minna, a security analyst, notices that Candace's computer has caught fire. Which fire extinguisher should she grab to put the fire out?

A. Class D

B. Class C

C. Class B

D. Class A

77. During the change management process, the process of scheduling the installation of a change should occur at which step?

A. Change approval

B. Change testing

C. Change documentation

D. Change implementation

78. Large US companies that do not offer data subjects the *right to be forgotten* may not do which of the following?

A. Operate business in the US due to OECD

B. Conduct business with Europe clientele due to GDPR

C. Operate business anywhere in the world due to OECD

D. Operate business in the UAE

79. Billy is a CISO and proposes to his security team the idea of using a virtual machine snapshot to deploy a virtual desktop infrastructure (VDI). The snapshot image is also known as a(n) what?

A. Gold master

B. Virtual machine cache

C. Least privilege

D. Application whitelist

80. Phyllis leads her software development team in an exercise that lists appropriate security mitigations for various threats. Which mitigations are preferred?

    A. Acceptance of the vulnerability

    B. Novel, state-of-the-art security controls

    C. Encryption

    D. Standard corporate security controls commonly used

81. Triple DES (3DES) has four modes. Which mode uses two keys – one for encryption and one for decryption?

    A. DES-EDE0

    B. DES-EDE1

    C. DES-EDE3

    D. DES-EDE2

82. Which of the following provides the *Least* protection to data in motion?

    A. WPA

    B. WEP

    C. L2TP

    D. PPTP

83. Tyler has been notified that she has just made a purchase of $150 from Tarmert that she does not recognize. Her email reports several messages regarding bad login attempts to other online stores. What is *MOST LIKELY* occurring?

    A. A hacker broke into her computer and stole all her online store credentials.

    B. Her Tarmert credentials were discovered on a pastebin, and hackers are attempting to use it elsewhere.

    C. There is no issue because she simply forgot about the purchase.

    D. Tarmert sent her the message in error.

84. Non-compete agreements are generally unenforceable because of which reason?

    A. Competition is covered in the non-disclosure agreement.

    B. Courts value a citizen's right to earn a reasonable income.

    C. Non-compete agreements are illegal.

    D. Non-compete agreements are always enforceable.

85. A centralized system that correlates, analyzes, and retains log files for the entire corporate network is known as which device?

    A. Kerberos

    B. LDAP

    C. TACACS

    D. SIEM

86. Perry is a security engineer who manages expired encryption keys. Where is the *BEST* place for him to put these expired keys?

    A. Key layaway

    B. Key escrow

    C. Secure key disposal

    D. Keychain

87. Locks share three components. Which of the following is *NOT* one of these components?

    A. Operating mechanism

    B. Switching device

    C. Locking device

    D. Latching device

88. Many social networking sites, such as Facebook, protect communications with which service to secure conversations from hackers?

    A. End-to-end encryption

    B. Data in use

    C. Data in motion

    D. Link encryption

89. Nigel is a new business owner who has just purchased 1,000 prospect leads from HotLeads. The prospects are guaranteed to be interested in business opportunities. What is his *Greatest* risk?

    A. That only 25% of prospects will have interest in business opportunities.

    B. That only 70% of prospects will have interest in business opportunities.

C. The lead list is stale because HotLeads has a poor reputation.

D. That only 5% of prospects will have interest in business opportunities.

90. Tom is an artist at *VeAr Corp*. His manager suspects he is giving away software licenses every Thursday to a secret contact that sells them online, and that they split the money. On Thursday morning, Tom is told to leave and not return for a week. This is known as which security method?

A. Voluntary vacation

B. Expulsion

C. Suspension

D. Mandatory vacation

91. Montrie is a network engineer who has been tasked with writing firewall rules that allow SYN-ACK-SYN communications. Which protocol does he set to permit?

A. UDP

B. TCP

C. IP

D. ICMP

92. Which of the following are *NOT* phases in the Microsoft SDL process? (Choose 2)

A. Training

B. Validation

C. Security

D. Requirements

93. The Risk Management Framework (RMF) is also known as which NIST Special Publication?

A. 800-35

B. 800-36

C. 800-37

D. 800-38

94. Agnes is a network administrator who has been assigned with installing wireless networks in the most secure way possible. Which of the following should she *AVOID*?

    A. Setting a maximum signal strength

    B. Setting WPA2 encryption

    C. Disabling SSID broadcasts

    D. Enabling MAC address filtering

95. Service organization control (SOC) reports related to security and privacy that are *NOT* focused on financial controls are classed as which of the following? (Choose 2)

    A. SOC 1

    B. SOC 2

    C. SOC 3

    D. SOC 4

96. James has just joined *PEL Products* as a new employee, and his accounts must be set up through identity proofing and enrollment. What is the correct order for providing his credentials?

    A. Validation, verification, authentication, resolution

    B. Resolution, validation, verification, authentication

    C. Resolution, verification, validation, authentication

    D. Verification, validation, authentication, resolution

97. Webber, a systems administrator, has installed a new service that requires port 59040 to be used. The service continually fails until he realizes that the firewall must be programmed to allow port 59040. When this new service is blocked, it is considered to be which of the following?

    A. True positive

    B. True negative

    C. False positive

    D. False negative

98. Some safes can detect heat rising; for example, from the tools that are used when breaking in to them. What is this feature called?

    A. Glass relocking

    B. Thermal relocking

    C. Passive relocking

    D. Fire safe

99. A system approach where the separation of elements mitigates accidental sharing of information is known as what?

    A. Weakest link

    B. Separation of duties

    C. Leverage existing components

    D. Least common mechanism

100. Nina, a security administrator, is in the process of installing fax machines on the corporate network. Where is the *BEST* place for her to install these for the best security?

    A. Computer room

    B. SOC

    C. Break room

    D. Utility closet

Answer key

1. C	16. B	31. B	46. B	61. B	76. B	91. B
2. C	17. A	32. A	47. A	62. B	77. D	92. B, C
3. B	18. B	33. A	48. D	63. B	78. B	93. C
4. D	19. A	34. C	49. B	64. D	79. A	94. A
5. B	20. C, D	35. B, D	50. B	65. B	80. D	95. B, C
6. B	21. B	36. A, C	51. B	66. D	81. D	96. B
7. C	22. A	37. D	52. B	67. A	82. C	97. C
8. A	23. D	38. C	53. B	68. D	83. B	98. B
9. B	24. B	39. C	54. B	69. C	84. B	99. D
10. A	25. B	40. D	55. D	70. D	85. D	100. B
11. B	26. B	41. C	56. B	71. C	86. B	
12. C	27. A	42. D	57. B	72. C	87. D	
13. C	28. D	43. B	58. A	73. A	88. A	
14. B	29. B	44. A	59. C	74. D	89. C	
15. D	30. A	45. D	60. B	75. A	90. D	

Domain key

Domain	Question
Security and Risk Management	1, 7, 11, 23, 31, 33, 40, 48, 50, 58, 59, 64, 74, 84, 93
Asset Security	8, 15, 26, 34, 44, 55, 67, 78, 88, 98
Security Architecture and Engineering	4, 9, 14, 24, 32, 46, 53, 61, 69, 76, 81, 86, 94
Communication and Network Security	6, 16, 18, 21, 29, 38, 47, 57, 65, 73, 82, 91, 100
Identity and Access Management (IAM)	5, 13, 19, 25, 35, 42, 51, 60, 66, 75, 83, 90, 96
Security Assessment and Testing	2, 12, 20, 30, 39, 45, 54, 63, 72, 85, 89, 95
Security Operations	10, 22, 28, 37, 41, 49, 56, 68, 70, 77, 79, 87, 97
Software Development Security	3, 17, 27, 36, 43, 52, 62, 71, 80, 92, 99

10
Full Practice Exam
Exam 2

This chapter contains practice exam questions from all eight domains and are weighted as if taking the real **Certified Information Systems Security Professional (CISSP)** exam, as follows:

- 15% from Security and Risk Management
- 10% from Asset Security
- 13% from Security Architecture and Engineering
- 13% from Communication and Network Security
- 13% from Identity and Access Management (IAM)
- 12% from Security Assessment and Testing
- 13% from Security Operations
- 11% from Software Development Security

Based on my experience in training hundreds of professionals to study and pass the CISSP exam, after thorough studying, if you score 85% or more on these practice exams, you are ready for the real exam. Please give yourself 2 hours (120 minutes) *maximum* to complete the exam.

At the end of the exam is an answer sheet and a listing of which questions belong to which domains. For any answers you get wrong, do more research and determine why you have the wrong answer. After further research, if you still have questions, feel free to contact me on Twitter at @jordanteamlearn or youtube.com/jordanteamlearn by commenting on one of my study videos.

Questions

1. Melinda just received an International Information Systems Security Certification Consortium (ISC)² certification. Per their *Code of Ethics*, her primary service is to?

    A. Users

    B. Management

    C. Shareholders

    D. All humanity

2. A key difference between a penetration test and a vulnerability scan would be which of the following?

    A. There is no difference between the two as they both search for vulnerabilities.

    B. Penetration testing is done only in logical environments to ensure firewalls are not vulnerable to attack.

    C. Vulnerability testing is done only in physical environments to ensure exit and safety doors are not vulnerable.

    D. A vulnerability scan searches for vulnerabilities, but a penetration test exploits vulnerabilities.

3. Phillip, a systems analyst, insists that he did not send an email requesting a ransom. Further analysis shows that the public key of the letter directly relates to Phillip's private key. This is an example of?

    A. Certificates

    B. Repudiation

C. Defense in depth (DiD)

D. Non-repudiation

4. After powering on a computer, it eventually boots the Linux operating system. Which of the following loads the kernel?

A. Basic input/output system (BIOS)

B. Master boot record (MBR)

C. User

D. Unified Extensible Firmware Interface (UEFI)

5. Terri is a security analyst seeking to improve authentication from using just a password, to a password and an authenticator that uses a time-based one-time password (TOTP). Which type of authentication is she implementing?

A. Two-factor authentication (2FA)

B. Three-factor authentication (3FA)

C. Something-that-you-know

D. Multi-factor authentication (MFA)

6. Emory is a security administrator setting up systems so that when users use a fully qualified domain name (FQDN), it is converted to Internet Protocol (IP) addresses. Which two technologies is he configuring?

A. Dynamic Host Configuration Protocol daemon (DHCPD)

B. Berkeley Internet Name Domain (BIND)

C. HyperText Transfer Protocol daemon (HTTPD)

D. Name server Daemon (NAMED)

7. Patty, a CISSP technician with *KNA Engr*, has discovered that Tom and Tim, also CISSPs, colluded and harmed a business associate. How should she report this ethics violation to (ISC)²?

A. Only with the sponsorship of another (ISC)²-certified individual

B. The (ISC)² ethics web page

C. By emailing ethics@isc2.org

D. In a typed or handwritten letter

8. Julie is setting up an intrusion detection system (IDS) that is rule-based. A rule-based IDS has which of the following attributes?

    A. Can recognize patterns and multiple activities

    B. Protocol recognition outside normal settings

    C. Produces `if` statements

    D. Recognizes new types of attacks

9. This computer security technique continuously and randomly repositions an application's data in memory to mitigate buffer overflows. Which of the following security techniques is being referred to here?

    A. Dynamic random-access memory (DRAM)

    B. Static RAM (SRAM)

    C. Erasable programmable read-only memory (EPROM)

    D. Address space layout randomization (ASLR)

10. Ken is a network engineer tuning the network to meet corporate standards. His supervisor informs him that the security measures are making the network perform poorly, and he must remove them. What must *BEST* be done for the security of the organization?

    A. Ken must remove the security measures.

    B. Ken should suggest his manager speak with the security manager.

    C. Ken should remove the security measures and re-enable them after his manager goes home.

    D. Make Ken's supervisor the security manager.

11. Akheela is required to destroy card verification value (CVV) codes after transactions have been completed. She is complying with which standard?

    A. The Committee of Sponsoring Organizations (COSO)

    B. The IT Infrastructure Library (ITIL)

    C. The National Institute of Standards and Technology (NIST)

    D. The Payment Card Industry Data Security Standard (PCI-DSS)

12. Jerry is an ethical hacker attacking *LUANG hospital* as authorized by their chief information security officer (CISO). Federal investigators notice the attack and raid Jerry's office and arrest him. Why was he *MOST LIKELY* arrested?

    A. All hacking is against the law, including ethical hacking.

    B. He was attacking the human resources (HR) department instead of the financial department, per the agreement.

    C. He was attacking HERT hospital instead of HART hospital, which was unapproved.

    D. He started the attack before getting his Get-Out-of-Jail-Free-Card document.

13. Jaquan is a security manager creating a corporate security document that states laptops must maintain the latest patches, use ClamAV malware detection software, LibreOffice suite, and Thunderbird email client. This document *BEST* fits which category?

    A. Policy

    B. Standard

    C. Procedures

    D. Guidelines

14. Aliyah, a software developer, is creating a chess-playing game. To make her job easier, she acquires a library of chess pieces recommended to her by a newsgroup. A week later, an overseas hacker is detected on her computer. What *MOST LIKELY* happened?

    A. The dynamic-link library (DLL) or shared object had a backdoor.

    B. The system was air-gapped.

    C. The malware protection was not updated.

    D. The application is written in the C language.

15. Identity management systems maintain user authentication information and include which two out of the following?

    A. Active Directory (AD)

    B. Lightweight AD Protocol (LDAP)

    C. A distinguished name (DN)

    D. A domain component (DC)

16. Toussaint, a network engineer, is asked to install a router to separate two networks within his local-area network (LAN) where there are no email or web services, instead of a firewall. After asking "why not a firewall", how does his network manager respond?

    A. Routers are stateful by default.

    B. Routers are less expensive.

    C. Firewalls are less expensive.

    D. Routers are stateless by default.

17. Robert, a software technician, develops an application in the C language allowing users to enter their home and business addresses. Which of the following is his primary concern?

    A. Lack of library support

    B. Users entering wrong addresses

    C. Buffer overflows

    D. Malware

18. Kristi is a security technician completing setups for the single sign-on (SSO) system. Which system should she utilize for the *MOST* secure authentication?

    A. Extensible Authentication Program (EAP)

    B. Message-digest 5 (MD5)

    C. Password Authentication Protocol (PAP)

    D. Advanced Encryption Standard (AES)

19. Prixy is a chef seeking to visit his daughter at the Federal Bureau of Investigation (FBI). He's instructed to go through a door, and the door in front and behind him are locked. While locked in the room, he hears over the speaker that metal is detected and he is being detained. What is the name of this room?

    A. Chroot jail

    B. Mantrap

    C. Panic room

    D. Temporary lockup

20. The practice of conducting timely network vulnerability scans helps to discover which two vulnerabilities?

    A. Unauthorized services

    B. File modifications

    C. Open ports

    D. Poor passwords

21. Brett is a network manager architecting a wired network through *Klout Co.* Part of the cabling will run above drop ceilings and through raised floors. Which of the following is his *BEST* recommendation?

    A. Use standard-grade cable because it is the least expensive.

    B. Use plenum-grade cable because, in the case of a fire, standard-grade cables emit deadly gas.

    C. Use standard-grade cable because it is fireproof.

    D. Use plenum-grade cable because of its encryption features.

22. Fake video cameras are a type of which security control?

    A. Deterrent

    B. Compensating

    C. Preventative

    D. Detective

23. Lisa's credit card information was stolen, and she realizes this occurred at the *Luke* petrol station. She believes the owner should go to prison. Which would *MOST LIKELY* occur?

    A. The PCI-DSS is a contractual agreement between the store owner and the credit card provider. At worst, the owners will lose the right to accept credit cards.

    B. PCI-DSS is an industry standard. At worst, the owner will lose their credit card license.

    C. PCI-DSS is a federal regulation punishable by up to 5 years in federal prison.

    D. PCI-DSS is a legal standard punishable by up to 5 years in state prison.

24. Computer system features such as the UEFI, a globally unique identifier (GUID) partition table, a universally unique ID (UUID), a trusted platform module (TPM), and SELinux are a part of which security feature?

    A. BIOS

    B. MBR

    C. Extensible Firmware Interface (EFI)

    D. Trusted computing base (TCB)

25. Lonnie is a security technician analyzing fingerprint scanners for access to the security operations center (SOC). Device 1 has a crossover error rate (CER) of 3.5. Device 2 has a CER of 3.1. Which of the following is true for *BEST* security?

    A. He should use device 1 because the CER is higher.

    B. He should use device 2 because the CER is lower.

    C. Since the CERs are similar, he should use the lower-cost device.

    D. Use both devices to simplify access to the system on a chip (SOC).

26. Diskless computers with memory and fast central processing units (CPUs), networked to obtain their operating system and data from a centralized server, are called?

    A. Backup servers

    B. Distributed computing

    C. Thick clients

    D. Thin clients

27. Complete mediation can be *BEST* described by which of the following approaches to security?

    A. Integrates authentication and authorization

    B. Layered security

    C. An approach that minimizes the opportunity to be circumvented

    D. An approach that uses DiD and least privilege

28. Which of the following predicts how long an electromechanical system will run until it fails and can be repaired?

    A. Mean time between failures (MTBF)

    B. Mean down time (MDT)

C. Mean time to failure (MTTF)

D. Mean time to recovery (MTTR)

29. Terminal Access Controller Access-Control System (TACACS) and TACACS+ systems contain which of the following two features?

A. 2FA

B. Encrypts passwords but not data

C. Communicates via User Datagram Protocol (UDP) protocols

D. Allows password changes

30. Several signs and emails warn staff not to pick up and use Universal Serial Bus (USB) drives found in parking lots or elsewhere. These types of security notices fall under which category?

A. Training

B. Education

C. Awareness

D. Professional development

31. Which of the following is *NOT* a directive control type?

A. Privacy policy

B. Beware of dog sign

C. Bollard

D. Terms of service

32. Which of the following is a framework that uses seven evaluation assurance levels to help assess the security of technology devices?

A. United Labs

B. Evaluation Assurance

C. Common Criteria (CC)

D. Functional Testing

33. Marcus has purchased laptops for his staff for US Dollars (USD) $4,000 each. Insurance will cover 50% if they are lost, stolen, or damaged. In an average year, five laptops are lost, stolen, or damaged. Calculate the annualized loss expectancy (ALE).

    A. $20,000

    B. $10,000

    C. $4,000

    D. $2,000

34. Anna's security manager asks her to provide data as to whether they should stay on their Remote Authentication Dial-In User Service (RADIUS) authentication, authorization, and accounting (AAA) server, or move to TACACS. What are two differences between RADIUS and TACACS?

    A. TACACS transmits data via Transmission Control Protocol (TCP), and RADIUS transmits data via UDP.

    B. TACACS transmits data via UDP, and RADIUS transmits data via TCP.

    C. TACACS encrypts all the data; RADIUS encrypts the password only.

    D. TACACS encrypts all the data; RADIUS encrypts the username and password only.

35. SSO systems have which characteristics?

    A. Provide a single username and password to access each system

    B. Provide multiple usernames and passwords to access resources

    C. Provide a single username with various passwords to access resources

    D. Provide a single username and password to access the entire network

36. Isolating test code from direct contact with in-production systems and data is which kind of process?

    A. Automation

    B. Isolation

    C. Revision control

    D. Sandboxing

37. *PGIN Corp* has detected an attack on their network where personally identifiable information (PII) was leaked to an overseas hacker. What is the next step in the incident management process?

    A. Preparation

    B. Response

    C. Detection

    D. Mitigation

38. Frank is a hacker seeking vulnerabilities to attack a bank and steal money electronically. Which electronic communication device is *MOST LIKELY* the weakest vulnerability?

    A. The bank website

    B. The internal corporate website

    C. Fishtank thermometer

    D. The firewall

39. From the following list, which is *NOT* a requirement of the PCI-DSS?

    A. Restrict physical access to cardholder data.

    B. Collect logins and passwords for each online customer.

    C. Protect stored cardholder data.

    D. Regularly test security systems and processes.

40. Which of the following represents an acceptable amount of data loss measured in time?

    A. Recovery point objective (RPO)

    B. Maximum tolerable downtime (MTD)

    C. Recovery time objective (RTO)

    D. Work recovery time (WRT)

41. Charles is a security administrator who convinced the chief security officer (CSO) that they should invest in an empty building as a recovery site because space becomes expensive in the case of a disaster. Which kind of facility is this?

    A. Hot site

    B. Cloud site

C. Cold site

D. Warm site

42. A type of role-based access control (RBAC) that allows for defining a subset of roles based on a superset role is named which of the following?

    A. Superuser

    B. Superset-based

    C. Subset-based

    D. Hierarchical

43. A popular source code repository (SCR) tool that archives, tracks the history, and maintains revisions of an application is known as which of the following?

    A. Pascal

    B. Git

    C. Java

    D. Fortran

44. Brig is a senior systems administrator looking to mitigate external threats into his Linux and Unix systems. What *BEST* mitigates brute-force attacks?

    A. Encrypt the hard drive.

    B. Implement stronger password policies.

    C. Hash passwords using Secure Hash Algorithm 256 (SHA-256).

    D. Change the root login name to `roto-root3r`.

45. Madge is a network manager whose team has recently installed 100 IP cameras. Practicing good security, all default logins and passwords were changed to strong credentials. It is later discovered that one of the cameras has been used as an attack vector to breach the corporate network. What did the team miss?

    A. They forgot to change the credentials on the breached camera.

    B. Malware is within the cameras that call back to the manufacturer.

    C. A team member installed a 101st camera with the default credentials.

    D. The camera had a hardcoded password.

46. Arie is a hacker who wishes to launch an attack with the least technology possible. Which attack does he *MOST Likely* perform?

    A. Social engineering

    B. Phishing

    C. Spam

    D. Trojan horse

47. Greg is a service manager ready to start his day. He opens his laptop but cannot access the internet. He notices that he has an IP address of `169.254.3.4` but still cannot access his online bank. What is *MOST LIKELY* the problem?

    A. The DHCP server is down.

    B. His network card is disabled.

    C. The bank's web server is down.

    D. The internet is down.

48. Arthur, chief executive officer (CEO) of *Funutek*, wishes to implement online purchasing via their website. The chief marketing officer (CMO) likes the idea because the new system can double sales. The CSO fears internet attacks and suggests *NOT* moving forward. How should Arthur proceed?

    A. Implement the website once he is certain there is no risk of attack.

    B. Implement the website after the CMO collects research on securing websites.

    C. Implement the website and secure it within acceptable risk levels.

    D. Listen to the CSO—do not implement the website.

49. Which of the following steps are *NOT* part of forensically protecting evidence from a hard drive?

    A. Hash the hard drive.

    B. Save critical files for the manufacturing department to a remote system.

    C. Duplicate the hard drive.

    D. Write-protect the hard drive.

50. Kilroy has just learned about hacking and attempts to hack into his school website to change his grades. This puts him in which class of hackers?

    A. Ethical hacker

    B. Script kiddie

C. Advanced persistent threat (APT)

D. Internal threat

51. *ZZX Corp* is under a widespread phishing attack, stating DHL cannot deliver a package and must click a link to fix the problem. Which is the *BEST* solution to this?

    A. Program a packet-filtering firewall.

    B. Install and program a circuit-level gateway within the corporate LAN.

    C. Install software-based firewalls on each PC.

    D. Security awareness training and phish auditing.

52. Matia is a software development manager, and her team is undertaking the final testing of software before releasing it to production. The final test will simulate the production environment. What is this test called?

    A. Penetration testing

    B. Production testing

    C. Simulation testing

    D. Sandbox testing

53. Nadia is a systems administrator given privileges above standard users, such as the ability to add and remove networks and printers. Senior systems administrators can also add and remove hard drives, which Nadia is not allowed to do. Which model does this *BEST* represent?

    A. RBAC

    B. Non-discretionary access control (NDAC)

    C. Discretionary access control (DAC)

    D. Mandatory access control (MAC)

54. Which groups are *MOST* responsible for data leaks of PII?

    A. Hackers and script kiddies

    B. Nation-sponsored hackers

    C. External hacktivists

    D. Employees and contractors

55. Compilation and derivation of data from databases is called?

    A. Aggregation and inference

    B. Compiling and deriving

    C. Compilation and derivation

    D. Certification and accreditation

56. Which of the following backup types make for the fewest number of tapes to restore after making several years of backups?

    A. Full

    B. Incremental

    C. Differential

    D. Partial

57. Routing IP (RIP) is a distance-vector routing protocol. Distance-vector routing protocols make routing decisions based on what?

    A. Physical distance measured in centimeters (cm) or kilometers (km), if preferred

    B. Number of hops, network load, and packet size

    C. A combination of physical distance and number of hops

    D. Minimum number of hops to reach the destination

58. Manne is conducting a risk assessment and needs to determine the percentage of risk his organization would suffer if an asset were compromised. Which of the following signifies this aspect of risk?

    A. Vulnerabilities

    B. Safeguards

    C. Exposure factors

    D. Risks

59. Nifta just completed a risk assessment with his team and they determined that the new planned office location was too dangerous, so they decided not to build there. Which risk response did they use?

    A. Mitigation

    B. Avoidance

C. Acceptance

D. Transfer

60. Mobile device management (MDM) helps security technicians manage security on smartphones. Which three features are managed using MDM?

A. Patch updates

B. Encryption

C. Remote wipe

D. Contact list updates

61. Catia is a hacker who can forge email messages to make them appear as if they are signed by a trusted person. Why will this fail for her?

A. Copying valid digital signatures to another document results in a different hash.

B. The public key must be identical.

C. The symmetric key must be identical.

D. A script kiddie would have no trouble forging messages.

62. What is an organization's largest security risk in using open source applications?

A. The operations department does not install version updates and patches in a timely manner.

B. The source code is visible by anyone in the world.

C. The creator(s) of the application may not have used secure software development procedures.

D. The creator(s) decides to discontinue further development of the application.

63. Two ways to monitor a website's utilization, storage, system loads, and users for effectiveness are with which utilities?

A. Alerts and logs

B. Metrics and logs

C. Events and logs

D. Thresholds and logs

64. Tanisia has discovered that her employer has been reading her emails. She approaches her boss, and her boss shows her that she signed the reasonable expectation of privacy (REP) agreement. Which steps can Tanisia take next?

    A. Report the supervisor to HR.

    B. Contact the police or federal authorities and open a criminal case.

    C. Nothing—she waived her rights to email privacy while at work.

    D. File a civil lawsuit.

65. Cheng, a networking engineer, is connecting two computers in a LAN. Computer A has an IP address of `10.0.4.7/24`, and computer B has an IP address of `10.0.5.8/24`. He tests the connections using `ping` but gets a `host unreachable` error message. They are both properly plugged into the switch. What is the *MOST Likely* problem?

    A. One of the cables is broken.

    B. Cheng needs to use a hub instead of a switch.

    C. The systems are improperly connected.

    D. The systems are on separate subnets.

66. A public key infrastructure (PKI) offers which type of trust to users?

    A. Peer-to-peer

    B. Transitive

    C. Trust metrics

    D. Coaching

67. Data that resides on a solid-state drive (SSD), optical disk, hard drive, or magnetic tape is also known as:

    A. Data in use

    B. Data on disk

    C. Data at rest

    D. Data in motion

68. *Bee-Ar Restaurant* suffers an incident where a male cook followed a woman into a bathroom, took a photo, and ran out. He is finally caught, and newspapers ask employees for answers. All staff, except for public relations (PR), should be trained to say which of the following?

    A. The attacker was apprehended, and the police will get back with answers to your questions.

    B. The attacker was apprehended, and the CEO will get back with answers to your questions.

    C. The attacker was apprehended, and PR will get back with answers to your questions.

    D. No comment.

69. A digital signature must have which two of the following attributes?

    A. Contain letters, numbers, and special characters

    B. Be unique

    C. Be easy to remember

    D. Be readable and legible

70. Karlton, a network technician, installs a firewall and opens ports 80 and 443. He can reach the website, but testing the Secure Shell (SSH) service from the Wide Area Network (WAN) results in access being denied. What *MOST LIKELY* caused this issue?

    A. The first rule of the firewall is deny-all.

    B. The first rule of the firewall is allow-all.

    C. The last rule of the firewall is deny-all.

    D. The last rule of the firewall is allow-all.

71. Which of the following describes an infrastructure of using asymmetric keys and certificates for mutual verification?

    A. GNU Privacy Guard (GPG)

    B. Pretty Good Privacy (PGP)

    C. Online Certificate Status Protocol (OCSP)

    D. X.509

72. Several administrators are getting phone calls at GD Company to make $3,000 investments in platinum. What likely caused this?

    A. Vishing

    B. PhoneSweep

    C. War dialing

    D. An administrator responded to an advertisement in a magazine

73. Roger is a security engineer reviewing log files and notices that from 9 P.M. to 3 A.M., the server reports attempted connections on network ports 0, 1, 2, 3...., and 1023 from an unknown system on the internet. Which type of attack is occurring?

    A. HPING

    B. Port scanning

    C. Network Mapper (NMAP)

    D. Distributed denial-of-service (DOS)

74. Bini has provided his phone number, email address, and home address to *Pay & Go Food Store* so that they can deliver groceries to his home. He is considered to be which of the following?

    A. Data owner

    B. Data auditor

    C. Data subject

    D. Data custodian

75. An example of a device that blocks cars from entering but allows people through is known as which device?

    A. Turnstile

    B. Mantrap

    C. Bollard

    D. Fence

76. Which command starts the computer management console on a Windows 10 system?

    A. `compmgmt.msc`

    B. `perfmon.msc`

C. eventvwr.msc

D. regedit.exe

77. Which of the following should *NOT* be put in a service-level agreement (SLA)?

    A. The types of media backup data is saved on

    B. Protocols to change metrics

    C. Metrics on how services will be measured

    D. Remedies for breach of the agreement

78. Dalip is president of *BAS Mail Order services* and is a vendor to firms that needs bulk letters sent to their clients. How would the General Data Protection Regulation (GDPR) define *BAS Mail Order services*?

    A. Data controller

    B. Data processor

    C. Data custodian

    D. Data steward

79. Casey, an information technology (IT) intern, opens a case with the corporate support department but they refuse to assist her. This is *MOST LIKELY* for which reason?

    A. Interns are required to get technological assistance from their supervisor.

    B. She is seeking assistance for software not on the whitelist.

    C. Interns are required to get technological assistance from their assigned peer.

    D. Part of being an intern is figuring out technology issues on your own.

80. Neicy is a software developer making a computer game. She has the option to reuse source code from previous video games to simplify the task. How should the manager respond?

    A. Never reuse code because it is poor practice.

    B. Never reuse code because it is inherently insecure.

    C. Test and validate the reused code as if it were new code.

    D. Never reuse code because it brings bugs into the application.

81. When comparing encryption systems, symmetric systems do *NOT* have which feature:

    A. Encryption algorithm

    B. Non-repudiation

    C. Decryption algorithm

    D. Key

82. Kim is a security analyst deploying a honeynet. Her manager suggests that once a hacker is identified, the system should automatically attack the hacker's system and wipe the hacker's hard drive. Why is this *NOT* recommended?

    A. It is technically impossible to launch a counterattack.

    B. Hackback is illegal.

    C. Hackback is too difficult to automate.

    D. There is not enough staff to conduct the remote hard-drive wipes.

83. Terry enjoys answering fun questions about himself on social media. His bank account was recently hacked and money stolen. What *MOST LIKELY* occurred?

    A. His credentials and other private data were stolen during a credit-union hack.

    B. Hackers obtained his credentials by launching a Structured Query Language injection attack on his computer.

    C. Hackers launched a DoS attack on the credit union to obtain his login credentials.

    D. Hackers used information from social media to discover his credentials and his mother's maiden name.

84. Matin is planning on hiring 25 new technicians. What should be his *FIRST* step when reviewing new candidates?

    A. Conduct thorough background checks.

    B. Make sure prospects pass lie-detector screening.

    C. Follow the employment candidate screening process.

    D. Perform drug screenings.

85. Denise is a website developer who has completed programming to accept credit cards. Which kind of testing is it when she simulates being a hacker attempting to steal credit card information?

    A. Static code analysis

    B. Misuse case testing

    C. Normal case testing

    D. Code review

86. SHA-1 hashing has a longer message digest than MD5 hashing. This makes SHA-1 less vulnerable to which kind of attack?

    A. Happy

    B. Correlation

    C. Collision

    D. Birthday

87. What is the *primary* purpose of configuring a computer room with hot and cold aisles?

    A. Reduce exhaust recirculation.

    B. Increase server capacity.

    C. Improve the availability of computing services.

    D. Reduce cooling costs.

88. Which of the following is *NOT* a trait of digital rights management (DRM)?

    A. Watermarking

    B. Product keys

    C. Automatic failover

    D. Copy restriction

89. Buffer overflow attacks occur because of poorly written applications. Attackers exploit the vulnerability and can potentially gain access to the entire computer. These attacks occur where?

    A. Space on hard drives where files have been marked for removal

    B. Main memory

    C. Unused space within files

    D. Unused space in applications

90. TACACS uses which communication protocol to support AAA?

    A. Internet Control Message Protocol (ICMP)

    B. TCP

    C. UDP

    D. A&P

91. Maria, a security technician, is testing methods to defeat the firewall. Which method does she find *MOST* effective?

    A. Changing the static IP address

    B. Firewalking

    C. Fragmentation

    D. Encryption

92. Microsoft has put which system together to help analyze common software threats?

    A. Self-Monitoring, Analysis, and Reporting Technology (SMART)

    B. Waterfall

    C. Denial, Rejection, Expectation, Acceptance, Dependency (DREAD)

    D. Spoofing identity, Tampering with data, Repudiation threats, Information disclosure, Denial of service, and Elevation of privileges (STRIDE)

93. Which of the following is *NOT* part of the qualitative risk analysis process?

    A. Cost versus benefit analysis

    B. Multiple experts

    C. Opinions considered

    D. Educated guesses

94. Gael is a system engineer setting up devices to reduce noise and power spikes entering the data center. Which system provides the *BEST* filtering?

    A. Generator

    B. Uninterruptable power supply (UPS)

    C. Power distribution unit (PDU)

    D. Dual power feed

95. Common vulnerabilities found during internal scans include which two of the following?

    A. Nessus results

    B. Unpatched systems

    C. Open network ports

    D. Wireshark results

96. Carla, a security technician, has installed a fingerprint scanner to authenticate users. The device has a relatively high false acceptance rate (FAR). Which result can she expect?

    A. Too many unauthorized users will be granted access.

    B. The false rejection rate (FRR) will be relatively high.

    C. The FAR will be equal to the CER.

    D. Unauthorized users will be blocked.

97. Geri is a CSO reviewing the International Organization for Standardization (ISO) *27002* security framework. She determines she can ignore the security controls related to parking because the organization has no parking lot. This process is known as what?

    A. Tailoring

    B. Scoping

    C. Baselining

    D. Supplementing

98. Fred, a security engineer, is notified that sketches of new boat designs have made their way to the internet and have been seen online. His office has no computers or other technology. What is his *BEST* next step?

    A. Enable encryption.

    B. Install dummy cameras.

    C. Deploy a firewall.

    D. Implement a clean desk policy.

99. Users who create passwords with multiple characters using lowercase, uppercase, and special characters, and a minimum of 16 characters, are using which security model?

    A. Mutual authentication

    B. Security through obscurity

    C. DiD

    D. Implicit deny

100. The Address Resolution Protocol (ARP) command notifies the user of which media access control (MAC) address a computer uses by providing the IP address of that system. ARP collects data from which layers of the Open Systems Interconnection (OSI) model?

    A. Network and data link

    B. Presentation and application

    C. Network and transport

    D. Physical and data link

Answer key

1. D	16. D	31. C	46. A	61. A	76. A	91. D
2. D	17. C	32. C	47. B	62. C	77. A	92. D
3. D	18. A	33. B	48. C	63. A	78. B	93. A
4. B	19. B	34. A, C	49. B	64. C	79. B	94. B
5. A	20. A, C	35. D	50. B	65. D	80. C	95. B, C
6. B, D	21. B	36. D	51. D	66. B	81. B	96. A
7. D	22. A	37. D	52. C	67. C	82. B	97. B
8. C	23. A	38. C	53. A	68. D	83. D	98. D
9. D	24. D	39. B	54. D	69. A, B	84. C	99. B
10. D	25. B	40. A	55. A	70. C	85. B	100. A
11. D	26. D	41. C	56. A	71. D	86. D	
12. D	27. C	42. D	57. D	72. D	87. C	
13. B	28. A	43. B	58. C	73. B	88. C	
14. A	29. A, D	44. D	59. B	74. C	89. B	
15. A, B	30. C	45. D	60. A, B, C	75. C	90. B	

Domain key

Domain	Question
Security and Risk Management	1, 7, 11, 23, 31, 33, 40, 48, 50, 58, 59, 64, 74, 84, 93
Asset Security	8, 15, 26, 34, 44, 55, 67, 78, 88, 98
Security Architecture and Engineering	4, 9, 14, 24, 32, 46, 53, 61, 69, 76, 81, 86, 94
Communication and Network Security	6, 16, 18, 21, 29, 38, 47, 57, 65, 73, 82, 91, 100
IAM	5, 13, 19, 25, 35, 42, 51, 60, 66, 75, 83, 90, 96
Security Assessment and Testing	2, 12, 20, 30, 39, 45, 54, 63, 72, 85, 89, 95
Security Operations	10, 22, 28, 37, 41, 49, 56, 68, 70, 77, 79, 87, 97
Software Development Security	3, 17, 27, 36, 43, 52, 62, 71, 80, 92, 99

Packt.com

Subscribe to our online digital library for full access to over 7,000 books and videos, as well as industry leading tools to help you plan your personal development and advance your career. For more information, please visit our website.

Why subscribe?

- Spend less time learning and more time coding with practical eBooks and Videos from over 4,000 industry professionals

- Improve your learning with Skill Plans built especially for you

- Get a free eBook or video every month

- Fully searchable for easy access to vital information

- Copy and paste, print, and bookmark content

Did you know that Packt offers eBook versions of every book published, with PDF and ePub files available? You can upgrade to the eBook version at packt.com and as a print book customer, you are entitled to a discount on the eBook copy. Get in touch with us at customercare@packtpub.com for more details.

At www.packt.com, you can also read a collection of free technical articles, sign up for a range of free newsletters, and receive exclusive discounts and offers on Packt books and eBooks.

Other Books You May Enjoy

If you enjoyed this book, you may be interested in these other books by Packt:

AWS Certified Security – Specialty Exam Guide

Stuart Scott

ISBN: ISBN: 978-1-78953-447-4

- Understand how to identify and mitigate security incidents
- Assign appropriate Amazon Web Services (AWS) resources to underpin security requirements
- Work with the AWS shared responsibility model
- Secure your AWS public cloud in different layers of cloud computing
- Discover how to implement authentication through federated and mobile access
- Monitor and log tasks effectively using AWS

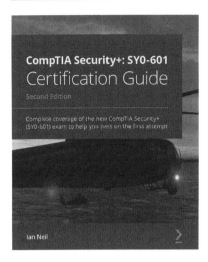

CompTIA Security+: SY0-601 Certification Guide

John Neil

ISBN: 978-1-80056-424-4

- Get to grips with security fundamentals, from the CIA triad through to IAM
- Explore cloud security and techniques used in penetration testing
- Discover different authentication methods and troubleshoot security issues
- Secure the devices and applications that are used by your company
- Identify and protect against various types of malware and virus
- Protect your environment against social engineering and advanced attacks
- Understand and implement PKI concepts
- Delve into secure application development, deployment, and automation concepts

Packt is searching for authors like you

If you're interested in becoming an author for Packt, please visit `authors.packtpub.com` and apply today. We have worked with thousands of developers and tech professionals, just like you, to help them share their insight with the global tech community. You can make a general application, apply for a specific hot topic that we are recruiting an author for, or submit your own idea.

Share Your Thoughts

Now you've finished *CISSP (ISC)² Certification Practice Exams and Tests*, we'd love to hear your thoughts! Scan the QR code below to go straight to the Amazon review page for this book and share your feedback or leave a review on the site that you purchased it from.

https://packt.link/r/1-800-56137-7

Your review is important to us and the tech community and will help us make sure we're delivering excellent quality content.

Index

Printed in Great Britain
by Amazon

68306730R00226